Government and Society in Nineteenth-Century Britain
Commentaries on British Parliamentary Papers

INDUSTRIAL RELATIONS

By the same author:

The Railwaymen: the history of the National Union of Railwaymen (London: Allen and Unwin, 1963)

The Railway Clearing House in the British Economy 1842-1922 (London: Allen and Unwin, 1968)

Britain and America: a Study of Economic Change 1850-1939 (with Professor G. E. Mingay) (London: Routledge and Kegan Paul, 1970)

'The Triple Industrial Alliance, 1913-22' *in Essays in Labour History 1886-1923* Asa Briggs and John Saville (eds.) (London: Macmillan, 1971).

By P. Ford

The Economics of Collective Bargaining (Blackwell, Oxford, 1958)
Social Theory and Social Practice (Irish University Press, 1968)

By P. & G. Ford

Hansard's Catalogue and Breviate of Parliamentary Papers, 1696-1834 (IUP British Parliamentary Papers, General Indexes, Volume 1)
Select List of British Parliamentary Papers, 1833-99 (Irish University Press, 1969)
A Breviate of Parliamentary Papers, 1900-16 (Irish University Press, 1969)
A Breviate of Parliamentary Papers, 1917-39 (Irish University Press, 1969)
A Breviate of Parliamentary Papers, 1940-54 (Blackwell, Oxford, 1961)
Luke Graves Hansard's Diary, 1814-41 (Blackwell, Oxford, 1962)
A Guide to Parliamentary Papers (3rd Revised Edition, Irish University Press, 1972)

By P. & G. Ford and Diana Marshallsay

Select List of British Parliamentary Papers, 1955-64 (Irish University Press, 1970)

Government and Society in Nineteenth-Century Britain
Commentaries on British Parliamentary Papers

INDUSTRIAL RELATIONS

Philip S. Bagwell

Introduction by P. and G. Ford

IRISH UNIVERSITY PRESS

IRISH UNIVERSITY PRESS

Irish University Press British Parliamentary Papers Series
CHIEF EDITORIAL ADVISERS
P. Ford
Professor Emeritus, Southampton University
Mrs. G. Ford

ISBN 0 7165 2215 2 (case bound) 0 7165 2216 0 (paper bound)
Library of Congress Catalog Card Number 73-93943

All forms of micro-publishing
© Irish University Microforms

Printed in Great Britain by
The Whitefriars Press Ltd., London and Tonbridge.

Contents

Abbreviations and Citations   vi

Introduction to Parliamentary Papers by P. and G. Ford   1

Industrial Relations by Philip S. Bagwell

Commentary

1. Introduction   7
2. Trade Unionism before the Repeal of the Combination Laws   9
    Select Committee on Artisans and Machinery, 1824, Select Committee on the Combination Laws, 1825: IUP Industrial Relations 1-2.
3. Industrial Relations in the Second Quarter of the Nineteenth Century   15
    Select Committee on Combinations of Workmen, 1837-38: IUP Industrial Relations 3.
4. New Model or Old Model Strengthened?   21
    Royal Commission on Trade Unions, 1867-68: IUP Industrial Relations 8-9.
5. The Development of Arbitration and Conciliation   26
    Select committees on the Settlement of Disputes between Masters and Operatives, 1856-60: IUP Industrial Relations 7.
6. The Royal Commission and the Labour Laws   34
    Royal Commission on Trade Unions, 1867-68, and Select Committee and Royal Commission on Master and Servant Act, 1865-66, and 1867: IUP Industrial Relations 8-10 and 18.
7. The Truck System   45
    Select Committees on Truck Acts, 1824-46, Railway Labourers, 1846, Payment of Wages Bill, 1854; Payment of Wages (Hosiery) Bill, 1854, Stoppage of Wages in Hosiery Manufacture, 1854-55, Royal Commission on Truck System, 1871-72 and Other Papers on the Truck System, 1887-97: IUP Industrial Relations 4-6, 11-12.
8. The Sweating System   56
    Select Committee of the House of Lords and Reports to the Board of Trade on the Sweating System, 1887-90: IUP Industrial Relations 13-17.
9. Co-operation and Profit Sharing   62
    Select Committee and other reports on Wages (Government Contracts) and on Profit Sharing, 1890-97: IUP Industrial Relations 22.
10. Employers' Liability   70
    Select Committee and other reports on Employers' Liability and the Insurance of Persons employed in mines, 1876-86: IUP Industrial Relations 19.
11. Unemployment   80
    Select Committee on Distress from Want of Employment, 1895-96: IUP Industrial Relations 23.
12. The New Unionism and the Royal Commission on Labour   88
    Royal Commission on Labour, 1892-94: IUP Industrial Relations 25-44.

The Documents   103

Bibliography   147

Index   161

Abbreviations

ASE	Amalgamated Society of Engineers	ILP	Independent Labour Party
ASRS	Amalgamated Society of Railway Servants	LRC	Labour Representation Committee
C., Cd., Cmd., Cmnd.	Command Paper	mins. of ev.	minutes of evidence
Ch.	Chairman	n.s.	new series
ev.	evidence	q.(qq.)	question(s)
GNCTU	Grand National Consolidated Trades Union	R. Com.	Royal Commission
		SDF	Social Democratic Federation
		Sel. Cttee.	Select Committee
HC	House of Commons	TUC	Trades Union Congress
HL	House of Lords		

Citations

The form used for House and Command papers is:

> session/paper no./volume no./volume page no.

Example:

> 1845 (602) xii, 331 or 1845 (602) XII, 331 or 1867 [3873] XXXII, 24

The number of a sessional paper appears in round brackets and that of a command paper in square brackets.

If the title has not been given in the text, the form should be preceded by the title and description:

> title and description/session/paper no./volume no./volume page no.

Examples:

> Game Law. Sel. Cttee. Rep.; 1845 (602) xii, 331
>
> London Squares. R.Com. Rep.; 1928-29 Cmd. 3196, viii, 111
>
> (5 geo. IV c. 96) refers to the 96th Act (or chapter) passed in the fifth year of the reign of George IV.

References are to the *House of Commons* bound sets, *except* where the paper is in the House of Lords set only. From this it follows:

a. Where the paper is the report of a Lords select committee (communicated to the Commons) it must be marked HL to indicate this and to distinguish it from a Commons select committee:

Example:

> Sale of Beer. Sel.Cttee.HL.Rep.; 1850 (398) xviii, 483.

b. Where the paper is in the Lords papers only, HL should be added to the paper number. This can be done in the form HL(259) or (HL.259).

c. For a reference to a statement on a particular page of a paper, the title and description should be followed by the *printed* page number of the paper:

> title etc./printed page no./session/paper no./volume no./vol. page no.

Example:

Finance and Industry. Cttee.Rep. p.134; 1930-31 Cmd.3897, xiii, 219

Where the reference is to the Irish University Press series the citation is:

IUP/subject/title/volume no.

Example:

IUP Monetary Policy: General 4.

Introduction to Parliamentary Papers

P. and G. Ford

A fully comprehensive definition of parliamentary papers would include all those which form part of the necessary machinery of parliamentary government, even those concerned with the procedures of the day-to-day business. But from the point of view of the researcher three groups are of primary importance. The first group, the Journals, record the things done in parliament. The second group, the Debates, record the things said in parliament (the publication of the House of Commons Debates became known as Hansard throughout the world and was at first not an official but a private venture receiving public subsidy). The third group, Papers arising in or presented to parliament deal with the formulation, development and execution of its policy. It is to this third group, for many years known as 'Blue Books' because of the blue paper with which most of them were covered, that the name Parliamentary Papers became particularly attached.

After 1801 the papers were gathered together and bound in two separate sessional sets, one for the House of Commons and the other for the House of Lords. These volumes include reports of select committees, composed of a limited number of members of either House appointed to examine particular problems, and reports of royal commissions and committees of enquiry appointed in form by the Crown though on the advice of ministers or by ministers themselves. These latter have the double advantage of comprising persons from outside the House thought to be experts on the subjects in hand, persons prominent in public affairs or representative of some body of opinion, experience or interest, and of not being limited in their work to the length of a parliamentary session. All these bodies reported the results of their enquiries together with the evidence taken to the authority which appointed them. The reports of select committees and the papers which departments were required by Act to send to parliament, because they originated *in* the House were grouped into a numbered series as House Papers. Royal commissions reported formally to the Crown — even submitting massive volumes of evidence for it to read — and committees reported to the minister concerned. Because these were the work of bodies *outside* the House, the papers were brought to the House and incorporated·in the Sessional Papers through the use of an historic formula which embodies much of the development of constitutional monarchy, 'Presented by Command'.

It was these committees and commissions which uncovered the evils of the work of children in factories and mines, the evils of bad housing and sanitation and of inadequate water supply in the new sprawling towns created by the Industrial Revolution, as well as the difficulties relating to monetary policy and the new phenomenon of recurrent trade depressions. The witnesses brought before the enquiring bodies included the victims of the new industrial conditions – little children who had worked in factories and mines, the exploited immigrants in the sweated trades, and the leaders of the early efforts to unionize workmen, such as John Gast 1815, John Doherty in 1838 and the whole of the top leadership of the great trade unions in 1867-69. What is more remarkable is that the oral evidence was printed verbatim. Even Marx was impressed by the commissions' plenary powers for getting at the truth, the competence and freedom from partisanship and respect of persons displayed by the English Factory Inspectors, the Medical Officers reporting on public health and the Commissioners of Enquiry into the exploitation of women and children, into housing and food. There is no parallel in the world for such a series of searching and detailed enquiries covering so long a span of years and embracing every phase of the transition from a rural aristocratic society to an industrialized democracy. It is the most significant of these reports on a century of investigation, the 'policy papers', that are embodied in the Irish University Press series.

The method of personal examination of witnesses had occasionally to be modified when central hearings were not practicable. Before the Benthamite conception of a unified central and local government machine had been realized in practice, the central authorities often knew little of what was going on in the localities. The many thousands of parishes administered the poor laws in their own ways so that the *Royal Commission on the Poor Laws* (1834) had to send round assistant commissioners to carry out and report on a detailed standardized plan of enquiry. The *Royal Commission on Municipal Corporations* (1835) had to make district enquiries on how the boroughs and 'places claiming to be boroughs' conducted their affairs. The effect of adverse forces on agriculture could be country-wide: the *Royal Commission on the Depressed Condition of the Agricultural Interests* (1881-82), on *Agricultural Depression* (1894-97) and the *Labour Commission* (1892-94) looking into agricultural labour, each made use of assistant commissioners to find out what was common and what was different in the problems of the various districts. These papers are a mine of information.

There are also the various famous reports by great civil servants, such as Horner's on the enforcement of factory legislation, Tremenheere's on the state of the mining districts, bound in the sets under the heading of commissioners' reports, and Southwood Smith's on the *Physical Causes of*

Sickness and Mortality to which the Poor are Exposed, tucked away in an appendix to an annual report.

Two aspects of these investigations — the membership of the committees and the importance of British constitutional procedure — are worthy of note. The fullness and considerable integrity of these penetrating investigations were remarkable in that in the first half of the century the members of the committees and commissions which made them were not, as they would be today, drawn from or representative of the great bodies of the working classes. On the contrary, they were from the wealthy and ruling groups, for the composition of the House of Commons reflected the fact that even after the Reform Act of 1832 the number of voters was still but a tiny fraction of the adult population. The Northcote-Trevelyan proposals for the reform of the civil service, by replacing recruitment by patronage with open competition, were approved by a cabinet all of whom, said Gladstone, who was a member of it, were more aristocratic than himself. No doubt they had their blind sides. For most of the century they assumed the existing class structure without much question; and there were fields in which their approach to problems and the conclusions they drew were influenced not only by the prevalent social philosophies, but class ideals and interests, as in the investigations into trade unions, game laws, etc. But the facts elicited in the examination of witnesses were not covered up or hidden — because apart from pressure by reforming groups, the constitutional procedure was that reports and evidence should be submitted and printed verbatim (see P. & G. Ford, *A Guide to Parliamentary Papers,* 3rd edition, IUP, 1972).

Further groups of papers are those which arose from the expansion of Britain overseas to control widely scattered colonial possessions and the development of areas of white settlement, Canada, Australia, and New Zealand. At the outset both kinds of territories were in some degree controlled from Whitehall. On the latter, beside formal committees of enquiry, there was a mass of despatches to and correspondence with colonial governors on the opening and sales of land for settlement, taxation, the administration of justice and the slow replacement of central control by primitive local representative bodies which eventually became the parliaments of self-governing dominions. In the case of the colonial possessions, after the Act abolishing slavery had been passed, the most striking feature was the immense body of papers which offer unique insight into the problem of enforcing this new political principle in widely scattered territories, differing in climate, crop conditions, land tenure, in the character and importance of slavery and in social structure. These are revealed in an immense volume of despatches, correspondence and instructions issued by the Colonial Office and the Foreign Office to colonial governors and their little Assemblies, which offered varying degrees of co-operation and resistance, and by the Admiralty in orders to commanders of naval vessels engaged all over the world in efforts to suppress the slave trade.

The great body of material for the nineteenth century occupies some 7,000 official folio volumes. At the outset the problem of making it available had to be met by the Printer to the House of Commons, Luke Hansard, who kept it in stock and numbered the House papers. He was frequently asked by MPs and others for sets of existing papers on particular questions then under discussion in the House or by the public. This led him to take two steps. He made special collections of papers arranged in subject order, and prepared a series of indexes to the papers, some in subject and some in alphabetical order. But the passage of a century has enlarged the number of papers to be handled and the scale of the problems; and at the same time we now have to meet the demand not only of the politician concerned with the problems of his time, but those of professional historians and researchers ranging over the whole century.

To deal with the papers on Home Affairs the Fords' *Select List of British Parliamentary Papers 1833-99* includes 4,000 policy papers arranged in subject order, so that researchers can follow the development lines of policy easily through any collection of papers. But complete collections are few and far between and even ample ones not common. The Irish University Press Parliamentary Papers series supplies this deficiency first by reprinting all the major policy papers, conveniently brought together in subject sets, e.g. 32 volumes on Agriculture, 44 volumes on Industrial Relations, 15 volumes on Children's Employment, 55 volumes on Education, and so on. Secondly, it has retained what was the great virtue of the original enquiries by reprinting with the reports all the volumes of evidence. Thirdly, in those fields where despatches, correspondence and instructions are vital as in the case of the papers on slavery, Canada, Australia, New Zealand, as far as possible all the papers on these matters found in the British Parliamentary series have been reprinted, e.g. 95 volumes on Slavery, 36 on Canada, 34 on Australia.

The series includes the most commonly used official general alphabetical indexes from which researchers can trace papers referred to in the footnotes of scholarly works and in the references in parliamentary reports themselves. In addition to the official indexes, a special index[1] to the 1,000 volumes has been prepared which will also provide cross references, so that the official indexes can be used either with the official sessional sets or with the IUP reprints.

1 *Checklist of British Parliamentary Papers in the Irish University Press 1000-Volume Series 1801-1899 (IUP, 1972)*

INDUSTRIAL RELATIONS

Philip S. Bagwell

Commentary

1. Introduction

A major preoccupation of British governments in the second half of the twentieth century has been the passage of legislation to delimit the power of trade unions. Industrial relations were also frequently the subject of legislation in the second half of the eighteenth century. One major difference between the two situations, however, was that whereas in the twentieth century the motive was to circumscribe the power of organized labour, which many considered had exceeded reasonable bounds,[1] 200 years earlier the purpose of legislation was the complete prohibition of all combinations of wage earners which had the aim of improving conditions of employment. In contrast with the situation in the 1960s and 1970s when both Labour and Conservative governments met with fierce opposition, both inside and outside Parliament, when introducing measures for the regulation of industrial relations, Whig and Tory governments in the age of George III passed, with impunity, a large number of Acts which were clearly hostile to organized labour.

The result was that in 1800 the overwhelming majority of wage earners were denied industrial — as well as political and cultural — rights. With the very limited exception of some of the more prosperous domestic out-workers and those who were electors in Scot and Lot boroughs, they were entirely disfranchised; they were forbidden to form trade unions; the new generation of factory workers were subject to the most fearsome dangers from moving machinery, and, when injured, stood very little chance of obtaining compensation from their employers; the mortality rate amongst coal miners was the heaviest of all; although the intensity of labour was possibly less than was the case in 1900, the hours of work were so long that little time or inclination remained for cultural pursuits. The workman could not even be sure of receiving legal tender when paid his wages: the truck system was widespread in many industries including coal mining, iron founding and textile manufacture — to mention only three of the most important. Thus the editor of one of the early radical newspapers was scarcely exaggerating when he wrote of the status of his class, 'Orphans we are and bastards of society.'[2]

1   Mr. Robert Carr, Secretary of State for Employment, moving the second reading of the Industrial Relations Bill in the House of Commons on 14 December 1970, maintained that liberty had in some areas degenerated into licence, that the Bill would put on record what the community believed to be fair and reasonable conduct, but that the right to combine, the right to strike and other rights, given to labour under the Trade Disputes Act, 1906, would continue to be guaranteed for registered trade unions. *Hansard,* 5th Ser., vol. 808, Cols. 963-64.

2   Asa Briggs, quoting from *The Pioneer,* 22 March 1834, 'The Language of Class in Early Nineteenth Century England', in *Essays in Labour History,* vol. 1, Asa Briggs and John Saville (eds.) (London: Macmillan, 1960), p. 68.

Towards the close of the nineteenth century the veteran Christian Socialist, J. M. Ludlow, who had studied the condition of the working classes longer than anyone then living, was asked by the eminent economist, Professor Alfred Marshall, to give his general impressions on how conditions had changed during his lifetime. In reply, Ludlow affirmed that, although there were still 'black spots' where wages were 'very low indeed', in general they had increased 'very considerably indeed'. The status of the working classes had 'changed immensely'. But what impressed him most was the change in public opinion about the rights of labour. He found 'boys and girls almost fresh from school' were more enlightened on the subject than were sympathetic adults in 1848.[3]

The improvement in the standard of living and the status of British labour in the nineteenth century was made possible through the completion of the process of industrialization — the proportion of the working population employed in agriculture declined from 26 per cent in 1841 to under 9 per cent in 1901. The bringing together of millions of wage earners in closely congested towns and cities made the physical problem of their organization into unions simpler, so that by the end of the nineteenth century just over two million workers were enrolled in trade unions. But, as J. M. Ludlow rightly emphasized, it was the change in public opinion and in the viewpoint of members of Parliament that was of great significance in altering the legal standing of trade unions. Taking a broad view of the century's legislation on industrial relations, it may be observed that before 1824 Adam Smith's opinion that there should be legal recognition of labour's right to combine was not accepted by Parliament. Thereafter two different policies gradually gained acceptance. One was the doctrine of 'collective laissez-faire' admirably summarized in Mrs. Barbara Castles's White Paper *In Place of Strife*:

> 'Trade unions should be accepted as lawful and given the right to organize. The State should recognize the right to strike and the right to bargain collectively to improve wages and conditions. But so long as the 'rules of the game' were roughly fair to both sides the State should not be concerned with its consequences. In effect the Government should provide facilities to help the parties agree, but should not interfere to impose a settlement upon them.'[4]

The other was the doctrine that it was necessary at times for the state to interfere to protect the interests of the community at large and to ensure the removal of evil aspects of industrial relations which free collective

3   *Fourth Report, Royal Commission on Labour, 1893-94,* p. 131. 1893-94 [c. 7063-1], XXXIX pt. 1, 157. IUP Industrial Relations 43, p. 157.

4   *In Place of Strife: A Policy for Industrial Relations,* 1969, p. 6, HC 1969 Cmnd. 3888.

bargaining seemed incapable of eliminating. Examples of major enactments which embodied the principle of 'collective laissez-faire' were the Combination Laws Repeal Act of 1824 (repealing the Combination Acts of 1799 and 1800), the Trade Union Act of 1871 and the Trade Disputes Act of 1906. Legislation based on the alternative doctrine included the Master and Servant Laws and the Criminal Law Amendment Act, 1871.

The enquiries, through select committees and royal commissions, which form the bulk of the material for the forty-four volumes of papers on industrial relations, reveal the gradual triumph of these two doctrines of 'collective laissez faire' in respect of trade union rights and state intervention to protect workmen from abuses like truck, sweated labour and inadequate compensation for industrial injuries, over the earlier ones of prohibition of trade unions and the non-intervention of the state with respect to working conditions.

2. Trade unionism before the repeal of the combination laws

It is well known that the occasion for the passing of the first Combination Act in 1799 (33 Geo. III c. 81) was the receipt by the House of Commons of a petition from the master millwrights of the City of London for a bill prohibiting combination amongst their journeymen. There was ample precedent for such action. There were already on the statute book more than forty acts to prevent workmen from combining in particular industries and most of these had been passed as a result of similar initiatives from the masters. For example, by 'An Act to prevent unlawful combination of workmen employed in woollen manufactures, and for better payment of their wages' (10 Geo. I c. 34), all combination of woolcombers and weavers were declared illegal. Those who were deterred from combination through specific legislative prohibition could be prosecuted under the common law for conspiracy. In 1783 Lord Mansfield ruled that 'everyone may work at what price he pleases but a combination not to work under certain prices is an indictable offence'. Three years later, when the London bookbinders struck for a reduction of working hours from twelve to eleven per day, five of their leaders were convicted on a charge of conspiracy and sentenced to two years' imprisonment. Those who were fortunate enough to escape prosecution for conspiracy could be charged under the thirteenth clause of the Statute of Artificers, 1563 (5 Eliz. c. 4) which decreed a month's imprisonment for persons guilty of breaking a contract by leaving their work unfinished. In the opinion of George White, Francis Place's agent who drafted the Combination Laws Repeal Act of 1824, this law was ninety-nine times more oppressive than the Combination Laws of 1799 and 1800 which were clearly less of 'a new and momentous departure' than the Webbs suggested.[5]

Since there were already numerous ways in which wage earners could be discouraged from attempting to combine, why was additional legislation necessary? The explanation lies partly in the war-time state of alarm of Parliament and partly in the ineffectiveness of earlier measures to deal with the problem. The combination laws must be seen alongside the Unlawful Oaths Act, 1797 (37 Geo. III c. 123) and the Corresponding Societies Act, 1799 (39 Geo. III c. 79) as motivated by government panic at the growth of radical societies sympathetic to republican France. The master millwrights in their petition to Parliament stressed the difficulties under the existing law of prosecuting offenders. Those who fell foul of the law could only be punished 'at the Sessions or Assizes after the commission of the offence' and they frequently used the gap in time between the summons and the meeting of the court to make good their escape to a different part of the country. The Combination Acts, then, 'did not make illegal what had before been legal'; they were 'measures of administrative reform designed to check a growing and illegal practice'.[6] The 1799 Act dispensed with the jury system and provided that 'one or more' magistrates, sitting as a court of summary jurisdiction, could sentence any workman who entered a combination to obtain higher wages, reduce the hours of labour or decrease the quantity of work, the penalty being imprisonment for a period of up to three months. The amending act, which was passed in the following year, required the presence of a minimum of two magistates to try the case and somewhat lessened the severities of the earlier measure by the addition of the qualifying phrases 'wilfully and maliciously' and 'without any just or reasonable cause' in respect of indictable offences committed by the workmen; but the essential purpose of the original act – expediting the administration of justice – remained unimpaired.

Despite the attempt to reduce the law's delays, trade unions continued to function throughout the quarter-century of their general prohibition. Asked by the members of the Royal Commission on Trade Unions in 1867 about the Ironfounders Society of which he was Corresponding Secretary, Daniel Guile conceded that the records of the Society went back to 1809. Proceedings were so secret that they 'had to dig holes in the floor and hide their books there' and meet 'out on the open moor'. Nevertheless

5   Mary Dorothy George, 'The Combination Laws Reconsidered', *Economic History*, (*Supplement to Economic Journal*), No. 2 (May 1927). Mary Dorothy George, 'The Combination Laws' *Economic History Review*, vol. VI, 1936. Arthur Aspinall, *The Early English Trade Unions* (London: Batchworth Press, 1849), pp. ix-xi. Sidney and Beatrice Webb, *The History of Trade Unionism* (London: Longmans Green & Co., 1920), p. 72.

6   A. Aspinall, *The Early English Trade Unions*, p. xii.

contributions continued to be received and strikes were conducted when the bargaining position of the union made them likely to succeed.[7] In general it was paradoxically true that 'in the very years the Combination Acts were in force trade unionism registered great advances', not only in trades where it had already existed before the new laws were passed, but even in those where the workmen were unorganized before the turn of the century.[8]

Although they were frequently ineffective and their influence was unevenly felt, the acts of 1799 and 1800 are to be distinguished from all preceding legislation restraining combinations because of their universality. They prohibited *all* combinations. Over the whole of the first quarter of the nineteenth century 'their general prohibitive influence was ever present'. They bore with most severity on those employed in factories or large workshops and in the out-work system. Combinations of skilled artisans employed by the small master class were less liable to prosecution, partly because a friendlier understanding often existed between employer and workman and because the small employer was often as resentful as was the skilled workman of the large employers' use of cheap, unskilled labour and new, but often defective, machinery to turn out goods of an inferior quality.[9]

Outlawing trade unions and denying working men constitutional means to redress their grievances undoubtedly prolonged the use of violence in industrial relations. Given the legal right to combine, cautiously managed and financially strong unions of the 'amalgamated' type, such as became well known in the 1850s, might well have developed earlier. Machine wrecking, the burning down of factories, vitriol throwing and other acts of violence long pre-dated the passing of the combination laws, but they reached a new intensity in an environment of war-time emergency, high food prices and the complete outlawing of trade unionism.

The Luddite outbreaks, which were concentrated in the centres of textile manufacture in Nottinghamshire, Derbyshire, Cheshire, Lancashire and the West Riding of Yorkshire between 1811-16, were, until recently, frequently described in terms of 'a brutish conflict between frightened workers and indignant authority'.[10] Only within the last decade has a

---

7   *5th Report Royal Commission on Trade Unions, 1867-68*, p. 19. 1867-68 [3980-1] XXXIX, 37. IUP Industrial Relations 9, p. 37.

8   Edward Palmer Thompson, *The Making of the English Working Class* (London: Gollancz, 1963), p. 503.

9   E. P. Thompson, *The Making of the English Working Class*, pp. 505-06.

10   John Steven Watson, *The Reign of George III 1760-1815* (Oxford: Clarendon Press, 1960), p. 571.

serious attempt been made to analyse in more detail the causes of Luddism and its relationship to trade unionism.

Before resorting to violence on any general scale the Nottinghamshire framework-knitters endeavoured to use constitutional means to redress their grievances. Gravener Henson organized the signing of a petition which was presented to Parliament in 1812. The farthest Parliament was prepared to go was to appoint the *Select Committee on the Framework-knitters' petition* whose *Report*,[11] published later that year, gave ample evidence of the depressing effects on living standards of the trade recession and the introduction of machinery. Here is to be found the all-important economic explanation of the outbreak of Luddism. With ordinary collective bargaining proscribed and Parliament unresponsive to petitions, wage earners resorted to 'collective bargaining by riot'.[12] By threatening (and sometimes carrying out) the destruction of factories of those employers who underpaid labour or who installed the hated new machinery they put pressure on their masters to pay higher wages and dispense with the larger frames from which the inferior 'cut ups' were manufactured. In the cotton areas of Lancashire and Cheshire, it has been noted, 'Luddism came in as a trade union technique when wage negotiations proved abortive'. It would be a fair generalization to state that where craft skills were in greatest demand and the masters therefore left trade clubs unmolested, Luddism was least in evidence, since collective bargaining was practised despite the combination laws. The skilled croppers of the West Riding woollen industry used normal wage negotiations in the neighbourhood of Leeds, where they were well organized, but resorted to Luddism in the villages where they were scattered and weak.[13]

Luddism changed its character over time. Whereas the earlier examples of machine wrecking had a greater element of spontaneity and impetuosity, the later attacks were more professionally, cold-bloodedly executed. There even appeared skilled machine wreckers who had a vested interest in the continuation of Luddism since they were the paid agents of the stockingers, croppers and others who employed them. Machine wrecking for purposes of industrial bargaining inevitably opened the way for

11   *Report from the Committee on the Framework-knitters' petition,* 1812, 1812 (247) II, 203-306.

12   Eric John Ernest Hobsbawm 'The Machine Breakers', in *Labouring Men* (London: Weidenfeld & Nicolson, 1964), p. 7.

13   Malcolm Ian Thomis, *The Luddites* (Newton Abbot: David & Charles, 1970), pp. 133-34. Roy Anthony Church and Stanley David Chapman, 'Gravener Henson and the making of the English working class', in *Land, Labour and Population in the Industrial Revolution,* Eric Lionel Jones & Gordon Edmund Mingay (eds.) (London: Edward Arnold, 1967), pp. 131-161.

professional criminals to take advantage of the disturbed condition of society and the absence of an efficient constabulary to engage in acts of violence and theft. Despite the alarm of the cabinet at the height of the disturbances in 1812, there is no conclusive evidence that the Luddites had wider revolutionary aims. They did not steal arms and use them against the employers until armed force had first been used against them. Whilst they gave general support to the cause of parliamentary reform 'acting politically for them meant striking a few blows, not organizing a political campaign, let alone a revolution'.[14]

Just as the emergence of Luddism in 1811-12 is to be explained largely in terms of extreme food scarcity, low wages and heavy unemployment, so its sharp decline after 1816 was the result of some improvement — if only temporary — in the price of bread, the reward of labour and the prospect of employment.

Machine wrecking in the second decade of the nineteenth century, as at other times, sometimes brought about a temporary improvement in the wages of those whose labour was being displaced by the new machinery. Its long term effects arrested, rather then accelerated, an improvement in living standards. But the Luddite movement did serve as a salutary reminder to Parliament that there were serious dangers in ignoring the voice of the working classes and denying them any say in the conduct of industry. The experience of the years 1811-16 may well have helped to influence MPs in 1824 to consider that allowing freedom of organization to wage earners was a less dangerous policy than that of crude suppression.

Francis Place, who led the movement for the repeal of all laws against trade unions, had a strong personal motive for the stand that he took. He felt the tyranny of the law in the 1790s when he was employed as an apprentice and a journeyman breeches-maker. Men of this craft came out on strike in 1793 and when most of them returned to work, defeated, Place found it impossible to obtain re-employment though he had taken no part in the organization of the strike. His first-born child died of smallpox at the time. He subsequently wrote in his autobiography: 'It is utterly impossible for anyone to tell how much we suffered during the six months which followed the conclusion of the strike without my having been in any way accessory to it'.[15]

But although he spoke from bitter experience when he stressed that the combination laws operated unjustly towards working men, Place held the view that once the obnoxious laws had been repealed 'combinations would

---

14 *Report from the Committee of Secrecy, 8 July 1812*, 1812 (335) II, 309-11. See also M. I. Thomis, *The Luddites*, pp. 94-95.

15 Mary Thale (ed.), *The Autobiography of Francis Place* (Cambridge: Cambridge University Press, 1972), pp. xiii, 116.

cease to exist'. The reason that trade unions had survived was that men had been kept together for long periods 'only by the oppression of the laws'. Once the laws were repealed combinations would lack any rational basis and would 'fall to pieces'. All would then be 'as orderly as a Quaker could desire'.[16] Workmen, he believed, would be foolish to attempt to defy the laws of political economy which made it clear that wages were determined by the conditions of demand and supply in the labour market. It was precisely because Place and Joseph Hume took the laissez-faire standpoint that they won a sufficient measure of support for their repealing Bill in 1824. By this time many more MPs had imbibed the doctrines of Adam Smith than had been the case in 1800.

Place's 'vetting' of the witnesses appearing before the select committee and his parliamentary manoeuvrings have made the campaign for the repeal of the combination laws one of the best known examples of political wire-pulling in the nineteenth century. And yet he admitted 'the workmen were not easily managed'. One reason for this difficulty was that he wished to see *all* laws for the regulation of labour swept away; the 'protective' laws governing conditions of apprenticeship and minimum wage rates as well as the 'oppressive' ones which outlawed trade unionism. He had already aroused the resentment of some of the leaders of the working men in 1812-13 when he campaigned for the repeal of the apprenticeship and wage fixing clauses of the Statute of Apprentices of 1563. In 1823 Gravener Henson, who was certainly more closely in touch with the textile workers of the north than was Place, sponsored a complicated Bill which provided for the repeal of the combination laws but at the same time prohibited truck payments, put strict limits to overtime working and encouraged resort to arbitration. It was a measure much in advance of its time and most unlikely to have passed into law. Place, condemning it as 'complicated and absurd', skilfully manoeuvred its suppression. It is therefore not surprising that the more astute leaders of the working classes, whilst accepting Place's Bill as a step forward, gave its sponsor only qualified support.[17]

Thus it was largely due to Place's unquestioning adherence to the teaching of Adam Smith, Ricardo and McCulloch that the *Act to repeal the laws relative to the Combination of Workmen 1824*, (5 Geo. IV c. 95) entered the statute book as the most perfect embodiment of the doctrine 'collective laissez-faire' of all the acts concerning industrial relations in the nineteenth century.

Much has been written of the alarming outbreak of strikes which

16 Graham Wallas, *Life of Francis Place* (London: Longmans & Co., 1898), pp. 210, 217.

17 E. P. Thompson, *The Making of the English Working Class*, pp. 518-19.

followed the repeal of the old laws on 21 June 1824. It remains doubtful whether industrial action did increase as alarmingly as contemporary newspaper reports suggest. What emerges from the hearings of the Select Committee of 1825 is that the wage earners, concluding that they had at last acquired the legal right to combine, at once proceeded to organize and to strike openly, whereas previously the state of the law had driven them to act in secret, keeping the newspapers in the dark as to the extent of their activity and influence.[18] Nearly all the evidence of the resort to violence came from the period between 1817 and 1820 and many of the incidents occurred in Dublin. Place was careful to put forward as witnesses employers who admitted that they had frequently combined together to keep down the rate of wages and had suffered no penalties, despite the illegality of such actions under the Combination Act of 1800.

The Combination Act of 1825 (6 Geo. IV c. 129) marked a retreat from the more comprehensive measure of the previous year but at least it brought some advance in the legal standing of trade unions. The principle of collective bargaining was conceded even though it was limited in application to negotiations over wages and hours of labour. The employers were given new safeguards in that pickets who were guilty of 'molesting' or 'obstructing' non-strikers were liable to imprisonment for up to three months.

3. Industrial relations in the second quarter of the nineteenth century

Parliament had decided to legalize collective bargaining for the settlement of wages and hours of work; but the majority of employers in 1825, and for long afterwards, were unwilling to give even this degree of recognition to organized labour. One of the foremost objectives of the trade unions in the second quarter of the nineteenth century was to eliminate the use of the 'Document' — the declaration of renunciation of trade union membership which the workman was required to sign as a condition of employment. They had not everywhere succeeded in this objective even by the end of the 1850s. The Document was widely used to break up building strikes in London, Leeds and elsewhere in 1833-34 and the cotton-spinners strike in Lancashire and in Scotland in 1837. On the occasion of the engineers lock-out in London and Manchester in 1851 it was used in an attempt to smash the recently created and potentially powerful Amalgamated Society of Engineers. On this occasion the men were advised by the officers of the union to comply with the employers' request but nevertheless to maintain their membership, on the grounds that a

18   George Howell, *Labour Legislation, Labour Movements and Labour Leaders*, vol. 1, 2nd edn. (London: T. Fisher Unwin, 1905), p. 54.

declaration exacted under duress was morally non-binding. On the last important occasion when this weapon was used in an industrial dispute, the London building strike of 1859, the employers eventually abandoned their demand that the strikers should sign the Document as a condition of their re-employment.[19]

In the absence of a clearly defined legal right to picket, the unions found it extremely hard to prevent the widespread use of blackleg labour to defeat strikes. Employers' Association multiplied in the 1830s and 1840s, making possible concerted action by firms to supply 'free' labour to take the place of strikers. In the textile industry of the 1830s a more than adequate, if disreputable living, was earned by 'nobs' (strike-breakers) who were first bribed by the employers to take the place of strikers and then bribed by the unions to leave the district. In April 1838 John M'Caffer, a Glasgow cotton operative, told the Select Committee on Combinations of Workmen that he knew of 'nobs' who by moving from one strike-bound part of the country to another, had made £100 a year by such tactics.[20]

If men went on strike without the backing of a union, chances of success were even slimmer. Following the extravagant promotions of the railway mania, the Eastern Counties Railway was in financial difficulties. The Board of Directors economized at the expense of labour, increasing the number of waggons per goods train and lengthening the working day. When the men went on strike the Board was offered replacements from the North British and the London and South Western Railways and circulated a black list of the offending strikers.[21]

The case of the six Tolpuddle labourers is a reminder that there were other ways of crushing incipient trade unionism apart from mobilizing 'free' labour and producing the 'Document'. The practice of oath-taking was widespread amongst the early generations of trade unionists. Its purpose was to instil a sense of unity and cohesion, to prevent any leakage of plans to informers and to intimidate potential defaulters at a time when unions lacked any legal remedy against embezzlement. The statutes of 1797 and 1819 prohibiting the administration of illegal oaths could well have been invoked many times before February 1834 to stifle combination in a host of different trades where oath-taking was still prevalent. They were brought into use in 1834 because of the rapid growth of trade union activity at the time and the determination of the Dorsetshire magistrates

19   G. D. H. Cole and Alexander Warnock Filson, *British Working Class Movements, Select Documents, 1789-1875* (London: Macmillan, 1965), pp. 270, 479.

20   *First Report from the Select Committee on Combinations of Workmen, 1837-8*, p. 76. 1837-38 (448) VIII, 80. IUP Industrial Relations 3.

21   *Herapath's Railway Journal*, 24 August 1850, p. 816.

and Lord Melbourne, the prime minister, to make an example of the agricultural labourers. The blow was scarcely designed specifically to crush the Grand National Consolidated Trades Union since the Friendly Society of Agricultural Labourers, which George Loveless and his friends had established, pre-dated the GNCTU by five months.

Although the success of the campaign for the pardoning and return of the six labourers owed much to the strength of public opinion against the iniquity of the sentences of seven years transportation, it also owed something to the government's awareness that its legal case against the six men was a shaky one. At the trial in Dorchester the full oath taken by the unionists was not quoted but only 'a few disjointed scraps' recalled from memory by witnesses. After the men had been sentenced the home secretary asked the law officers of the crown for an opinion. In reply, they considered that not all oaths were illegal, but that it depended upon the purpose for which they were administered. Since they could discover no firm evidence that the labourers were planning to commit any illegal act they could give no definite assurance that the oath itself was illegal. It is now clear that if the six men had been provided with better legal advice they might well have been found not guilty, as were the oath-taking Exeter bricklayers who had been charged a month before the arrests were made at Tolpuddle.[22]

The attempts which were made during this period to establish nationwide groups, both within a single trade and among groups of trades, sprang from a growing awareness of the futility of purely localized effort. Thus it was the failure of separate strikes of cotton spinners at Stockport and Manchester in 1828 which persuaded John Doherty (1797 or 1799-1854) to establish the Grand General Union of all the Operative Spinners of the United Kingdom in 1829. He soon realized that even this organization was not wide enough in scope. Before the spinners' union faded out in 1831 he set up the first important *trades* union, the National Association for the Protection of Labour, in 1830. For two years it brought together wool textile workers, mechanics, potters, miners and builders within a radius of one hundred miles from Manchester. But it failed through opposition to Doherty's attempt to move the office of the *Voice of the People* to London and through the exhaustion of its funds by a series of unco-ordinated strikes. The best known of all attempts at general union, the Grand National Consolidated Trades Union of 1834 was a much less substantial organization than its name and the writings of the Webbs would suggest: it is doubtful, as Professor Clegg has shown,

22   W. H. Oliver, 'Tolpuddle Martyrs and Trade Union Oaths', *Labour History* (Sydney) No. 10 May 1966, pp. 5-12. W. H. Oliver, 'The Consolidated Trades Union of 1834', *Economic History Review,* 2nd Ser. vol. XVI No. 1, 1964, p. 77.

whether, at its peak, it recruited as many as 20,000 members but certainly not 'half a million . . . including tens of thousands of farm labourers and women'. Recent research has shown that the organization was essentially the creation of London artisans and craftsmen who had little success in recruiting members from the textile trades of the north-west. The outstanding reason for its failure, as well as that of its predecessors, was a financial one. Although the leaders understood that localized organization was ineffective and they therefore endeavoured to centralize funds, they lacked the authority to restrain local leaders from impetuous strike action. The last of the attempts at general union in the first half of the nineteenth century, the National Association of United Trades for the Protection and Employment of Labour, survived for over twenty-two years and had some successes as a political pressure group, but it came little nearer to solving the problem of financial control than had the pioneering organizations of the early 1830s.[23]

For the wage earners these were years of growing class-consciousness and political awareness. Many of the leaders of the trade union and radical movements were enthusiastic for 'self-improvement' through education. Through the Hampden Clubs, Secular Sunday Schools and co-operative societies they sought to acquire 'useful knowledge' which would enable them to master their destiny instead of being entirely at the mercy of their employers. Above all they wished to understand the laws which governed the working of the economy. In the mechanics institutes, particularly in London, a battle was fought between the ideas of Thomas Hodgskin (1787-1869) author of *Labour Defended against the claims of Capital* (1825) and the orthodox theories of James Mill and McCulloch, for the minds of large working class audiences. To Francis Place, Hodgskin's teaching, that the capitalist exploited the labourer by depriving him of the full fruits of his labour, was anathema. At his instigation Hodgskin was replaced as lecturer in political economy by the far less radical, but also less intelligible, Wilmot Horton. In the provinces the middle class radicals learned from the experience of their metropolitan contemporaries. From the start they endeavoured to ensure that only 'sound' economic doctrines were taught. In less well endowed establishments up and down the country the ideas of Robert Owen, John Bray, Thomas Hodgskin and William Thompson continued to circulate. But the victory of the orthodox school of economics in the all important mechanics institutes was a significant

---

23 S. and B. Webb, *History of Trade Unionism*, p. 120. Hugh Armstrong Clegg, Alan Fox and Arthur Frederick Thompson, *A History of British Trade Unions since 1899*, vol. 1. (Oxford: Clarendon Press, 1964), pp. 2, 8. W. H. Oliver, 'The Consolidated Trades Union of 1834', *Economic History Review*, 2nd Ser. vol. XVI No. 1., 1964, p. 77.

influence in the growth of moderate views in the trade union leadership of the 1840s and 1850s.[24]

In so far as they too came to accept the views of the classical economists, writers such as Charles Dickens, Elizabeth Gaskell, Benjamin Disraeli and Thomas Carlyle helped to create, among their vast reading public, a generally unsavoury image of trade unionism. In the case of three outstanding episodes in the history of British labour relations — the Glasgow cotton spinners strike of 1837, the Preston strike of 1854 and the Sheffield outrages of 1866 — the reports of parliamentary select committees and a Royal Commission provided real life material for the novelist's pen. The Glasgow dispute alone provided violent or fearsome scenes for *Mary Barton, Barnaby Rudge* and *Sybil* besides Carlyle's references to 'Glasgow Thuggery' in his *Chartism*. Although the generally humanitarian approach of these writers and their readiness to point out the shortcomings of employers, as well as working men, may have given some early encouragement to the movement for industrial conciliation, their emphasis on the violent and coercive elements in trade unionism delayed the advance of full union recognition and collective bargaining. According to responsible witnesses such as James Ludlow and John Doherty, trade union violence was on the wane after the repeal of the combination laws, but some blood-curdling incidents continued to occur, and these made more colourful raw material for the novelist than the dull business of building up provident funds through regularly collected subscriptions.[25]

Raymond Postgate, a pioneer of British trade union history, wrote in his *Builders' History* in 1923 that building trade union documents were 'sharply divided about the year 1860', the first half being 'a devastated area' the second 'a jungle'. Before 1860 the documents are 'rare and vague' but thereafter they are abundant. Those who followed Postgate and wrote the history of other unions, found much the same story.[26] It is for this reason that the historian of industrial relations can only regret that Parliament made but one major enquiry into the subject of trade unions between 1825 and 1867. The minutes of evidence and reports of the

---

24   Brian Simon, *Studies in the History of Education, 1780-1870* (London: Lawrence and Wishart, 1960), pp. 152-59. G. D. H. Cole, *A History of Socialist Thought* vol. 1. *The Forerunners, 1789-1850* (London: Macmillan, 1953), Chaps. ix-xii.

25   P. Brantlinger, 'The Case against trade unions in early Victorian fiction', *Victorian Studies,* vol. XIII No. 1. September 1969, pp. 37-52.

26   Raymond Postgate, *The Builders' History* (London: Labour Publishing Co., 1923), p. xv. See also James Bavington Jefferys, *The Story of the Engineers* (London: Lawrence & Wishart, 1945), p. 299.

Select Committee on Combinations of Workmen, 1837-38, have a greatly enhanced value because of this fact.

As was almost invariably the case throughout the nineteenth century, the appointment of the select committee was prompted by particularly severe and prolonged industrial unrest, in this case in the textile industries of Glasgow, Manchester, Dublin and Belfast. The strike of cotton-spinners in and around Glasgow, which began on 8 April 1837, was accompanied by attacks on mills and on the homes of blacklegs and the murder of one 'nob'. Although the leaders of the Glasgow Cotton Spinners Association denied complicity with the worst acts of violence and although there had been much provocation, the five accused men were sentenced to seven years transportation. Mr. Wakley, the radical MP for Finsbury, demanded a parliamentary enquiry into the spinners' case but was countered by Daniel O'Connell who condemned the restrictive practices of the Dublin book binders and of trade unionists in general. Hence the select committee had a briefing which was, ostensibly at least, of wider scope than the trade unionists had bargained for.[27] Nevertheless, the enquiry was mainly concentrated on the state of industrial relations in the textile industry with no attention being given to any other industries except printing and the lumber trade and no examination of trade unionism outside the above-mentioned cities.

It is clear from the evidence of John Doherty that the Grand General Union of All Operative Spinners of the United Kingdom and the Glasgow Cotton Spinners Association had had the backing of the smaller masters against the aristocratic methods of the large firms; in fact, in Glasgow, partial strikes had occurred in at least six instances at the suggestion of these masters. It is also clear that some of the policies, such as the preference for arbitration, generally held to have originated with the 'New Model' unions of the 1850s, were already being followed by the cotton unions in the 1830s. A unique feature of the Glasgow strike was the appeal from the leaders of the unions to the churchwardens to act as mediators between the spinners and their employers.[28]

For the development of trade unionism outside the textile industry during this period the historian is obliged to turn to other parliamentary papers, local newspapers and, wherever possible, the records of individual unions for the necessary evidence. The miners are a case in point. David Swallow, who became the first general secretary of the Miners' Association

27   S. and B. Webb, *History of Trade Unionism,* pp. 153-57. Archibald Swinton, *Report of the Trial of Thomas Hunter and other operative cotton spinners in Glasgow in 1838* (Edinburgh: 1838).

28   *First Report from the Select Committee on Combinations of Workmen, 1837-38,* pp. 250-67. 1837-38 (488) VIII, 254-271. IUP Industrial Relations 3.

in November 1842, gave important evidence to the Royal Commission on Mines on the working conditions which gave rise to the union.[29] The union's progress can be traced through the files of its newspaper *The Miner's Advocate,* through local newspapers such as *The Newcastle Journal* and through the Chartist *Northern Star.* During the six years of its existence it was the strongest union of its time with 60,000 paid up members in 1844. It was distinguished by its early realization of the importance of parliamentary lobbying to achieve the passage of safety legislation and by its employment of W. P. Roberts, the 'miners' attorney general' to resist every individual act of oppression. Since its members appreciated the importance of parliamentary action it is not surprising that many of them were Chartists or that there were five North Staffordshire miners and five other miners from Northumberland on the Chartist General Council of 1842. Working conditions in the coalfields were such that questions of accident prevention and workmen's compensation often figured as importantly as did those of wages and hours of labour in the formulation of union policy. It was early realized that collective bargaining alone would not secure the reduction of the terrible mortality rate in coal-mining and thus the Miners' Association blazed a trail, to be followed by other miners' unions later in the century, in reinforcing industrial bargaining with political activity.[30]

4. New model or old model strengthened?

In their magisterial *History of Trade Unionism,* first published in 1894, the Webbs drew a sharp distinction between the 'revolutionary' period of trade unionism between 1829-42 and the 'New Model' of more cautious, more businesslike, organization in the 1850s and 1860s. A number of distinguished modern labour historians, including Professors Hobsbawm and Harrison, have endorsed these generalizations, though with some modifications. Others, including Professor Clegg and Dr. Musson, maintain that there was less revolutionary fervour and more practical realism in the early period than the members of the Webb school of thought would have us believe. According to this revisionist school of thought there was no radical change in organization, not even in the creation of the Amalgamated Society of Engineers in 1851 — the New Model itself — since this

29   *Appendix to the First Report of Commissioners for Mines, 1842,* p. 277. 1842 [381] XVI, 285. IUP Industrial Revolution: Children's Employment 7.

30   Raymond Challinor and Brian Ripley, *The Miners' Association* (London: Lawrence & Wishart, 1968), pp. 7-14. A. J. Taylor, 'The Miners' Association of Great Britain and Ireland, 1842-48', *Economica,* February 1955, p. 47.

was based on the Journeymen Steam Engine and Machine Makers Society. What happened in the 1850s and 1860s, then, was 'not the creation of a "New Model", but a strengthening of the old'.[31] It is therefore worth again questioning how novel were the unions such as the Amalgamated Society of Engineers, the Amalgamated Society of Carpenters and Joiners and the Ironfounders Society which had acquired a prominent position in the trade union scene by the sixties?

It is certainly difficult to discover any institutional features or rules in the new unions of this period which were complete innovations. There were unions before 1850 which concentrated their activities on friendly society benefits rather than on strikes; there were others, like the Miners' Association, which endeavoured to centralize funds; and yet others, like the Glasgow Cotton Spinners Association, which favoured resort to arbitration. In one important respect, however, the New Model Unions differed from the large majority of their predecessors: they survived. Whereas most of the earlier unions fell victims of industrial recession or mismanagement, they went on from strength to strength. Long survival extended the experience and negotiating skill of the now 'permanent' general secretaries. It would be hard to find in the 1830s, or even 1840s, such sophisticated policies for controlling forward movements among union branches as were practiced by Robert Applegarth and explained by him to the Royal Commission in 1867. His union, the Amalgamated Society of Carpenters and Joiners, kept detailed statistics of the rates of pay in all parts of the country. The executive kept a firm rein on all expenditure and only sanctioned strikes when the rates of pay of members in the district concerned were noticeably behind the national average.[32] The leaders of the New Model were undoubtedly helped by the comparative prosperity of the fifties and the sixties – though there were financial panics in 1857 and 1866 – the spread of the railway network and the cheapness and speed of the posts after 1840. But they *were* more cautious in respect of strikes than had been the leaders of the earlier generation and for this very reason their financial position, and therefore their chances of survival, greatly improved. Over a period of ten years to 1867 the Amalgamated Society of Engineers, with 33,000 members, spent only 6 per cent of its income on trade disputes; the Ironfounders, with

31   E. J. Hobsbawm, 'The Labour Aristocracy in nineteenth-century Britain, *Labouring Men*, pp. 272-315. Royden Harrison, *Before the Socialists* (London: Routledge and Kegan Paul, 1965), pp. 11-13. Albert Edward Musson, *British Trade Unions 1800-1875* (London: Macmillan, 1972), pp. 49-53. H. A. Clegg, A. Fox and A. F. Thompson, *A History of British Trade Unions since 1889*, p. 7.

32   *First Report, Royal Commission on Trade Unions, 1867-8*, p. 6. 1867 [3873] XXXII, 14. IUP Industrial Relations 8, p. 24.

10,000 members, squandered $2\frac{1}{2}$ per cent of subscription revenue on strikes and the Shipwrights had virtually no strike expenditure at all.[33]

However much the attempt is made to whittle down any difference between the objectives and conduct of the unions of the early Victorian and mid-Victorian years, the fact remains that the leadership of the New Model unions was often prompted by a completely different ideology from that which had motivated many of the leaders of labour in the 1830s and 1840s. In 1856 Mr. William Newton, a leading member of the Amalgamated Society of Engineers, told the Select Committee on Masters and Operatives that the earlier unions had 'more of a political character' than they then had.

When asked,

'Now they are regarded as benefit associations; have they not much more that character than they had?'

He replied:

Yes; as regards the association with which I am connected, we do not allow any political matter to be discussed at all, nor entertained among us.'[34]

J. C. Buckmaster, who had had substantial experience as secretary of a carpenters and joiners union with 4,000 members, told another select committee that, in the early 1840s, 'political feeling was certainly an element in all sorts of unions', but that by 1860 'the feeling was much more healthy'. The men were 'more amenable to reason' than they had been and they looked for 'social progress' rather than 'political change'.[35] It was because Messrs. Newton and Buckmaster noted what was clearly a new trend of opinion amongst working class leaders in the 1850s that more members of the government and more employers began to think in terms of the feasibility of establishing conciliation machinery. The greater moderation in the leaders of the working class was reflected in their serious reading. Whereas the earlier generation had been fed on the strong meat of Thomas Hodgskin's *Labour Defended* (1825) or John Francis Bray's *Labour's Wrongs and Labour's Remedies* (1838-39) their successors

33   *Eleventh and Final Report Royal Commission on Trade Unions, 1867-68* Statement referred to in third dissent, pp. xliv-xlv, 1868-69 [4123] XXXI, 278-79. IUP Industrial Relations 10, pp. 52-53. Richard Clements' citation of D. Guile's opinion on strikes in his 'British Trade Unions and Popular Political Economy', *Economic History Review*, 2nd Ser. vol. XIV No. 1., should be seen in the light of these statistics.

34   *Report from the Select Committee on Masters and Operatives (Equitable Councils of Conciliation), 1856*, p. 138. 1856 (343) XIII, 160. IUP Industrial Relations 7, p. 138.

35   *Report from the Select Committee on Masters and Operatives, 1860*, p. 52. 1860 (307) XXII, 504. IUP Industrial Relations 7.

were content with John Stuart Mill's *Principles of Political Economy,* the first edition of which appeared in 1848. Although Mill declared that he and Harriet were to be classed 'decidedly under the general designation of socialists', it was a form of self-help, co-operative socialism, not national-ization, which was favoured. This matched exactly with the aspirations of many of the trade union leaders.[36]

On the other hand G. D. H. Cole was right to point out the dangers of generalization about the character of the unions in the third quarter of the nineteenth century. Whereas the name 'Amalgamated' generally became attached to that type of union in which the funds were highly centralized and the leadership apolitical and industrially moderate, this was far from being the case with the miners and the textile workers. Thomas Halliday's Amalgamated Association of Miners, founded in 1869, combined the centralization of funds with an aggressive industrial policy such as had generally been associated with the highly decentralized unionism of an earlier period. On the other hand Alexander Macdonald's National Association of Coal, Lime and Ironstone Miners of Great Britain (1863), an organization whose name was shortly afterwards mercifully shortened to National Miners Union, combined a decentralized power structure with a cautious policy in industrial bargaining. However, both unions were fully appreciative of the need for political action in the miners' interests and directed this side of the work through their head offices.[37]

There were two main types of overtime working in the nineteenth century. In some of the better paid skilled occupations the workmen had less urgent necessity to work in excess of ten or twelve hours in the day but the conditions of the trade — such as the need to execute orders promptly — and some men's hope of achieving earnings above the average, prompted the continuance of the practice. In the case of the underpaid, unskilled workers on the other hand, hours were long because the competition for work was so great and the remuneration for it so low that a great deal of labour had to be done to earn a very slender livelihood.

William Newton, the engineer, had as one objection to excessive overtime the fact that it destroyed all efforts at the men's self-improvement. His society's branch at Greenwich had had to abandon the attempt to establish a mutual instruction class because the members lacked the free time to attend. But another significant reason for the dislike with which overtime was regarded was its repercussions on union funds. If some

36   John Stuart Mill, *Principles of Political Economy* (London: Pelican Classics, 1970), Introduction by Donald Winch, p. 37.

37   G. D. H. Cole, 'British Trade Unions in the third quarter of the nineteenth century', in *Essays in Economic History,* vol. III, Eleanora M. Carus-Wilson (ed.) (London: Edward Arnold, 1962), pp. 202-219.

members 'hogged' the available work others were more likely to be in receipt of the union's donation (out of work) benefit. Those who were out of work would be tempted to accept offers of work from the employers at less than agreed rates and the whole basis of wage bargaining would be undermined. It was also a matter of self-respect. The author of a prize essay on 'The Evils of Systematic Overtime Working' published by the Journeymen Steam Engine Makers Society (the forerunner of the ASE) in 1846, hit the nail on the head when he wrote that 'men are slaves when they receive no equivalent for their labour, and no equivalent can compensate the ruin of health or the destruction of the moral and intellectual powers for want of application.'[38]

The self-esteem of the workman was also at the back of the unions' objection to piecework. The foremost nineteenth century authority on the subject, who was not a working man, noted that 'piecework unquestionably leads, in many cases to scamping'. Any man who kept some pride in his work might object to piecework for this reason. The theory of a limited 'lump of labour' led to the belief that if a man on piecework strove too hard he would 'do a brother out of work'. George Howell, the bricklayers union leader, had strong trade objections to piecework. He was convinced that the scamping of work and the undue amount of competition which it engendered ultimately had the effect of breaking down wages.[39]

The employers' attitude to overtime working and piecework was often the obverse of that of the wage earners'. The practice of overtime, especially if it was not paid at enhanced rates, ensured a more flexible labour supply. In times of brisk trade it would increase aggregate profits as more orders could be fulfilled. It might indirectly generate a pool of reserve labour which would weaken the bargaining strength of the trade unions. In 1851 the engineering employers in London and Manchester quite rightly saw the decision to ban overtime, made by the recently formed Amalgamated Society of Engineers, as a serious undermining of the employers' control of the labour market. They quickly formed the Central Association of Employers of Operative Engineers and locked out the men in an attempt to smash the union. Although the men were obliged to return to work without any promise of a change in the practice regarding overtime, the union survived and quickly became stronger than ever.[40] In the case of another major industrial dispute of the 1850s, the

38 John Binns, *The Evils of Systematic Overtime Working* (London: Journeymen Steam Engine Makers Society, 1846).

39 *First Report, Royal Commission on Trades Unions*, p. 64. 1867 [3873] XXXII, 72. IUP Industrial Relations 8, p. 82.

40 James Bavington Jefferys, *The Story of the Engineers* (London: Lawrence and Wishart, 1945).

London building trades lock out of 1859, the conflict arose from the same basic cause – the strong desire to cut down excessive hours of work. But in this case the demand was for a reduction of the regular working day to nine hours. Once more the men had to return to work defeated, the only consolation being that the employers abandoned the attempt to compel signature of the 'Document' as a condition of reinstatement.

It was manifest from the attitude of the large majority of the employers in the industrial disputes of the 1850s and 1860s that they were unprepared to accept a situation of 'collective laissez-faire' even though the government had agreed to tolerate it, at least partially, ever since 1824. From the persistence with which the 'Document' was used in an endeavour to smash trade unionism in the engineering industry in 1852, in the Preston textile industry in 1853-4 and in the London building trade in 1859, it is clear that the masters were determined to maintain individual bargaining as long as possible. The leading employers advanced a variety of reasons for taking the stand they did. Some, like James Nasmyth, the famous engineer, adopted an extreme form of individualism. Any employer wishing to employ an individual workman should be free to do so 'without the intrusion of any third party' since such an intervention would be 'derogatory to the interests of society at large and to trade in particular'. Others, like the well known building contractor, G. F. Trollope, mixed an adherence to the laws of political economy – 'wages if left to themselves would always find their natural level' – with a benevolent paternalism. The objection to trade unions was that they loosened 'the tie between workmen and employer'. As these were characteristic attitudes of members of the employing class it is not surprising that, with the exception of a few trades such as printing, where from time to time unions could exploit a labour shortage, there was little evidence of genuine collective bargaining in the third quarter of the nineteenth century.[41]

5. The development of arbitration and conciliation

Events in the Preston textile industry lock out, which lasted seven months through the autumn and winter of 1853-54, drew public attention to the growing power of the unions and the stubbornness of the employers who repeatedly declined all offers of conciliation and arbitration. Charles Dickens, after visiting Preston in January 1854, declared that the strike

---

41 *First Report, Royal Commission on Trades Unions 1867,* pp. 106-07. 1867 [3873] XXXII 112-13. IUP Industrial Relations 8, pp. 124-25.

was a 'deplorable calamity'. He understood very little of the aspirations
and way of life of the factory workers, and in *Hard Times,* published later
in 1854, drew a picture of an imaginary union leader, Slackbridge, which
Bernard Shaw declared to be completely unlike trade union leaders 'even
at their worst'.[42] But the publicity which his writings and Mrs. Gaskell's
North and South gave to the waste of human and material resources in this
prolonged dispute helped to turn the thoughts of government towards the
encouragement of more peaceful methods of resolving industrial conflict.

That more disputes were not settled peaceably was, in the first half of
the century at least, less frequently the fault of the unions than of the
employers. The party in the weaker bargaining position over wages and
working conditions is generally more willing to resort to arbitration or
conciliation than is the party that feels it is strong enough to come out
victorious in a strike or lock out. Before the 1860s few unions were in a
position to dictate terms to the employers: on the other hand they
considered that they would be gainers rather than losers from arbitration
awards. They therefore often included provisions in their rules that there
should be resort to arbitration before the issue was put to the arbitrament
of a strike. The Boilermakers Society had a rule in 1839 that disputes
should be submitted to arbitration before resorting to strike action. The
110 trade unions delegates attending the inaugural conference of the
Association of United Trades for the Protection of Industry in March 1845
favoured 'the establishment of Local Boards of Trade ... composed of
masters and operatives, to whom all matters affecting the regulation of
wages, duration of labour, disputes etc. shall be referred, and their
decisions have the authority of law'.[43]

The employers, on the other hand, were still reluctant to regard unions
as an established part of the industrial scene. It was expected that they
would shortly be suppressed by the use of the Document, or the lock-out,
or by invocation of the law. In 1854 the Preston employers proclaimed
that to accept mediation would be to acknowledge 'a principle most
dangerous and mischievous in its tendency − a principle alike subversive of
the rights of the working man in the disposal of his labour, and the rights
of the master in the employment of his capital'. Hence although there
were isolated instances in the early part of the century of conditions of
employment and rates of payment being jointly agreed, as, for example,

42   George Bernard Shaw, *Introduction to Hard Times* (London: Waverley, 1912)
reprinted in *Hard Times*, George Ford and Sylvere Monod (eds.) (New York: Norton
Critical Editions, 1966), p. 337.

43   Ian Gordon Sharp, *Industrial Conciliation and Arbitration in Great Britain*
(London: Allen & Unwin, 1950), p. 2. *Northern Star,* 29 March 1845.

the list of prices for piecework in the silk trade jointly negotiated at Hawick in 1833, these were completely unrepresentative of the time.[44]

In the light of the continuing reluctance of the large majority of the employers to recognize trade unions as appropriate bodies with which to discuss the conditions of employment, it is not surprising that the report of the Select Committee on Masters and Operatives (Equitable Councils of Conciliation) 1856, contained few revolutionary proposals. It had been appointed to examine the expediency of establishing 'equitable tribunals' for settling industrial disputes and to discover how far the existing law needed amendment. Since the beginning of the eighteenth century there had been statutory provision for the settlement of disputes between masters and workmen in particular trades. The 'Act to Consolidate and Amend the Laws relating to the Arbitration of disputes between Masters and Workmen, 1824' (5 Geo. IV c. 96) made general the arrangements which had hitherto been specific for particular industries. Whenever there was a dispute between master and workmen on the interpretation of a contract, the payment of wages, etc., the matter could be brought before the local magistrate as arbitrator. The select committee found that the act was utilized very seldom. The principal reason why the workmen largely ignored it was that they were reluctant to appear before a justice of the peace since, however straightforward a man's intentions, 'there was some disgrace about it'. But there was also the fear that any trade unionist who brought a complaint before a magistrate would soon be victimized by his employer.[45]

The committee made no reference to the biggest defect of all previous legislation: the limitation of arbitration to disputes about work which had been *completed* and for which wages were due, or differences about the interpretation of contracts (verbal or written) previously agreed. No provision was made for arbitration of disputes concerning proposed *future* rates of pay or hours of work. These were questions which were considered to be within the exclusive jurisdiction of the employer who

44   Victor Leonard Allen, 'The Origins of Industrial Conciliation and Arbitration', *International Review of Social History*, vol. IX pt. 2. (Amsterdam: 1964), p. 242. I. G. Sharp, *Industrial Conciliation and Arbitration*, p. 1. E. Humphries, a member of the committee of the National Association of United Trades, declared that 'most trade societies made it an invariable rule when a dispute occurs to have it settled by arbitration'. *First Report, Select Committee on Masters and Operatives (Equitable Councils of Conciliation), 1856,* p. 47. 1856 (343) XIII, 69. IUP Industrial Relations 7, p. 69.

45   George Howell, *Labour Legislation, Labour Movements and Labour Leaders,* 2nd Edn. vol. II (London: Fisher Unwin, 1905), pp. 434-36. Evidence of Thomas Winters, *First Report, Select Committee on Masters and Operatives (Equitable Councils of Conciliation), 1856,* p. 10. 1856 (343) XIII, 32. IUP Indusrial Relations 7.

ought to be master in his own house. The committee were warned, by Mr. Sidney Smith, one of the spokesmen for the employers, of the dangers of establishing voluntary Boards of Conciliation with powers of enforcement concerning future contracts. Where a dispute arose within a particular firm and resort was made to a board of conciliation, the settlement would be binding on that firm alone and might be of a character to place it at a disadvantage in relation to its competitors who would remain exempt from control.[46] In its report, the committee recommended the setting up of courts of conciliation particularly in the large commercial, manufacturing and mining districts, with elected representatives of both employers and workmen. But their terms of reference were to be strictly limited to the interpretation of *existing* contracts and it was entirely up to the parties in dispute whether they chose to make use of the conciliation machinery. The reluctance of the majority of the employers to accept even this small degree of limitation on their powers was reflected in the fate of Bills, based on the recommendations of the select committee, which were introduced in parliament in the late 1850s but failed to pass.

The Select Committee on Masters and Operatives, 1860, which considered one of the proposed bills, endeavoured in its report to allay the fears of the more conservative employers. It assured parliament that there was 'nothing in the Bill that gives power to any Council to regulate the rate of wages in any prospective manner whatever'.[47]

By the middle 1860s, in a number of trades, the strength of the employers and the unions was more evenly matched and the prospects for industrial conciliation improved. Although every attempt was made by means of legislation, as in 1867 and 1872, to promote settlement of disputes by peaceful means, the movement was largely a voluntary and spontaneous one. Neither employers nor workmen were to be coerced into settling their differences peaceably. The psychological moment for the introduction of conciliation machinery came 'when the unions had sufficient strength to convince the employers that conciliation and arbitration were necessary, but insufficient power to make an openly militant policy more attractive for themselves'.[48]

In hosiery this stage was reached in the course of 1860. In this year of booming trade, different groups of the workers came out on strike on no

46   Evidence of Mr. Sidney Smith, *First Report, Select Committee on Masters and Operatives (Equitable Councils of Conciliation), 1856*, p. 116. 1856 (343) XIII, 138. IUP Industrial Relations 7.

47   *Report from the Select Committee on Masters and Operatives, 1860*, p. iii. 1860 (307) XXII, 445. IUP Industrial Relations 7.

48   J. H. Porter, 'Wage Bargaining under Conciliation Agreements, 1860-1914', *Economic History Review*, 2nd Ser. vol. XXIII, No. 3. December 1970, p. 461.

less than four separate occasions in an attempt to secure a greater share of the industry's prosperity. The masters were greatly inconvenienced as important American orders could not be met on time. Here was the opportunity for A. J. Mundella, who employed more than a thousand persons in all branches of the industry, to persuade his fellow employers to set up a standing committee for regulating relations between employers and workers in the Nottingham hosiery trade. It included ten representatives of the workers, was backed by the trade unions and brought ten years of industrial peace. Although Mundella claimed that he had been much influenced by the experience of the Conseils de Prud'hommes, established in France from 1806 onwards, neither his scheme for the hosiery trade nor that of Sir Rupert Kettle for the Wolverhampton building trades, initiated in 1864, bore more than a slight resemblance, at least in practical details, to the French example.[49]

Mundella's advocacy, and the success of the experiments in Nottingham and Wolverhampton, paved the way for the 'arbitration craze' of the years 1867-75 during which a large number of boards were set up, on a regional basis, in the five major industries of hosiery and lace making, boot and shoe manufacture, cotton spinning, iron founding and coal mining. At this stage in the development of industrial relations, arbitration was resorted to rather than conciliation, since, after long years of fierce antagonism, labour and capital found compromise solutions difficult to reach and it was easier to throw the burden of responsibility for the settlement of a dispute on to the shoulders of the lawyers, politicians or businessmen who acted as arbitrators.[50]

When asked to explain his success in bringing industrial peace to the hosiery trade Mundella declared 'We could have done nothing without the organization of the union'. He found the participation of the union leaders on the standing committee doubly advantageous. In the first place they could be taught some of the uncomfortable realities of a highly competitive industry:

'We produce on the table the articles made in France and Germany, and the men are convinced by their own senses of the justice of what we say . . . Their system had been a complete educational process for our men; they know as well as we do whether we can afford an advance or not'.[51]

It was also the case that the rank and file were much more likely to accept

49   John Richard Hicks, 'The Early History of Industrial Conciliation in England', *Economica,* vol. X, 1930 p. 25.

50   J. H. Porter, 'Wage Bargaining Under Conciliation Agreements', p. 462.

51   *Tenth Report, Royal Commission on Trade Unions, 1868,* p. 75. 1867-68 [3980-VI] XXXIX 525. IUP Industrial Relations 9, p. 537.

a disappointing award if it came with the recommendation of their own leaders than they were if it was announced directly by the employers.

No doubt those masters who followed Mundella's example in establishing a more permanent negotiating machinery were persuaded that it would be a means of teaching working men the immutable laws of political economy. As Sir Rupert Kettle expressed it at the time: 'An arbiter would be able to keep before the disputants those great fundamental rules of commercial economy by which service contracts are governed.' Wildcat strikes were then less likely.[52]

There can be no denying the interest which the leaders of the New Model unions had in the extension of arbitration and conciliation. As hostile witnesses before the Royal Commission on Trade Unions in 1867 were at pains to point out, their unions were both friendly societies providing 'social security' benefits *and* trade societies whose purpose was to negotiate better working conditions for their members. If strikes were avoided the 'industrial' expenses of the unions would be correspondingly reduced whilst the provident funds would be in a healthier state. This is one reason why the two trade union moderates, George Odger and George Howell, helped Lord St. Leonards to frame his Conciliation Bill (enacted as 30 and 31 Vict., c. 105) in 1867 and why five years later, the parliamentary committee of the TUC employed Mr. R. S. Wright to draft the Arbitration Bill which, after amendment, became law as the Arbitration Act, 1872 (35 and 36 Vict., c. 46).[53]

As the nineteenth century drew to a close, rank and file trade unionists became increasingly disillusioned with the process of arbitration. In the great depression of 1873-96 both prices and profit margins fell and it followed that most of the awards made by arbitrators involved reductions in the money rate of wages. Of sixty-one decisions reached in five main industries in these years only nine brought improvement in wage rates. There were complaints from the workmen that when arbitration awards were being determined too much emphasis was given to commodity selling prices and too little to increased productivity. Profit trends were not considered at all because of the employers' strong objections to their inclusion. Most of all there was discontent at the sliding scale agreements whereby wage rates were automatically adjusted to the selling price of products. They were established in the iron trade of the North East from as early as 1869 and in the coal mining industry of South Wales from 1875. It is true that these could be seen as a natural stage of development after arbitration awards in which the prime consideration in determining

52   Rupert Kettle, *Strikes and Arbitrations* (Wolverhampton: Simpkin, 1866), p. 6.
53   George Howell, *Labour Legislation, Labour Movements and Labour Leaders*, vol. II pp. 437-38.

wage levels had been commodity prices, and that less resentment was felt against them in the iron industry than in coal mining. But they were unpopular because for the greater part of their years of operation they involved downward adjustments in money wages.[54]

It has been maintained that the sliding scale system debilitated trade unionism; for if wages were fixed by an automatically operating scale the trade union seemed to be largely superfluous. Where the men's leaders took the view that 'prices should rule wages' they tended to lose sight of the more important objective of achieving a decent minimum wage. In coal mining where prices and hence wage packets were subject to violent fluctuations, it was difficult for lodge treasurers to collect the regular weekly union subscriptions. According to one authority, the introduction of the sliding scale on the South Wales coalfield 'caused trade unionism to die for the best part of two decades'.[55]

The discontent of many of the younger generation of trade unionists, with the whole compromising system of arbitration awards and sliding scale agreements, found expression through the growth of unofficial strikes and the upsurge of the 'New Unionism' in the late 1880s and early 1890s. The total number of strikes (official and unofficial) averaged only 278 a year between 1872-80 but rose to 509 in 1888 and 1,145 in 1889. One consequence of the best known of these disputes, the London dock strike of August-September 1889, was a renewed campaign for conciliation, rather than arbitration, as a method of achieving industrial peace. Within three months of the success of Cardinal Manning and Sydney Buxton as mediators in ending the dock strike, the council of the London Chamber of Commerce appointed a Conciliation Committee for the trades of the London area. A few months later the government set up the Royal Commission on Labour with, among its many responsibilities, the task of examining the respective merits of conciliation and arbitration.[56]

The industrial reformers of the day were certainly not shy in suggesting to the commission how the 'labour problem' might be resolved. Among the many proposals advanced were the establishment of state-sponsored boards of arbitration; the creation of a consultative committee comprising an equal number of 'labour' MPs and employers; the setting up of conciliation boards by town councils; the appointment of two judges to settle all disputes and the creation of a board of arbitration 'so influential,

54   J. H. Porter, 'Wage Bargaining under Conciliation Agreements', p. 465.

55   V. L. Allen, 'The Origins of Industrial Conciliation and Arbitration', *International Review of Social History,* vol. IX Pt. II, p. 253. S. and B. Webb, *History of Trade Unionism,* pp. 323-24.

56   I. G. Sharp, *Industrial Conciliation and Arbitration in Great Britain,* p. 290. George Howell, *The Conflicts of Capital and Labour Historically and Economically Considered,* 2nd Rev. Edn. (London: Macmillan, 1890), p. 439.

so authoritative and so dignified that no body of employers or workmen would dare not to submit their case to it'. But although the commission reported in favour of 'some more rational and less barbarous method of settling industrial disputes rather than strikes and lock-outs', it turned down all proposals for the compulsory reference of disputes to state or other boards of arbitration. It felt that 'less faith should be put in legal sanction in these matters so that more might thereby by expected from the moral sanction'. The government of the day followed this advice. It abandoned any attempts such as had been made in the Arbitration Act of 1872, to devise 'a universally applicable means of settling disputes with a legal sanction'. Instead, by the Conciliation Act 1896 (59 and 60 Vict. c. 30) it repealed all former Acts concerning conciliation and arbitration, including those of 1824, 1867 and 1872, and in their place gave the President of the Board of Trade the power to intervene where an industrial dispute existed or seemed likely to occur. He could search out the causes of the dispute, take steps to bring the parties together, appoint a conciliator if requested to do so by either side, or appoint an arbitrator if both sides agreed to him doing so. Regional or national conciliation boards were invited to register with the Labour Department of the Board of Trade.[57]

British industry's adherence to the policy of voluntaryism is reflected in the aftermath of the Act. There was no rush of conciliation boards to register. A negligible number – only 19 out of a possible 325 – had notified the Labour Department of their existence by 1913.

Industrial conciliation and arbitration in nineteenth century Britain touched but a substantial fringe of the problem of labour conflict in a rapidly industrializing nation. Whole sectors of the economy including engineering, shipbuilding and agriculture were largely unaffected by the movement, and the Lord James arbitration award for the employees of the North Eastern Railway in 1896 was the only example of its kind on British railways before 1907.

Until the 1860s the employers were disinclined to resort to compromise in their dealings with labour. They were still reluctant to recognize that trade unions had a justifiable role in society. The hey-day of arbitrations was in the 1870s and 1880 when the forces of labour and capital were more evenly matched. Thereafter the leaders of the new Unionism tended to eschew the path of compromise pursued by the older generation of trade union leaders. Legislation throughout tended to take second place in importance to the development of voluntary agreements. In any case,

---

57   H. A. Clegg, A. Fox and A. F. Thompson, *A History of British Trade Unions since 1889,* pp. 177, 263. I. G. Sharp, *Industrial Conciliation and Arbitration in Great Britain,* pp. 290-92.

every act before 1872 had the great defect that it concerned the interpretation of existing contracts and made no attempt to cover disputes concerning the formulation of new ones. It required the impact of two world wars to bring about a much greater participation by government in the settlement of industrial disputes.

6. The Royal Commission and the labour laws

The ten years 1866-75 marked a watershed in the history of industrial relations in Britain. At the beginning of this decade membership of trade unions was increasing rapidly and the leading organizations possessed a stability and financial strength which was unprecedented. In 1866 the eighteen largest societies had over 200,000 members and there were possibly 300,000 others enrolled in the smaller organizations. The *General Trades Union Directory,* published in 1861, made it clear that the movement was nationwide in extent: it listed names and addresses of secretaries of unions in no less than 408 towns and cities in the United Kingdom.[58] Although union leaders felt a strong resentment about the unjust operation of the master and servant laws they had growing confidence that their legal position in other respects was becoming more secure. It was widely believed that the funds of unions registered under the Friendly Societies Act, 1855, were protected against embezzlement. Section one of the Molestation of Workmen Act, 1859 (22 Vict. c. 34) had ruled that 'no workman or other person, whether actually in employment or not, shall . . . by reason merely of his endeavouring peaceably, and in a reasonable manner, and without threat or intimidation, direct or indirect, to persuade others to cease or abstain from work . . . be deemed or taken to be guilty of "molestation" or "obstruction" . . . and shall not therefore be subject or liable to any prosecution or indictment for conspiracy'. If this did not make clear that peaceful picketing was legalized then words had no meaning.

Some of the leading employers were either like A. J. Mundella and Samuel Morley in the hosiery trade, accepting trade unions as negotiating bodies, or like Thomas Brassey, the railway contractor, appreciating the economy of high wages.

The growing industrial strength of labour in the early 1860s was matched by a political awakening which was in marked contrast with the relative quiescence of the 1850s. When the Italian hero Garibaldi arrived at Nine Elms station, London, in April 1864 a crowd of 50,000 persons lined

58   John Malcolm Forbes Ludlow and Lloyd Jones, *The Progress of the Working Classes 1832-67* (London: Strahan, 1867), p. 205.

the streets to greet him.[59] In the meantime huge meetings of trade unionists had pledged support for the Union cause in the American Civil War, and persuaded working class newspapers like the *Beehive* and the *Glasgow Sentinel* that, in supporting the Confederacy, they were out of touch with the views of a large body of their readers.[60] Most significant was the revival of the demand for the extension of the franchise to the working classes. In 1861-62 Messrs. Howell and Odger failed to persuade the London Trades Council to abandon its opposition to the discussion of political issues. But in 1866 the Council committed itself enthusiastically in support of the Liberal government's Reform Bill. The story of the huge reform demonstration of 23 July 1866, when large numbers of police, reinforced by Foot Guards, failed to keep the demonstrators out of London's Hyde Park is a well known episode of British labour history.

To many MPs and to the majority of the employers the growth of trade union membership and the demand for the franchise were seen as a double threat to the established order. Robert Lowe voiced their fears when he spoke in the House of Commons in the debate on Mr. Baines' motion for reform:

'I shall not refer to the subject of strikes, but it is, I contend, impossible to believe that the same machinery which is at present brought into play in connection with strikes, would not be applied by the working classes for political purposes. Once give the men votes and the machinery is ready to launch those votes in one compact mass upon the institutions and property of the country.'[61]

Had it not been for contemporary fears about the growing political influence of labour it is more than possible that the renewed manifestations of rattening and acts of violence in the Sheffield cutlery and tool trades in 1866 would have received only passing notice in the national press, as earlier incidents had done in 1854, 1857, 1859 and 1861. But coming as they did during the height of controversy over reform, it was inevitable that not only the small unions in Sheffield, but trade unionism in general, should be subjected to vituperative attacks in the press. What had come into question was 'the survival of trade unions as such'.[62]

Before the enquiry into the Sheffield outrages and the Royal Commission hearings on the trade union had begun, the financial security and legal standing of the unions were thoroughly undermined through the

---

59   Julius Jacobs, *The London Trades Council, 1860-1950: a History* (London: Lawrence and Wishart, 1950), p. 32.

60   R. Harrison, *Before the Socialists*, pp. 69-77.

61   *Hansard,* 3 Ser. vol. CLXXXII, Cols. 2100-2102, 26 April 1866.

62   Sidney Pollard, Introduction to *The Sheffield Outrages* (Bath: Adams and Dart, 1967), p. vi.

judgement given on 16 January 1867 in the case of *Hornby vs. Close* in the Court of Queen's Bench. The defendant, Close, fully admitted wrongfully withholding £24. 18s. 5½d from the United Order of Boilermakers and Iron Shipbuilders. But the unanimous verdict of the four judges was that the union could not recover the money because 'the purposes of a trade union were not analogous to the purposes generally included in a friendly society'. Trade unions, whose rules were 'in restraint of trade' were illegal under the common law. The assumption that they acquired a legal personality by registering under the Friendly Societies Act, 1855 was wholly invalid.[63] The judgement amounted to an open invitation to branch treasurers and others to abscond with union funds. At the same time as trade unionists in Sheffield and to a lesser extent, Manchester, were being denounced for practicing rattening in order to secure adherence to union rules, one of the highest courts in the realm had given a decision which amounted to the open encouragement of theft of union property.

Within six months of this first body blow came a second, equally serious to the union's position. In the case *Reg. vs. Druitt* the Central Criminal Court found three working tailors guilty of criminal conspiracy for picketing the workshops of master tailors in the West End of London. It had been assumed that peaceful picketing had been made legal under the Molestation of Workmen Act, 1859. Baron Bramwell, in summing up, gave a completely different interpretation of the law:

> 'Even if the jury should be of the opinion that the picket did nothing more than his duty . . . still, if that was calculated as to have a deterring effect on the minds of ordinary persons, by exposing them to have their motions watched, and to encounter black looks, that would not be permitted by the law of the land . . . If the jury were satisfied that this system, though not carried beyond watching and observation, was still a serious molestation and obstruction as to have an effect on the minds of the workpeople, then they ought to find the three men guilty.'[64]

In the meantime the disabilities which workmen suffered under the master and servant laws were aggravated in the course of the early 1860s. The law was unequal in its severity as between masters and men in that a breach of contract by the workman rendered him liable to criminal prosecution and imprisonment, whereas a similar offence committed by the employer was subject to a civil action for damages and was punishable by fine only. It was not merely the difference in punishment which offended the self-respecting working man but also the contrast in the way

63   Edward William Cox, *Criminal Law Cases,* vol. X, Pt. VI (London: 1864-67), pp. 393-401.

64   E. W. Cox, *Criminal Law Cases,* vol. X, p. 592.

he was treated when brought to trial. As George Newton, the engineer saw it:

'The process . . . by which the one is brought before the court is very different indeed to that by which the other is brought before the court; while the servant may be dragged as a criminal to the bar, and not infrequently is dragged there in that way; while he may be taken there manacled, the employer is taken into court as a gentleman; he is simply summoned there and treated with the respect that is due to mankind generally.'[65]

The abuse was not a minor one. Between 1858-75 an average of 10,000 prosecutions of workmen for breach of contract took place each year in England and Wales alone. The irony of the situation was that the campaign for the reform of the laws, launched in 1863 by Alexander Campbell, the leader of the Glasgow building trade workers, through the *Glasgow Sentinel* and the Trades Council of the city, and taken up enthusiastically in Sheffield, London and elsewhere, had the immediate effect of aggravating the evil it sought to eradicate. This was particularly the case in the building trade where the management of the labour force presented much greater problems than in most other industries because of frequent changes in the location of work. The labour force, particularly the large unskilled element, lacked local roots. Where a man had no permanent address, successful prosecution for breach of contract proved much more difficult. In the aftermath of the London building dispute of 1859 the master builders nationally endeavoured to lengthen the contracts of employment as a counterweight to union influence. The effect of the campaign to reform the master and servant laws was to draw the attention of many employers for the first time to the opportunities provided by the existing law for the disciplining of the labour force. Mr. A. Mault, a spokesman of the General Builders Association, which included many master builders from Birmingham and the north, was questioned about this by the Select Committee in 1866:

'I presume that there are not many prosecutions under the Act? Latterly a great many more cases have occurred than ever before.

Why is that? Because we have introduced longer contracts and because we have paid more attention to the subject. There has been, till recently, the greatest ignorance prevailing among builders as to the provisions of the law; they had no idea, or if they had any idea they never acted upon it, that a man could be followed who had broken through a contract even on a matter of piecework, much less on a matter of time.'

65   *Report, Select Committee on Contracts of Service between Master and Servant, 1866,* p. 1. 1866 (499) XIII, 11. IUP Industrial Relations 18, p. 47.

Mr. C. Williams, the general secretary of the National Association of Operative Plasterers, confirmed that prosecutions were on the increase and gave the same explanation. He said that 'employers were not aware how far they could stretch the Act till the agitation came on'.[66]

It is important to see the controversy over the reform of the master and servant laws, not as a separate issue, but as part of the larger question as to whether trade unions should be accorded a recognized role in industry and society. The increase in prosecutions under the master and servant laws in the mid 1860s was part and parcel of the campaign to curb the rising power of the unions. It was a recognized tactic of the employers, particularly in dealing with smaller strikes, to cause all the strikers to be arrested for breach of contract and then to confront them with the alternatives of returning to work on the employers' terms or suffering up to three months imprisonment. Furthermore, as the law stood, a troublemaker might be silenced not just once, but repeatedly. When a man left prison after serving his sentence under the master and servant laws he could be summoned and imprisoned again if he failed to complete the original contract.[67]

In view of the convergence of these many challenges to organized labour, the care that the trade union leaders gave to the presentation of their case to the Royal Commission in 1867 may well be appreciated. If trade unions were to achieve any legal standing at all they needed to destroy the image, built up in the press, of trade unionists as malevolent intriguers only too willing to resort to violence to achieve their nefarious ends.

The unions could not have had a more telling first witness to appear before the commission than Robert Applegarth, the general secretary of the Amalgamated Society of Carpenters and Joiners. A man of great integrity, quiet and inoffensive self-assurance and considerable astuteness, he convinced his questioners that his union was of a completely different genre from the Sheffield Sawgrinders Union whose members were being accused of rattening and more serious acts of violence.[68] He emphasized the stability his union brought to industrial relations through the national spread of the branches and financial strength of the central organization. As ratepayers, the otherwise hostile members of the commission must have

66   Daphne Simon, 'Master and Servant', *Deomocracy and the Labour Movement* (ed. John Saville) (London: Lawrence & Wishart, 1954), p. 160. *Report, Select Committee on Contracts of Service between Master and Servant, 1866*, pp. 124, 48. 1866 (449) XIII 134, 58. IUP Industrial Relations 18, pp. 170, 94.

67   Evidence of W. P. Roberts, 'the miners' advocate', *Report, Select Committee on the Contracts of Service between Master and Servant, 1866*, p. 103. 1866 (449) XIII, 113. IUP Industrial Relations 18, p. 149.

68   Asa Briggs, *Victorian People* (London: Penguin Books, 1965), pp. 176-204.

been impressed by the eight shillings a week retirement pension paid to long serving members of the union, thus relieving the poor law of expense for the care of the elderly. (The carpenters' and joiners' pension was three shillings a week more than the amount paid by the state more than forty years later under the first Old Age Pensions Act.) The union also acted as an unofficial labour exchange. Foremen from all parts of the country made application to branch secretaries for spare men, knowing that they would be 'good workmen and of good moral character'.

A succession of witnesses of like calibre reinforced the impression of cautious, responsible, leadership. William Allan of the Engineers, Daniel Guile of the Ironfounders and Edwin Coulson and George Howell of the Operative Bricklayers, though defending strikes as a regrettable last resort and not denying that their organizations were first and foremost trade societies, were conciliatory in approach and expressed a strong preference for settling with, rather than battling against, the employers. There was nothing impetuous in the Operative Stonemason's rule, explained by Richard Harnott, their general secretary, that permission to conduct strikes had to be obtained not only of the general committee, but also of each branch, before the men were allowed to withdraw their labour.

It was due to the evidence of such witnesses and the support that they received from three of its members, Frederick Harrison, Thomas Hughes and the Earl of Lichfield, that the commission, in its final report, recognized the unequal bargaining strength of the individual workman and the individual employer (section 61) and therefore considered that, provided the combination was voluntary and that the non-unionist's right to work was recognized, men should be given the full legal right to combine in unions (section 60).

In the meantime the hearings of the separate three-man commission which met in the Council Hall in Sheffield did less damage to the cause of trade unionism than was at first feared. The anti-unionists, such as Fearnehough, who provided evidence of rattening and the blowing up of houses, were seen to be 'not the most engaging witnesses'. Reading the minutes of evidence no doubt reinforced the main commissioners opposition to picketing and intimidation: it could not controvert the contention of the moderate Junta leaders that violence was confined to the older, smaller, local trade groups and that it found no place in the great national organizations. Even in Sheffield, the very centre of the outrages, four fifths of the unions had never used violent methods.

The Trade Union Act, 1871 (34 and 35 Vict. c. 31) embodied the main Commission's recommendations. The interim protection of funds from embezzlement provided under The Trade Unions (Protection of Funds) Act, 1869 (32 and 33 Vict. c. 61) was made permanent and the unions were given full legal personality and the right to register themselves with the registrar of friendly societies.

However, the concepts of laissez-faire and the right of the employer to have free access to the labour market and of the workman to continue at work during a strike were firmly embedded in the minds of the majority of the commission. Hence their recommendation in respect of picketing to a considerable extent undermined the concessions they had made to the unions in the earlier part of the report. Parliament followed suit. On the same day as the Trade Union Bill was enacted there was passed the Criminal Law Amendment Act 1871 (34 and 35 Vict. c. 32) which made the molesting, obstructing or persistently watching or following of non strikers by pickets a criminal offence. The government had at first brought forward only one bill including the obnoxious clauses concerning picketing with those giving unions legal recognition; but the newly formed parliamentary committee of the TUC, on instructions from the third congress which met in London in March 1871, persuaded the government to split the Bill into two.[69]

The challenge which adverse legal judgements, the summoning of the royal commission and the passage of the Criminal Law Amendment Act presented to the trade unions ultimately resulted in the bringing together of hitherto discordant elements within the movement. Before 1867 the London Junta leaders Applegarth, Guile, Coulson, Odger and Allan had been at loggerheads with George Potter, manager of the *Beehive* newspaper and acknowledged leader of the smaller and generally more militant trade groups. Congresses of trade unions were separately summoned in Glasgow in 1863, London in 1864 and Sheffield in 1866 but none of these was completely representative. In 1867 two rival bodies, the Junta-dominated Conference of Amalgamated Trades and the Potter-dominated St. Martin's Hall Conference Committee, were both claiming to represent the trade union movement before the royal commission and they were lobbying parliament on the same issues on separate occasions. At the end of February 1868, however, the Manchester and Salford Trades Council decided that in May of that year there should be summoned to Manchester a Trades Union Congress whose object would be not to deal with particular single issues, such as the master and servant laws, as the earlier congresses had done, but to form the first of a series of annual congresses to consider all questions of interest to labour. By this time there was more general recognition of the need for trade unionists to close their ranks. Although the Junta still held aloof, the fifty-seven delegates present at Manchester between 2-6 June 1868 (a later date than that originally

69   Fred Marc Leventhal, *Respectable Radical: George Howell and Victorian Working Class Politics* (London: Weidenfeld & Nicolson, 1971), pp. 50-51.

intended) resolved that 'the trades of the United Kingdom should hold an annual congress for the purpose of bringing the trades into closer alliance and to take action in all parliamentary matters pertaining to the general interests of the working classes'. Thus the TUC was born.[70]

The Junta leaders gave only half-hearted support to the Congresses of 1869 and 1870. Their alarm when they finally learned the terms of the government's original trade union bill finally persuaded them to sink all their differences with their London and provincial rivals. Hence the congress which met in Marylebone, London, early in March 1871 was the most representative so far assembled, with delegates from 49 societies representing 289,430 members. By the time the fifth congress of the TUC met in Leeds in January 1873 unity was further strengthened through the indignation aroused over the harsh effects of the Criminal Law Amendment Act.

The severity of the challenge to basic trade union rights was revealed within two months of the passing of the Act. At Aberdare police court on 15 August 1871, six women, the wives of striking colliers, were each sentenced to a week's imprisonment for shouting 'Hurrah' and making a loud noise by banging kettles as John Howells, a strike breaker, left the Navigation Colliery, Mountain Ash. The magistrate gave this sentence despite the fact that Howells was unable positively to identify the accused as they had been separated from him by the lines and waggons of the Great Western Railway.[71]

The case of the London gas stokers (*Reg vs. Bunn and others, 1872*) provided an even sharper reminder of the precarious legal position of trade unionists in the early 1870s. Clause two of the Trade Union Act, 1871 stated:

> 'The purposes of any trade union shall not, by reason merely that they are in restraint of trade, be deemed to be unlawful so as to render any member of such a trade union liable to criminal prosecution for conspiracy or otherwise.'

But J. Brett, the judge involved in the gas stokers case, told the jury that the accused men could be convicted of conspiracy (a criminal offence) if, by withdrawing their labour 'they interfered with the masters by molesting them' and prevented them obtaining the labour they needed. The jury accordingly sentenced the men to a year's imprisonment.[72] It was the

---

70   Albert Edward Musson, *The Congress of 1868* (London: TUC. 1955). Benjamin Charles Roberts, *The Trades Union Congress, 1868-1921* (London: Allen and Unwin, 1958) Chap. 1.

71   *Western Mail,* 15 and 16 August 1871. S. and B. Webb in *The History of Trade Unionism* (1920 Edn.) p. 284, state that the women called out 'Bah', but the newspaper report states that they shouted 'Hurrah'.

72   E. W. Cox, *Reports of Cases in Criminal Law,* vol. XII, 1875 p. 316.

clearest possible reminder, both that the Trade Union Act had not given legal protection for the unions' industrial action and that the master and servant laws, despite their amendment in 1867 to preclude imprisonment as a punishment except in 'aggravated' cases, could still be invoked as an additional reason for imprisoning strike leaders.

The background to the appointment of the Royal Commission on the Labour Laws in 1874 was the failure of the parliamentary committee of the TUC over the years 1872-4 to persuade the Liberal government to make any substantial concessions to the unions. The home secretary, H. A. Brace, was opposed to making any alterations, either to the master and servant laws or to the Criminal Law Amendment Act. In the general election campaign in 1874, rank and file unionists gained more favourable answers from Conservative candidates than they did from Liberal candidates, to the questions on the labour laws which the parliamentary committee of the TUC suggested should be asked of all those standing for election. But after the Conservative victory Disraeli shelved an immediate decision by announcing the appointment of a royal commission. George Howell, the secretary of the parliamentary committee, and Frederick Harrison, the Positivist supporter of the TUC campaign, were suspicious. They believed that the appointment of the royal commission was a concession to the Federation of Employers, a pressure group which was opposed to new legislation. The parliamentary committee therefore refused to co-operate and recommended its members not to serve on the commission. However, just as R. A. Cross, the new home secretary, was despairing of finding any representative of labour to serve, Alexander MacDonald, the miners' leader, accepted the invitation. He was joined by Thomas Hughes, the Christian Socialist and Liberal MP, and thus the case for the trade unions did not go by default.

The report of the commission, published in February 1875, was a great disappointment to the trade union leaders. With the exception of Alexander MacDonald, who signed a minority report, the commissioners favoured a modification of the existing laws rather than their repeal. Although Disraeli and Cross could see that it would be political suicide for the government merely to adopt the very limited recommendations of the commission, the ensuing weeks were to show how much could be achieved by skilful parliamentary lobbying. During the committee stages of the Conspiracy and Protection of Property Bill the Liberals R. Lowe and A. J. Mundella exacted important concessions from the government. Even more changes were made to the working of the Bill after Cross had consulted with Howell.[73]

With the passage of both the Conspiracy and Protection of Property

73   F. M. Leventhal, *Respectable Radical*, pp. 173-5.

Act (38 and 39 Vict. c. 86) and the Employers' and Workmen's Act (38 and 39 Vict. c. 90) in the summer of 1875 the bargaining strength of the trade unions in industrial relations was immeasurably increased. Under the former Act an action by two or more persons in the course of a trade dispute would not be liable to criminal penalties if the same action when committed by a single individual was not criminal. The likelihood of prosecutions for conspiracy was thereby greatly reduced. Although acts of violence and intimidation were still to be penalized, peaceful picketing was legalized, and the obnoxious and dangerously vague words 'molest' and 'obstruct' found no place in the new law. The Employers and Workmen's Act gave effect to the intention Richard Cross had expressed when introducing the Bill in the House of Commons:—

'that in all breaches of contract between master and servant, the whole of the old law, so far as it is coercive, shall be swept away, and that they shall be treated simply by a civil proceeding.'[74]

Henceforward there was to be no imprisonment for breach of an engagement by a workman. The effects of the change in the law on the workman's sense of security to participate in trade union activity and to quit his employment when conditions seemed to him intolerable may be measured by the fact that in 1872, after the Act of 1867 was supposed to have improved the worker's position, 17,100 persons were prosecuted and, of these, 10,400 were given convictions.[75]

While through the years 1871-75 union leaders and cabinet ministers were bargaining over the reform of the labour laws, at the grass roots there was a remarkable growth of trade unionism, particularly in industries hitherto virtually exempt from its influence. In its report for the year 1873 the parliamentary committee of the TUC noted that the advances in membership had been 'unparalleled' particularly 'in those branches of industry which had hitherto been but badly organized'. Although there were particular reasons for the spread of union organization to the agricultural workers, the railwaymen, the teachers — to mention only the outstanding examples — all these groups benefited from the remarkable expansion of economic activity with its accompanying labour scarcity and all took full advantage of the Trade Union Act 1871 which gave the new organizations legal protection. In the case of the railwaymen they were goaded in 1871 into forming a protective association, the Amalgamated Society of Railway Servants, by the excessive hours of work they were called upon to perform during the hectic months of the boom. The formation of the National Union of Elementary Teachers, the forerunner

74 *Hansard*, 3rd Ser. vol. 225 Col. 678 28 June 1875.

75 Kenneth William Wedderburn, *The Worker and the Law* (London: Penguin Books, 1965), p. 49.

of the National Union of Teachers, marched in step with the passage of the Elementary Education Act, 1870. The Revolt in the Field leading to the foundation of the National Agricultural Workers' Union in 1872 was made possible by a remarkable, if temporary, shortage of labour.[76]

The movement was undoubtedly helped by the improvement in communications. The last of the taxes on knowledge, the paper duty, was removed in 1861, and there was a remarkable expansion in the circulation of the daily press and in weekly trade union newspapers. A reporter employed by one of the new publications, *The Graphic* explained what was happening in the countryside at the time of the farm labourers' strike of 1872:

' "Late this morning" says master, looking sour and crabbed.

"Yes, Sir, I had to wait five minutes for ma paper."

"What do you want wi' a paper?" he says.

The fact is they can't bear education, but it's come.'[77]

Hodge would not of course have obtained his paper as easily and as cheaply as he did had it not been for the rapid expansion of railway branch lines in the 1860s.

Indicative also of the growing strength of the labour movement at this time was the success of the nine hours movement, particularly in engineering and the building trades in 1871-72. The earlier attempt made by the London building trades in 1859 to persuade the employers to concede the nine hour day had ended in defeat. This time the gains were more permanent. One reason for the success of the campaigns of the early 1870s was that they were better co-ordinated through trades councils. The London Trades Council was founded in 1860 because it was felt that the experience of the building dispute had shown the need for a more permanent body to dovetail the campaigns of the various trades. At that time the only other trades councils of major importance were those of Glasgow, Sheffield, Liverpool and Edinburgh. By the end of 1867 there were about a dozen, including the important Birmingham Trades Council, founded in 1866. Seven years later this number had been doubled. What was significant was that although trade union membership declined in the depression which followed the boom years of the early 1870s, the trades councils remained to pilot the renewed industrial activity in the boom of 1889-90.[78]

The development of employers' associations more than matched the growing organization of labour in the third quarter of the nineteenth

76   Philip Sidney Bagwell, *The Railwaymen* (London: Allen & Unwin, 1963), Chap. 2. Asher Tropp, *The School Teachers* (London: Heinemann, 1957).

77   *The Graphic*, 23 March 1872, p. 274.

78   S. and B. Webb, *History of Trade Unionism* (1894 Edn.). pp. 225-26.

century. Confronted with the demand for an ending of piecework and overtime, some of the leading masters in the engineering industry in Manchester and London formed the Central Association of Employers of Operative Engineers. The success of the Masters Association of Preston in the prolonged lock out of textile workers in 1853-54 is well known. Later in 1854 the Blackburn Power Loom Weavers Association spoke for most of the masters in this section of the textile industry. Consolidation was carried a stage further in 1866 when the Preston and Blackburn employers formed a United Association to formulate 'one Uniform Standard List as the basis for the rate of wages within the district'.[79] It was a combination among London master builders which locked out the London building trade workers in 1859-60. In 1865 the building employers further consolidated their strength in a General Builders Association, national in scope, with local associations in 75-80 towns. In 1867 the Glasgow Master Brickbuilders Association had as one of its objects 'the establishment of certain rules to be observed by members in the payment of wages to those in their employment'. At the same time the North of England Iron Manufacturers Association helped those of its members whose employees were on strike by levying the remainder who were not directly involved.[80] These are but a few examples of many more that might be cited.

There is less evidence of employers in different trades associating together on a regional basis as the trade unionists did increasingly through trades councils; but they did meet through local chambers of commerce. Also the employers were slower in forming a national federation to match the TUC. The National Federation of Associated Employers of Labour established on 30 April 1873 to resist the union's campaign for the reform of the labour laws, disintegrated after 1875.[81] The Association of Chambers of Commerce of the United Kingdom was formed in 1860 but this body did not as a rule concern itself with industrial relations.

7. The truck system

At the beginning of the nineteenth century the truck system, under which wages were paid in goods, or in any other form than coin of the realm unconditionally given, was a 'mischief of old standing' in Britain. Parliament had long recognized the evil, for there were already eighteen

79   H. A. Clegg, A. Fox and A. F. Thompson, *A History of British Trade Unions since 1889*, p. 28.

80   *First Report, Royal Commission on Trade Unions, 1867*, p. 145. 1867 [3873] XXXII, 155. IUP Industrial Relations 8, p. 163.

81   G. Howell, *Labour Legislation, Labour Movements and Labour Leaders*, (2nd Edn. 1905) vol. II Chap. XXX.

Truck Acts in the statute book, the earliest dating back to 1465. The evidence produced by the select committees on the Truck Acts (1842) and the Railway Labourers (1846) suggests that truck payments were on the increase for the greater part of the first half of the century. The system was prevalent in coal mining, iron founding, nail-making, the hosiery trade, hand-loom weaving, in the manufacture of lace, gloves, hats and locks, in railway building and in lead mining. It was practiced from the fishing industry of the Shetland Islands in the far north of Scotland to the quarrying of Portland Stone in Dorsetshire; but it was most widespread in South Wales (including Monmouthshire), Staffordshire, parts of Lancashire and Derbyshire and in Lanarkshire. It was most oppressive in the handicraft branch of the nail-making industry in the area around Dudley, Staffordshire, where in the 1840s a man needed to work not less than fourteen hours a day five days a week to earn a total of fourteen or fifteen shillings. 'To work like a nailer' was a well known expression in the Black Country. Although the perquisites which have formed a substantial part of the incomes of agricultural labourers have sometimes not been considered as truck, the Select Committee on the Truck Acts in 1842 heard the rector of Clyst St. Lawrence, Devonshire, declare that the payment of truck to agricultural labourers was 'very general' and that compulsory deductions of two shillings a week for cider, as well as one shilling weekly for the rent of a tied cottage, were the rule.[82]

As late as 1871 the Truck Commission found that more than half a million persons were directly, or indirectly, through the bread winner, dependant on the truck system. Thirty years earlier the numbers must have been substantially greater.

The forms taken by the truck system were almost as varied as the industries in which it appeared. Before the passing of the Truck Act in 1831 when the practice was made illegal, payment of wages in kind was very common. It still continued, though less extensively, after legal prohibition. In the textile towns and villages of the West Riding of Yorkshire, more than a decade after the practice had been declared illegal, weavers were being paid part of their wages in worsted cloth. In the village of Windhill, near Bradford, only three out of twenty cloth manufacturers paid their workers entirely in cash. Sometimes Bradford weavers were paid in what was locally called 'jot', a term for a variety of groceries including coffee, meal and flour. As late as 1870 a pawnbroker in the town of Prescott, Lancashire, had 800 watches pledged at his shop because 500 of the employees in the local watchmaking industry were paid partly in the

---

82 *Report from the Select Committee on the Payment of Wages, 1842,* p. 133. 1842 (471) IX, 137. IUP Industrial Relations 4, p. 137. George Woodman Hilton, *The Truck System* (Cambridge: Heffer & Sons, 1960) p. 17.

surplus stocks of the local manufacturers. In the calico industry of Burnley surplus stocks of milk, and in the worsted industry near Bradford loads of potatoes, liberally mixed with dirt, were fobbed off in part payment of wages.[83]

Nevertheless the most common form of truck found after 1836 was the obligation, strongly implied, if not formalized and included in a contract, to trade at the company store. If the manufacturer did not himself own the store it would be run by a relative or leased to an associate. Since the 1831 Act had prohibited the issuance of tickets (except in railway building, where there was no prohibition of truck) most workers subject to the truck system were paid in coin of the realm. But there was still no freedom of choice. The extent of change was revealed in the cynical comment of a collier: 'Since then (i.e. 1831) we have had the pleasure of hugging our money about forty yards to the shop, and there paying for such goods as they thought fit to give us.' Any wage earner who tried to escape with his money to spend it in an unattached shop was known as a 'sloper' and as such, was a marked man, liable to discharge from the works, if not immediately, then as soon as trade slackened. At Carnbrae in Scotland, double crosses were marked in the books of a company store against the name of the man who 'sloped' twice. If the company store sold goods at the same prices as charged in the other shops of the neighbourhood then its existence might have been regarded as a convenience rather than as an imposition on the wage earners who were under strong pressure to patronize it. However, the comment of the Truck Commission in 1871 that 'the company's shop constantly, though not universally, sells dearer than the surrounding shops' was undoubtedly true.[84]

The truck system tended to spread in times of trade depression and to diminish in importance in more prosperous years. When orders for the products of the factory or mine were short, the screw was put on the workers to trade at the tommy shop, enabling the employer to make up low industrial profits, or even losses, with greater profits on retail trade. When industrial production was at a low level it was often easier to obtain extended credit on the trade of a retail store supplying the people's basic

---

83 *Report from the Select Committee on the Payment of Wages, 1842*, pp. 10, 26. 1842 (471) IX, 138, 154. IUP Industrial Relations 4, pp. 20, 26. *Report from the Select Committee on Payment of Wages Bill and Payment of Wages (Hosiery) Bill, 1854*, p. 21. 1854 (382) XVI, 33. IUP Industrial Relations 5, p. 45. *Report of the Royal Commission on the Truck System, 1871,* p. xxxv. 1871 [C 326] XXXVI, 35. IUP Industrial Relations 11; p. 47. *Report from the Select Committee on the Payment of Wages, 1842*, pp. 153, 74. 1842 (471) IX, 281, 202. IUP Industrial Relations 4, pp. 153, 74.

84 *Report from the Royal Commission on the Truck System*, 1871, p. 165. 1871 [C 326] XXXVI, 447. IUP Industrial Relations 11, p. 459.

necessities than it was on a factory or mine. Browbeating employees into trading at the tommy shop was, in effect, an alternative to wage cutting. H. S. Tremenheere's estimate that a truck shop gave a colliery owner a cost advantage of at least seven per cent was a conservative one and supports the statement, made by the economist Alfred Marshall, that 'the truck system was a device for employers getting back by underhand ways part of the wages they normally paid away'. On the other hand, when times were prosperous and jobs more abundant the self-respecting workman would feel more free to defy the truck-paying employer. William Jennings, a master manufacturer from the Bradford district, summed up the situation succinctly when he said: 'I know what will cure the truck system — a good trade'.[85]

Generally speaking it was the masters who operated on a small scale who depended upon the tommy shop to lower effective wage rates, secure bank advances and supplement the profits of the workshop or pit with the profits of retail trade. Often these were men who clung to handicraft methods of manufacture when these were being superceded by machine production. The outstanding example was the petty fogger or middleman in the domestic nail-making industry. Machine-made nails sold at but two thirds of the price of the hand made variety, and whereas a hammer nailer might produce a thousand nails in the course of fourteen hours labour a machine would turn out many times that amount in the same space of time. The tommy shop depressed the already meagre wages of the nailer to even lower depths, but it was the salvation of the factor who kept it. But there were big firms which clung to the truck system. Among them was the Cambrian Iron and Spelter Works whose managers made the excuse that there was no independent shop within two miles of the works and that therefore the company store was a boon to the workmen.[86]

Long pays, i.e. long intervals between pay days, served to perpetuate the truck system. The labour force for building the railways was made up, in part, by itinerant labourers who often arrived at the scene of the excavations virtually penniless. Since wages were often paid only fortnightly, or even monthly, these men were obliged to obtain advances at the tommy shop or public house where payments were made. Not suprisingly many of them remained permanently in the debt of their employer.[87] The Truck Commission in 1871 confirmed that the system

85   G. W. Hilton, *The Truck System*, p. 40. *Report from the Select Committee on the Payment of Wages, 1842*, p. 26. 1842 (471) IX, 154, IUP Industrial Relations 4, p. 30.

86   *Report from the Select Committee on the Payment of Wages, 1842*, p. 146. 1842 (471) IX, 274. IUP Industrial Relations 4, p. 150.

87   *Report from the Select Committee on Railway Labourers, 1846*, p. v. 1846 (530) XIII, 428. IUP Industrial Relations 4, p. 534.

began 'at the point where the workman, unable to support himself till pay day by the help of his draw alone, finds it necessary to obtain a further or intermediate advance between the draws'. In parts of the textile industry workers believed that there were advantages in being in the 'ribs' of the master, i.e. in his debt, since in times of slack trade he would keep them in employment. The record for length of pays in the 1840s must surely have gone to the men who quarried stone at Fortuneswell on the Island of Portland. Here the men worked in 'companies' of five to eight persons and were never paid more frequently than once in six months. Delays of between two and three years were not unknown. The excuse given was that a great deal of time-consuming preparatory work had to be done before the valuable stone could be extracted and it was not always known until the end of the operation what the total market value of the saleable product would be. Although long pays certainly helped to keep men in bondage they were not the only cause of impoverishment under the truck system. In the case of the nail-makers and chain-makers, for example, the uncompetitiveness of the hand-made with the machine-made product was the prime cause of pauperization.[88]

As the select committee revealed in 1854-55, the truck system in the midlands hosiery industry had very distinctive features. There were frequently no less than four types of deduction which the middleman made when he settled accounts with the framework knitter. The most important was the rent for the hire of the frames. But he also charged for winding the yarn, for his trouble in bringing to the workman the materials to be manufactured, and, where the stockinger worked away from home, a rent for the use of the workplace. The workman rarely made complaints about the last three of these deductions; his big grievance was that he was overcharged for the use of the frames. In the 1850s, a stocking frame which cost £14 brought in £5. 4s. a year in rent. Since it lasted twenty years its owner gained a net profit of £57 from its rents. In this industry clearly it was the charging of excessive rents on the hire of the stocking frames, rather than the profits of a tommy shop, which provided the middleman with a large part of his livelihood.[89]

As was the case in other trades, it was in times of business depression that the abuses multiplied. When orders were low, the hard pressed middleman would let out the maximum number of frames and charge the full week's rent for their hire at the same time as distributing a smaller than usual quantity of materials. Thus the framework knitter would be

88 *Report from the Royal Commission on the Truck System, 1871*, p. iv. 1871 [C 326] XXXVI, iv. IUP Industrial Relations 11, p. 16.

89 *Report from the Select Committee on Stoppages of Wages in the Hosiery Manufacture, 1854-55*, p. iii. 1854-55 (421) XIV, 3. IUP Industrial Relations 6, p. iii.

earning smaller wages but would still be subject to the full deductions. Particularly resented was the practice resorted to by some employers of charging frame rent even when the stockinger was on his sick bed.[90] In hosiery, as in the metallurgical and mining industries, it was the small man rather than the large, prosperous employer who found it necessary to resort to the severest exactions in order to survive in the business. Thus Samuel Morley and A. J. Mundella who headed the biggest firms in stocking manufacture had good reputations as employers. They resented the activities of the undercutting middlemen and favoured legislation to suppress malpractices.

Whether truck took the form of excessive prices charged at a tommy shop, excessive rents charged for the hire of knitting frames, or the payment of wages partly in the form of goods or raw materials, it had the effect of weakening the bargaining strength of the wage earners. Hence the involvement of the trade union movement in campaigns against the truck system. It was noted by the commission in 1871 that trade unionism never flourished 'side by side with truck'. Where the truck system prevailed, stopping all purchases from the tommy shop was an alternative to prosecution for conspiracy or breach of contract, as a method of strike breaking. Mr. James Baird MP, an ironmaster, noted with obvious satisfaction, that the truck shop was 'a very powerful engine against strikes' since 'the moment they stopped working the store stopped advancing'. Alexander MacDonald, the miners' leader, cited a case of a successful strike at Annbank for weekly pays in place of the three monthly ones which were tied up with the truck system. More frequently the payment of truck was an aggravating cause of industrial unrest rather than the sole reason for a body of men leaving their work. John Frost, the leader of the Monmouthshire rising of the Chartists, was not alone in canalizing resentment against the tommy shop in support of other industrial and political ends. Those who had a vested interest in its continuation did not hesitate to raise the bogey that opposition to the truck system was all due to the activity of 'paid agitators'. Mr. R. Walker, who hired out 130 frames in hosiery manufacture, considered the 'whole of the agitation' was for the sake of two paid union organizers, Buckley and Elliot, 'getting a living out of the men' by receiving one penny a frame per week from those supporting the campaign for the abolition of frame rents. All the evidence points to the conclusion that a precondition for effective

90 *Report from the Select Committee on Stoppages of Wages in the Hosiery Manufacture, 1854-55,* pp. 84, 310. 1854-55 (421) XIV, 108, 334. IUP Industrial Relations 6, pp. 107, 334.

collective bargaining in coal mining, the iron trade and the textile industry was the abolition of the truck system.[91]

It would be misleading to suggest that those who suffered from the extortions of the tommy shop always joined eagerly in the campaign to destroy it. Some victims of the system were so impoverished and exhausted by their toil that they developed a languid indifference to any industrial or political agitation. The cash paying nail-masters carried on a more vigorous and sustained campaign against truck masters than did the nailers' union. The agitation in favour of more effective truck acts was more generally supported by a motley combination of trade union leaders, aggrieved local shop keepers, enlightened churchmen and even poor law officials. William Jennings, a worsted manufacturer who paid his men solely in good coin of the realm, confessed that he had no great love for the truck-paying masters. 'We do not very often shake hands together, very seldom', he said.[92]

The supporters of laissez-faire, from Ricardo and Joseph Hume in the 1820s and 1830s to G. W. Hilton in the 1960s, have argued that parliament was mistaken in attempting to suppress the truck system by means of legislation. In opposing the Framework Knitters Bill in 1812 Hume use the naive argument that if payment in truck was inconvenient or injurious to any man he would 'not work a second time' for the master who paid him in that manner.[93] By resorting to this form of payment the bag hosier, or middleman, was able to employ more men than would otherwise have been possible, thus reducing the charges on the poor rates. The classical economists argued that the objections voiced by the opponents of the truck system, that it undercut the prices of the other producers, was, in fact, a powerful reason in favour of its continuance since the consumer benefited from cheaper goods. The argument of the shop keepers, that the tommy shops deprived them of business, was also turned on its head: the labour of a handful of assistants in the tommy shop, where there was a large and rapid turnover of stores, was far more productive than that of the small shopkeeper who spent a large part of the day chatting with neighbours.[94]

91   *Report from the Royal Commission on the Truck System, 1871* pp. xxii et seq. 1871 [C.326] XXXVI, 22. IUP Industrial Relations 11, pp. 34 et seq. *Report from the Select Committee on the Payment of Wages Bill and Payment of Wages (Hosiery) Bill, 1854*, p. 137. 1854 (382) XVI, 149. IUP Industrial Relations 5, p. 149. *Report from the Select Committee on Stoppages of Wages in the Hosiery Manufacture, 1854-5*, p. 141. 1854-5 (421) XIV, 165. IUP Industrial Relations 6, p. 165.

92   *Report from the Select Committee on the Payment of Wages, 1842*, p. 28. 1842 (471) IX, 156. IUP Industrial Relations 4, p. 32.

93   *Hansard*, vol. XXIII (1812), Cols. 1175-76.

94   G. W. Hilton, *The Truck System*, pp. 57-58.

The weakness of the classical view of the labour market was that it assumed a greater mobility of the wage earner than was possible through most of the nineteenth century. The truck system was at its most virulent when trade conditions were most depressed and unemployment was at its peak. It was not true that the workman was free to leave the employment of a truck master if he found conditions too onerous. More often than not he had no alternative but to cling to the only employment within his knowledge and reach. There was no perfect market and no perfect mobility of labour. The alternative to the truckmaster keeping men in employment need not have been the absolute destitution of the wage earners. It was a matter of policy. What was needed was a humane system of poor relief combined with a speedier re-deployment of labour into expanding industries.

The classical enonomists' view overlooks the wider depressing social and economic consequences of the truck system. Far from ensuring the greatest efficiency in the production of goods, the system acted as a debilitating drag on the progress of the economy. In important sectors of British industry labour was rendered less mobile than would otherwise have been the case. An important reason why there were still 25,000 men employed in the domestic nail-making industry of the Midlands as late as 1871, when machine manufacture had for long been more efficient, was that between 14,000 and 16,000 of them worked for truck paying masters. The impoverished labourers did not dare to trade other than in the shop of the petty-fogger. They feared that when slack times came they would be 'paid off' if they did not buy their goods from the tommy shop. There was similar situation, though the workers were not quite so impoverished, in other trades. John Fisher, a worsted weaver, told the select committee in 1842 that he only stopped with Mr. Walker, his truck-paying employer, because 'work was scarce'.[95]

Professional men who made a close study of the districts where the truck system was prevalent were unanimous as to its adverse effects on the habits and morale of entire communities. Since payment in truck was a form of wage cutting, the purchasing power of the community in which it held sway was thereby reduced. In 1854, H. S. Tremenheere, who for the past ten years had been employed by the government to report on the truck system, found that in South Staffordshire where it was widespread, workmen could not afford to send their children to school or to make contributions to friendly societies. In North Staffordshire, where wages were paid in cash and the tommy shop was rarely seen, the children

95   *Report from the Select Committee on the Payment of Wages, 1842*, p. 17. 1842 (471) IX, 145. IUP Industrial Relations 4, p. 21.

attended school regularly, homes were better furnished and savings clubs prospered. Seventeen years later his evidence about savings was corroborated by W. P. Pattison, actuary of the important Commercial Union Assurance Company. In truck paying districts he found that friendly and building societies 'did not exist at all'. Elsewhere they were everywhere on the increase. In cash-paying Swansea there were twenty building societies: in nearby Rhymney and Ebbw Vale, where truck still held sway, he had found none. Dr. P. M. M. MacDouall, a doctor from Bury, Lancashire, found that in the part of his district where wages were paid in cash his remuneration was 'generally pretty regular'; but in the other part, where truck prevailed, the men squandered any money they received 'with a reckless spirit, like schoolboys' and he was consequently poorly rewarded for his services.[96]

The wives of drunken husbands were among the few defenders of the truck system. When wages had to be spent at the tommy shop they queued up on 'turnbook days' (i.e. days of extra credit) to buy the necessary food for their families. But as contemporary observers noted, this state of affairs 'subjected large numers of workmen who had no intention of spending their money on alcohol to a sumptuary control for the restraint of a minority of drunkards'.[97] In so far as the truck system reduced incentives to save it is, in any case, doubtful whether it did act as a check on drunkenness.

If the effect of truck on the labour force was to immobilize and impoverish it, the effect on the entrepreneur was to discourage enterprise. The frame rents system in hosiery encouraged the bag hosier to obtain 'the greatest possible amount of rent from the least possible amount of produce'.[98] In nail-making, the middleman clung to the domestic system of manufacture because labour was so cheap; and the low wages of the domestic sector of the industry depressed wages of those employed in making nails by machinery. Had the truck system not existed in these, and other industries, wages would have been higher and labour and capital would have been more speedily transferred from domestic to factory pro-

---

96 *Report from the Select Committee on the Payment of Wages Bill and the Payment of Wages (Hosiery) Bill, 1854*, p. 53. 1854 (382) XVI, 65. IUP Industrial Relations 5, p. 65. *Report from the Select Committee on the Payment of Wages, 1842*, pp. 100-101. 1842 (471) IX, 224-5. IUP Industrial Relations 4, pp. 100-101. *Report of the Royal Commission on the Truck System, 1871*, p. 898. 1871 [C. 326] XXXVI, 1180. IUP Industrial Relations 11, p. 1192.

97 G. W. Hilton, *The Truck System*, pp. 26-27.

98 *Report from the Select Committee on the Stoppage of Wages in Hosiery Manufacture, 1854-55*, p. 47. 1854-55 (421) XIV, 47. IUP Industrial Relations 6, p. 23.

duction. The comments made in the report of the select committee in 1854 in respect of the hosiery trade have relevance to practically all the domestic industries affected by truck and they form a fitting conclusion to the effects of the system on the economy and hence on the prospect of improved industrial relations through collective bargaining:

> 'A much larger body of persons are committed to and detained in the manufacture, through successive generations, than can be adequately supported by it, while the gradual working of the ordinary remedy by the withdrawal of superfluous hands is intercepted and frustrated.'[99]

The decline of truck in the second half of the nineteenth century can scarcely be attributed to the effects of legislation. Apart from the Hosiery Manufacture (Payment of Wages) Act, 1874 (37 and 38 Vict. c. 48), which dealt with only a part of the problem, no legislation was passed for fifty-six years after 1831 despite the acknowledged ineffectiveness of the law. In the early years of the century Parliament was prodded into action by disturbances in the truck paying districts. But it was not prepared to abandon the principles of laissez-faire sufficiently to pass effective legislation once the immediate occasion for concern had passed. Thus unrest, in the form of pillaging of truck shops, in the coalfields of South Wales in 1816-17 led to the Truck Act, 1817 (57 Geo III c. 122), which extended earlier legislation to include employment in coal mines. The activities of the Weavers Association of Gloucestershire in 1829 in attempting to ban the allocation of more than two looms to each weaver, and the signature of a petition in favour of the payment of wages in money, led to the passage of E. J. Littleton's Truck Act in 1831 (1 and 2 William IV c. 37).[100]

There were two principal reasons why the 1831 Act was largely ineffective. The penalties for its violation were totally inadequate to deter a truck-paying master from persisting in his offence. For the first offence the fine was a mere £10, for the second £20 and for the third £100. Littleton had wanted these to be much stiffer, but he was over-ruled by the Commons Committee.[101] Much more serious was the fact that prosecution was left to the initiative of individuals who would bring the accused before two local magistrates who had the power to impose the fines nominated in the Act. The great difficulty, which was the principal cause of the ineffectiveness of the Act, was that very few men would come

99   *Report from the Select Committee on the Stoppage of Wages in Hosiery Manufacture, 1854-55,* p. iv. 1854-55 (421) XIV 4. IUP Industrial Relations 6, p. iv.

100   G. W. Hilton, *The Truck System,* p. 95.

101   G. W. Hilton, *The Truck System,* pp. 109-13.

forward to give information.[102] The reward offered to informers under section 18, of half the penalty imposed on the offender, up to a maximum of £20, was insufficient to offset the loss of employment which would inevitably follow. The Truck Amendment Act, 1887 (50 and 51 Vict. c. 46), overcame this major drawback in the earlier legislation. In 1842 a solicitor's clerk, Isaac Oldfield, had advocated the appointment of a public prosecutor to summon all masters who attached a shop to their workplaces.[103] The Truck Commission in 1871 had recommended that 'the institution of prosecutions should be entrusted to some public officer'.[104] Only in 1887 did parliament follow this advice. Under section 13 of the Act of that year enforcement was delegated to inspectors of factories and mines. But by this time it was almost a case of shutting the stable door after the horse had bolted. At the end of the 1880s there were probably less than 5,000 men employed in the hand-made nail trade compared with 60,000 in 1818. The competition of machines had virtually eliminated the hand frames in the stocking industry and the growth of miners' trade unionism and the effects of the Mines Regulation Act of 1872 helped to eliminate some of the worst abuses in the coal-mining industry.

The Truck Act of 1896 (59 and 60 Vict. c. 44), the last of its kind in the century, was designed to eliminate the exaction of unjust fines from the wage earner. Particularly in trades where women were employed for low wages, e.g. in pen nib manufacture, it was a common practice for the employer to deduct fines for bad workmanship. This practice was sometimes prosecuted with such zeal that the total of deductions exceeded the normal wage at the end of the working week. In railway employment fines were imposed as an aid to the enforcement of a rigid military-style discipline. The Act did not forbid all deductions as had been the case for the hosiery industry under the Act of 1874. But it required the employer to publish the fines that were payable, or to secure the written agreement of his staff, and to limit these to instances where it could be shown that management had sustained increased costs through loss or damage.[105]

By the end of the century, then, Parliament came to accept the necessity of protective legislation to deal with abuses in the methods of wage payments but by this time the occasion for the legislation had largely passed.

102 *Report from the Royal Commission on the Truck System, 1871,* p. xxvi. 1871 [C.326] XXXVI, 26. IUP Industrial Relations 11, p. 38.

103 *Report from the Select Committee on the Payment of Wages, 1842,* IX p. 82. 1842 (471) IX, 210. IUP Industrial Relations 4, p. 86.

104 *Report from the Royal Commission on the Truck System, 1871,* p. xlvi. 1871 [C.326], XXXVI, 46. IUP Industrial Relations 11, p. 58.

105 G. W. Hilton, *The Truck System,* pp. 147-48.

8. The sweating system

Witnesses before the House of Lords select committee in 1888-90 offered a wide variety of definitions of the term 'sweating'. Some emphasized the role of the sweater as a person, while others stressed the economic and social conditions which made sweating possible. Mr. Parnell, the secretary of the West End branch of the Alliance Cabinet Makers Association, was in the first category. The sweater, he said, was the person who lived on the labour of other persons, whether he took work and sub-contracted it or whether by any other means he managed 'to live without working'. More vaguely, Mr. Arnold White contended that the sweater was anyone 'who grinds the face of the poor'. Beatrice Potter (later Mrs. Sidney Webb) felt that this concentration on the role of the middleman sweater was misleading. In her view the crux of the evil was the putting-out system of completely unregulated home-work. The Lords Committee, in its Report, selected three outstanding features: unduly low rates of wages, excessive hours of labour and the insanitary state of the workplace; but it attempted no definition of 'unduly low' or 'excessive'. Mr. D. F. Schloss added a fourth: 'driving'.[106]

Whichever definition be accepted, it is clear that these conditions of industrial life were not new. Henry Mayhew in two articles which appeared in the *Morning Chronicle* in December 1849 wrote about the conditions of London's working tailors. In the second of the Tracts by Christian Socialists *Cheap Clothes and Nasty*, Parson Lot (i.e. Charles Kingsley) noted that 'at the honourable shops the master deals directly with his workmen, while at the dishonourable ones the greater part of the work, if not the whole, is let out to contractors of middlemen "sweaters" as their victims significantly call them'. But although the Christian Socialists opened a number of co-operative tailoring shops, including one in Castle Street, near Oxford Circus, in an attempt to eliminate sweat shops, they did not survive very long and, in any case, only tackled the barest fringe of the problem.[107] In 1876 there was a brief-lived scare about the danger of wearing clothes made in insanitary workplaces; but this soon died down. The evil continued.

Why, then, the sudden concern in the late 1880s about the sweated industries? It may be partly explained by an awakening social conscience

106   David Frederick Schloss, *Methods of Industrial Remuneration*, vol. I (London: Williams & Norgate, 1892). pp. 279, 35. *Fifth Report, House of Lords Select Committee on the Sweating System, 1890*, p. xlii. 1890 (169) XVII, p. 298. IUP Industrial Relations 16, p. 700.

107   'Parson Lot', *Cheap Clothes and Nasty, Tracts by Christian Socialists* II, (London: Working Printers' Association, 1851), p. 2.

about the problem of the condition of the poor. In 1883 Andrew Mearns, the Congregationalist, created a stir with the publication of his *Bitter Cry of Outcast London* and a short while later Charles Booth began his monumental survey into London life and labour. Mr. Lewis Lyons, a free-lance journalist, wrote numerous articles in the *East London Observer, The Jewish World* and the *Star* before starting his own paper *Anti-Sweater.* The other newspapers were more concerned with the influx into London, between 1882-86, of between 20,00 and 30,000 Russian or Polish Jews, the victims of the anti-semitism of the Tsarist regime. Many of these immigrants were obliged, through their poverty, to find employment in the sweated trades. Although by 1887 the tide of immigration had ebbed, the government of Lord Salisbury yielded to the press campaign and instructed John Burnett (1842-1914), a former secretary of the Amalgamated Society of Engineers, who was the first labour correspondent of the Board of Trade, to make reports on conditions in the worst of the sweated trades. The publication of the first of these early in 1888 was the occasion for Lord Kenry's resolution in the House of Lords on 28 February 'that a Select Committee be appointed to enquire into the Sweating System of the East End of London, and to report thereon to this House'.[108]

Charles Kingsley claimed that it was the British government which was responsible for introducing the sweating system when it put out to contract the making of military uniforms. In March 1847, when informed of the miserable wages of those employed by the contractors and sub-contractors and urged to put a stop to the abuse, the Admiralty flatly declined to alter its policy and disclaimed any responsibility for having caused the depression of wage rates. It took refuge behind economic laws. The tailors' wages, it blandly declared, depended upon 'the amount of competition for employment'.[109]

However, sweating was not confined to the tailoring trade. In the late 1880s John Burnett found it present in the cutlery trades, in nail- and chain-making, in boot and shoe manufacture and in the furniture industry. No government department could be held responsible for initiating anti-social methods of employment in these industries.

The readers of the popular and even the middle class press were given to believe that it was the influx of aliens, especially Jewish people, that was the cause of oppression of the native worker. The immigrants, it was asserted, either undercut the wages of the established workers in the trade,

---

108   Fabian Society, *Sweating: its Cause and Remedy* (Fabian Tract 50) (London: Fabian Society, 1894), p. 6.

109   Parson Lot, *Cheap Clothes and Nasty*, p. 14, quotes the letter from the Admiralty.

or exploited them by acting as sub-contractors who let out work at cut rates. In March 1888, just at the time the Lords' committee was beginning its hearings, *Punch* carried a full page cartoon depicting a Jew, with a contract bulging from his pocket, as a bloated man-spider sucking the life blood out of men and women who were working around him. In her evidence before the committee Beatrice Potter endeavoured to destroy this conception. In the worst cases of sweating, she said, the middleman did not appear. This was the situation in the coat trade where wholesalers put out the work direct. She claimed that the 'raw greener' immigrant could not be used in the tailoring trade until he had had some experience. If the government attempted to check immigration by imposing a poll tax, as was currently being suggested, the employers would simply go down to the docks and pay the poll tax and then 'the immigrant would be entirely in his power'.[110]

The Lords' committee report was much influenced by the earlier reports of John Burnett who emphasized the key role of the sub-contractor as the chief cause of oppression of the worker. He defined the sweating system as 'one under which sub-contractors undertake to work in their own houses, or small workshops, and employ others to do it, in making a profit for themselves by the difference between the contract prices and the wages they pay their assistants'. Predisposed into thinking that sub-contracting was the root cause of the ills being investigated, they summoned witnesses who claimed to be the victims of the sub-contract system and cross examined many middlemen contractors; but they heard no evidence from wholesalers who let out work to be done in people's homes and they were not interested in contractors and sub-contractors who did *not* exploit others. Inevitably the report over-emphasized the role of the middleman and failed to appreciate the growing importance of the large firms as perpetuators of the sweating system. Thus one of the crucial reasons for the survival of the evil, in the words of the final report, was 'that in these occupations an excessive number of small masters were competing with each other, to an extent which made it necessary for each of them, in order to live himself, to reduce the cost of production to the utmost'. The second crucial reason given was the existence of an 'overcrowded and unorganized mass of workpeople ... competing with one another for employment'.[111]

110   *Punch,* 17 March 1888.

111   *Fifth and Final Report of the Royal Commission on Labour, 1894,* p. 19. 1894 [C.7421] XXXV, 27. IUP Industrial Relations 44, p. 27. D. F. Schloss, *Methods of Industrial Renumeration* (3rd Edn. 1898), p. 218. Beatrice Potter, 'Tailoring' in *Labour and Life of the People* vol. I. *East London,* Charles Booth (ed.) (London: Williams and Norgate, 1889), pp. 209-241.

It was a misleading over-simplified version of the situation in the sweated trades where there were many variations in the forms of exploitation and many different agencies responsible for 'grinding the faces of the poor'. In the coat trade in London tailoring, the worst sweating occurred where the women employed went direct to the wholesale house for their assignments of work. In the trouser trade also the work was handed out direct by the wholesalers. It was often the case that the conditions of employment in the workshop belonging to small retail shops were every bit as oppressive as in those of the sub-contractor. In shirt making there had been a transition from the sub-contract system to one in which the wholesaler gave out work from his warehouse. Under the former system the sub-contractor paid the shirt maker tenpence and pocketed the twopence difference between this and the wholesaler's price of one shilling. When the wholesaler took over, he still paid only tenpence to the worker while he kept for himself the twopence formerly retained by the sub-contractor. Thus it was the middleman as well as the seamstress who was being squeezed by the more powerful wholesalers. In the trunk and saddlery trades the growth of strong trade unions was bringing to an end the exploitation of the workers but pressing the middleman out of existence.[112]

The Fabian Society maintained that it was the survival of home-work into an age when the competition of factory-made goods was increasing rapidly which was the most significant feature of the sweating system. Wholesalers, as well as all types of middlemen (including butty-men in the metallurgical trades) all helped to keep the system alive. They preferred to hand out materials to people to 'make up' in their own homes or in hired corners of small workshops, for in so doing they were relieved of all responsibility for the conditions under which the work was done. The sweaters' insanitary dens and the overcrowded garrets of the home-workers were completely outside the jurisdiction of the factory inspectors. Furthermore, work under the putting-out system was so fragmented that individual bargaining over payment was inevitable. A wholesale clothing contractor in East London had hundreds of different families looking to him for work. It was a well-nigh impossible task for trade unions to organize such a motley and dispersed labour force. What is surprising is the valiant attempts made by Jewish clothing workers to organize their trade despite these formidable difficulties. Between 1889-1891 fifteen local

112   Fabian Society, *Sweating: its Cause and Remedy*, p. 5. *First Report, Select Committee of the House of Lords on the Sweating System, 1888*, p. 324. HL 1888 361) XX, 344. IUP Industrial Relations 13, p. 382. Beatrice Webb, *How best to do away with the Sweating System*. Paper read at the 24th Annual Conference of Co-operative Societies, Rochdale, June 1892 (Manchester: Co-operative Union, 1892), p. 9.

unions were formed in London, Leeds and Manchester. The main reason for the impermanence of these organizations was the shifting character of the Jewish labour force – the Jewish Board of Guardians repatriated many thousands, and thousands more emigrated to the USA – rather than any reluctance on the part of people of this race to join trade unions.[113]

The Lords' committee recognized the Fabians' case to the extent of including in its recommendation the proposal that there should be a compulsory registration of all home-workers. This was the one recommendation of the report that was included in the Factory Act, 1891 (54 and 55 Vict. c. 75, Section 27). However, the government made Section 27 practically inoperative by imposing on the contractor or sub-contractor the obligation of registration only if he was specifically required to do so by the Secretary of State. The Act incorporated practically all the demands of the well organized cotton factory operatives but set aside most of the proposals in Mr. Sydney Buxton's bill (No. 61 of 1891) for making the landlord of premises used for industrial purposes responsible for the sanitary conditions of the premises and making him also responsible for notifying a factory inspector when his property was being used as a place of manufacture.[114]

Many trade unions were too preoccupied with the problems closer to hand to recognize the importance of campaigning for the elimination of sweating in industry. The National Union of Boot and Shoe Operatives and The Scottish Tailors' Society were notable exceptions. In the 1890s they put the abolition of homework in the front of their programme. However, many trade unionists accepted the demand for a stricter control over immigrant labour and in 1892 the TUC passed a resolution calling for the exclusion of 'foreign pauper labour' from Britain. A similar resolution was passed in 1894. Had trade unionists endorsed Beatrice Webb's view that 'the removal of all Jews from the sweated trades would be but a partial and temporary relief', they might have given more powerful support to the Fabian programme for the control of home-work contracts.[115]

Despite the publicity given to the problem and the opportunity provided for the registration of outworkers under the Factory Act of 1891, sweating continued to be a feature of British industrial life for at least a further two decades. In 1897 Edith F. Hogg discovered the most appalling conditions of insanitation and overwork persisting amongst the

113   Fabian Society, *Sweating: its Cause and Remedy*, pp. 7-9 H. Clegg, A. Fox and A. F. Thompson, *A History of British Trade Unions since 1889*, p. 182. S. and B. Webb, *Industrial Democracy* (London: Longmans Green, 1902), p. 435.

114   B. Webb, *How best to do away with the Sweating System*, pp. 11-12.

115   S. and B. Webb, *Industrial Democracy*, p. 540. B. C. Roberts, *The Trades Union Congress, 1868-1921*, p. 182.

women fur-pullers in South London. Working in an atmosphere impregnated with the millions of fine hairs of the skins it was their task to process, they earned sixteen and a half pence in the course of a twelve hour working day. Although the atmosphere in the paper bag makers' homes was cleaner, their earnings were every bit as meagre, and the contractor did not even know the addresses of his outworkers. Nearly ten years later those who attended the *Daily News'* Sweated Industries Exhibition could see that the problem still awaited solution.[116]

In the meantime steady if unspectacular progress was made by central government departments and local authorities in establishing fair wages contracts. One positive outcome of the publicity surrounding the enquiry by the Lords' Select Committee on the Sweating System was the passing of a resolution by the House of Commons on 13 February 1891:

'That in the opinion of this House, it is the duty of the Government in all Government contracts to make provision against the evils recently disclosed before the Sweating Committee, to insert such conditions as may prevent the abuse arising from sub-letting, and to make every effort to secure the payment of such wages as are generally accepted as current in each trade for competent workmen.'

The resolution was interpreted very cautiously for several years after its adoption. On 3 August 1893 Mr. Sydney Buxton explained to the House of Commons that the government simply aimed at ensuring there would be 'no bar to prevent trade unionists doing work under Government contracts'. There was certainly no approach towards a closed shop. Seven years after the House of Commons resolution had been approved, the Select Committee on Statutory Contracts heard evidence from C. W. Bowerman, the secretary of the London Society of Compositors, that in some houses of the Government printing firm of Eyre and Spottiswoode they did not pay the trade union rates of the district although most of the daily newspapers, with the exception of *The Times* the *Globe* and *The Sportsman,* were union houses.[117]

Meanwhile the London County Council had agreed on the payment of standard union rates as far back as 1898. The Council's Standing Orders ruled that for skilled workers the recognized standard rate of wages, for unskilled male workers the minimum rate of sixpence an hour and for adult women a minimum of eighteen shillings a week, should be paid.[118]

116 Edith F. Hogg, 'The Fur Pullers of South London', *Nineteenth Century,* November 1897, reprinted in *Nineteenth Century Opinion,* Michael Goodwin (ed.) (London: Penguin Books, 1951), p. 19.

117 *Report from the Select Committee on Government Contracts (Fair Wages Resolution),* 1896, p. 27. 1896 (230) XIII, 469. IUP Industrial Relations 22, p. 471

118 Fabian Society, *The Economics of Direct Employment* (Fabian Tract 84; London: Fabian Society, 1898), pp. 2-3.

In a rapidly increasing number of other towns and cities local authorities decided to pay only 'Fair' or 'Trade Union' rates of wages. No less than 150 of them had decided to do this by 1893.[119]

However, the local authorities did not as a rule employ labour in industries like furniture manufacture, chain-making and the all important tailoring trade. Improvement in these industries had to await the Liberal government's Trade Boards Act of 1909 which made provision for the setting up of trade boards comprising representatives of employers, workpeople and independent members nominated by the government, for the chain-making, ready-made tailoring, machine-made lace finishing and cardboard-box making trades. The boards were empowered to fix minimum rates of wages which became enforceable when ratified by the minister. By the outbreak of the first World War this enforced collective bargaining had brought substantial improvements in working conditions and rates of pay in these long-neglected industries.[120]

Thus the problem of the sweated trades only came near a solution when it was finally recognized that this was an area of industrial relations where 'collective laissez-faire' had not operated because of the exceptional difficulty of organizing those domestically employed into trade unions. Over the twenty years 1890-1910 it was gradually recognized that the state would have to intervene. When the Trade Boards Bill was being debated in the House of Commons the Liberal member of parliament for Bury, Mr. Thoulmin, summed up very well the viewpoint of those on the government benches when he said 'We must as far as possible follow the natural growth of labour in this country, the orderly development of trade unionism. Where this natural evolution stops or lags the state must step in'.[121]

9. Co-operation and profit sharing

Schemes for the co-operative production and distribution of goods pre-date the nineteenth century. The dockyard workers of Woolwich and Chatham established co-operative corn mills, in an attempt to beat a local corn miller's monopoly, as early as 1760. In the early years of the nineteenth century the number of co-operative experiments increased very rapidly as more and more families began to experience the effects of industrialization and were influenced by the writings of Robert Owen, William Thompson and other reformers. At least 250 co-operative

119   House of Commons Return No. 435 of 1893.

120   Richard Henry Tawney, *Minimum Rates in the Tailoring Industry* (London: L.S.E., 1915).

121   *Hansard,* 4th Ser. vol. 184 Col. 1198 21 February 1908.

societies, most concerned solely with retailing, but a substantial number also engaged in manufacturing, are known to have existed between 1826-35 — a decade before the well-known Rochdale Equitable Pioneers Society set up its famous Toad Lane store. At the height of the Owenite movement in Britain in 1832-33 there were more than 400 societies functioning. The great majority were very short-lived.[122]

The influence of Robert Owen was so powerful in the second quarter of the century that many of the co-operative ventures were designed to achieve much more than a cheaper distribution of groceries and a distribution of any profits in the form of a dividend. Together they were designed to be the nucleus of a new co-operative commonwealth. The Rochdale Society is remembered principally for its grocery store; but its objects extended further than a more efficient system of retail trading. They included the statement:

'That as soon as practicable the society shall proceed to arrange the powers of production, distribution, education and government; or, in other words, to establish a self-supporting home community of united interests, and to assist other societies to establish such colonies.'

The origins of these communities were very diverse. Some, like the Rochdale society, were started by groups of Owenites of different trades. Others were established by small groups of men of the same trade as was the Co-operative Dyeing Manufactory in Manchester in 1832. Yet others were founded by particular trade unions or federations of unions. In 1852 the Amalgamated Society of Engineers bought the Atlas Ironworks at Southwark after its executive had decided that 'all . . . future operations should be directed in promoting the system of self-employment in associative workshops'. In 1848 the National Association of United Trades supported 'a system of self employment upon the principle of associated labour'. It advocated producers' co-operatives in 'shoe making, carpentering, manufacturing and agricultural arrangements'.

Throughout the first half of the nineteenth century there survived a large number of skilled craftsmen who were either self-employed or worked in small-scale establishments. It was from among this substantial class of operatives that there were to be found some of the strongest backers of co-operative undertakings. This movement was well past its peak in the late 1840s.

When there was a revival of the movement for co-operative production in the 1850s it owed much more to the middle class patronage of the leaders of the Christian Socialist Movement including J. M. F. Ludlow,

122   G. D. H. Cole, *A Century of Co-operation* (London: Allen & Unwin, 1944) pp. 13, 25. Benjamin Jones, *Co-operative Production* (Oxford: Clarendon Press, 1894) vol. I Chap. 6. The following paragraphs are largely based on these two works.

Charles Kingsley, E. V. Neale and F. D. Maurice. In 1850 there were three working Shoemakers' Associations, a Working Tailors' Association, a North London Needlewomen's Association and Working Builders and Working Bakers' Associations in the Central London area. Those employed by them were housed in the most sanitary conditions and were paid the best standard rates of wages, plus a share in the profits, after payment of a fixed interest on any capital lent, of four per cent. They were all very small concerns and the setting up of a Society for Promoting Working Men's Associations, with proposals for a standardizing the rules and practices of each associative group, did little to solve the problems of their organization. The Working Tailors Association, Working Bakers Association, etc. each wished to be self-contained, but lacked the resources for growth in isolation from the general movement. Not all the workmen were happy to remain in a position of tutelage under their middle class sponsors until their debts had been repaid.[123]

In 1852 the Christian Socialists scored a success with the passage of the Industrial and Provident Societies Act under which co-operative societies were given an assured legal status. But their sponsoring of industrial co-operation proved to be of short duration. One of their number, E. V. Neale, wished to link up with the Leeds Redemptionists 'who were subscribing a penny a week to a fund for the redemption of labour' by its employment on the land and in self governing workshops. He founded the Central Co-operative Agency in London in 1851 to act as wholesaler for co-operative organizations throughout the country. However, F. D. Maurice was always more dubious of the wisdom of joining hands with the more purely secular side of the co-operative movement, and after the failure of the Pimlico Working Builders Association in 1853 and the engineers' withdrawal from their three ironworks ventures in London, the formal association of the Christian Socialists with schemes for co-operative production came to an end in 1853-54. However, two of their leaders, J. M. F. Ludlow and E. V. Neale, gave subsequent service 'of inestimable value' to the co-operative movement.

Throughout the nineteenth century there was a constant interplay of influences between the co-operative movement and the surrounding industrial society organized on the basis of private enerprise. As the numerous producer and consumer co-operatives passed from their pioneering days into years of steady expansion and financial stability, their success helped to influence the more liberal-minded employers to think more kindly about schemes of profit-sharing with their employees. But the influences in the reverse direction were more powerful. In an environment

123   The Society for Promoting Working Men's Associations, *Tracts on Christian Socialism, No. V* (London: Working Printers' Association, 1851).

of general acceptance of laissez-faire the ideals of the co-operative pioneers were either forgotten or set aside. Later nineteenth-century co-operation took the form of consumers self-help within a private enterprise economy, rather than that of a nucleus of socialism which was eventually to replace the competitive system entirely. Nowhere was this change more manifest than in the developments in Rochdale itself, where, in the organization of the Equitable Pioneers Society and its offshoot the Rochdale Co-operative Manufacturing Society there was:

'At no time ... a deliberate break with the past, but the ideals of justice, of fair dealing, of banishing poverty and want, were gradually transferred to the day-to-day operation of distribution, and before long, production ... while the ultimate ideal of community life receded ever farther into the dim future, even among the leaders.'

The change was epitomized in the Manufacturing Society's abolition of the 'bounty on labour' in 1862. Before that date the Society's factory operatives, in addition to receiving the market rate of wages for their labour, received a proportion of the profits of the enterprise. After 1862 their position as wage earners was indistinguishable from that of the other factory workers of their day.[124]

In the last quarter of the nineteenth century when profit sharing and welfarism were on the increase in private industry, co-operation lost some of its impetus and self-confidence. The activities of the societies expanded and the number of members continued to grow; but some of the fire had gone out of the movement. The growth of scale of operation in private business — particularly from the mid 1880s when there was a rush of firms to become limited liability companies and the department stores and the multiples figured more prominently in the typical High Street — undermined the movement's faith in its ability to go on expanding indefinitely. The great increase in factory acts and other ameliorative legislation largely obliterated the distinction between co-operative employment and employment in private industry. The spread of literacy after 1870 tended to reduce the significance of the educational activities of the co-operative movement. Finally the emergence of the New Unionism in the late 1880s and early 1890s, with its emphasis on state socialism, seemed to many to offer a more promising road to salvation.[125]

That in the course of the nineteenth century the co-operative movement had changed its principal concern from community building to shopkeeping is shown by the situation in 1892. There were then 170

124   Sidney Pollard, 'Co-operation from Community Building to Shopkeeping', in *Essays in Labour History,* vol. 1. Asa Briggs and John Saville (eds.) (London: Macmillan, 1960), pp. 96-98.

125   Bert James Youngjohns, *Co-operation and the State, 1814-1914* (Loughborough: Co-operative Union Ltd., 1954), p. 53.

producers societies with 24,056 members compared with 1,471 distributive societies with 1,143,962 members. The value of the turnover of the producers societies was only one-twelfth that of the distributive societies.[126]

In a class by themselves as experiments in industrial organization, from the 1860s onwards, were the 'Oldham Limiteds' in cotton spinning. These were limited liability companies which had taken full advantage of the Companies Acts of 1856-62 and had recruited about half their total capital from the working classes 'in the immediate vicinity'. This was neither co-operative production nor profit sharing. It was the loan capital bearing fixed rate of interest that was subscribed by the working classes while the share capital was almost all held by the middle classes. In 1892 Mr. D. F. Schloss found that none of the seventy-six Oldham Limiteds gave any share of their profits to any of their employees, a situation which was repeated in the textile factories of other towns which copied the Oldham example.[127]

Later nineteenth-century profit-sharing took a variety of forms, but each scheme contained the common feature that the staff employed in a concern were to receive in addition to normal salary or wages some pecuniary advantage, either immediate or prospective, to be paid out of the firm's profits. The principal varieties of profit-sharing included an end-of-year bonus, the allocation of a part of the profits to a provident fund for sickness or old age benefit payments, an allocation of shares in the company and a cash payment out of profits proportionate to the output and productivity of labour.

In some cases the introduction of profit-sharing schemes was motivated by a genuine concern on the part of management to raise the living standards and improve the morale of their employees. Influenced by the economic teachings of John Ruskin in *Unto this Last* (1862) and by the writings of Sedley Taylor, who recorded the success of profit sharing experiments in France by the Maison Leclaire, M. Bord and the Paris-Orleans Railway, Mr. T. W. Bushill, head of a Coventry firm of cardboard box manufacturers, initiated a scheme of profit-sharing with his 185 employees in 1888. Other examples can be cited of employers such as Richard Tangye, head of the Birmingham engineering firm, who were motivated by Christian principles to concede a share of profits to the workmen they employed. But the evidence suggests that in most cases less altruistic motives dictated the spate of profit-sharing experiments over the

---

126 *Report by Mr. D. F. Schloss on Profit Sharing, 1894,* p. 14 et seq. 1894 [C.7458] LXXX, 596 et seq. IUP Industrial Relations 22, pp. 74 et seq.

127 *Report by Mr. D. F. Schloss on Profit Sharing, 1894, p. 14.* 1894 [C.7458] LXXX, 596. IUP Industrial Relations 22, p. 74.

period 1888-92.[128] Concern for the amelioration of labour bore a direct relationship to the extent of labour unrest. In each of the years 1889 and 1890 there were more industrial disputes than in any year before 1913. In these same two years more schemes for profit-sharing were launched than in any comparable period in British history. Forty-eight out of seventy-one projects mentioned by Timothy Bushill as having been launched between 1873 and 1892 inclusive were established between 1888-1892.[129]

Some profit-sharing schemes owed their origin directly to the existence of industrial disputes. In the Thames Ironworks, a prolonged dispute between the company and certain classes of its workers between 1889-90 induced the managing director, Mr. A. F. Hills, to think that management must 'do something to stop it'. The first plan that came to mind was 'some scheme of profit-sharing'. In 1889 the South Metropolitan Gas Company plan included the condition that the staff of 3,000 men would forfeit their right to share in the profits 'in the case of a strike or wilful injury to the company'. Although this condition was subsequently withdrawn, in the gas workers' opinion it condemned the scheme as a device to prevent the growth of trade unionism. They were confirmed in their opinion when, following a strike later that year, a clause was added excluding members of the Gas Workers' Union from membership. Nearly a quarter of a century earlier Briggs Collieries of Whitworth, Lancashire, had hoped that their profit-sharing scheme of 1865 would be accepted by the miners 'as a substitute for union organization'. However, the men decided to retain union membership. When in 1874, in common with other employers of the district, Messrs. Briggs announced a reduction in wages, the miners resisted by coming out on strike and the shareholders, in disgust, put an end to the profit-sharing scheme in the following year.[130]

Trade Union leaders were divided in their views about profit-sharing. Moderate leaders such as Thomas Burt MP, secretary of the Northumberland Miners Association, backed the efforts of Thomas Bushill to extend the scope of profit sharing within British industry. The parliamentary committee of the TUC was of a different opinion. In its report for the year 1890 it warned that profit-sharing was 'no sure preventive of industrial conflicts' and that it might have 'a certain tendency to weaken the power

128 Sedley Taylor, *Profit Sharing between Capital and Labour* (London: Kegan Paul, Trench & Co., 1884), pp. 1-30, 77-86. Thomas William Bushill, *Profit Sharing and the Labour Question* (London: Methuen & Co., 1893), pp. 25, 48. John Ruskin, *Unto This Last* (London: Smith Elder & Co., 1862), p. 156.

129 *Abstracts of Labour Statistics*. T. W. Bushill, *Profit Sharing and the Labour Question*, pp. 122-25.

130 *Report by Mr. D. F. Schloss on Profit Sharing, 1894*, p. 30. 1894 [C.7458] LXXX, 612. IUP Industrial Relations 22, p. 90. H. Clegg, A. Fox and A. F. Thompson, *A History of British Trade Unions since 1889*, p. 67.

of trade union combination especially in trades and districts where it did not possess much strength.'[131] This view was supported by D. F. Schloss who noted that:

'Forms of profit-sharing, such as "anti-union" and "deferred" participation make it not unlikely that the employee will find it difficult to obtain an advance in wages, which he might have insisted upon had he been unfettered by participation in profits; so that, in effect, his share in profits may very possibly turn out, in the end to be, pro tanto, in lieu of, and not wholly in addition to, normal or ordinary wages.'[132]

Employers who introduced profit-sharing schemes claimed that they brought substantial benefits to both labour and capital. Thomas Bushill found that the costs of supervision in his factory were reduced once the staff were given the incentive, through the profit-sharing plan, to avoid waste of labour and materials. He maintained that employees were devising cheaper methods of production which benefitted both themselves and their employers. Where it was the practice to set aside a part of the shared profits as contributions to a benevolent fund this helped to increase the staff's attachment to the firm. Although it is impossible to measure the goodwill of the staff in money terms, it was asserted that profit sharing greatly improved the relationships between workers and management.

If these substantial claims made by the exponents of profit-sharing were at all true it is necessary to explain why arrangements of this kind covered such a very tiny fraction of the labour force. In 1893 only 19,109 wage earners in Britian were participating in profit-sharing schemes. Since the total occupied labour force exceeded ten million persons, 0.2 per cent of the workers were involved in projects which gave them a fraction of the profits they had helped to earn.[133]

The sluggish response of the majority of the employers to the blandishments of Messrs. Bushill and Taylor was in part due to hesitations about the impact of profit-sharing on the attitude of the working-classes. W. T. Shaw, of the firm of Messrs. De La Rue Company of London, feared that profit sharing would lead wage earners 'to assume that the share in the results of an enterprise dispensed in the form of wages weekly was not a just and adequate share and that, consequently, equity called for a further distribution of money to the workers at the annual balancing'. Other employers were reluctant to concede their workers a share in the profits in good years if there were no arrangement for them sharing the burden of

131   Parliamentary committee of the TUC, *Report for the Year 1890*, p. 24.
132   D. F. Schloss, *Methods of Industrial Remuneration*, p. 257.
133   T. W. Bushill, *Profit Sharing and the Labour Question*, pp. 41, 59, 122-25.

losses in years of trade depression. Inertia and the continuing reluctance of most employers to concede the principle that labour had any right to participate in the returns of capital, were no doubt the most formidable obstacles to the further spread of schemes of profit sharing.[134]

Apart from the engineers' suspicion that profit-sharing was the hated piece-work in another guise and the TUC's belief that it was an antidote to union organization, even the non-unionist was not always convinced that he was better off when tied down to schemes of this kind. Messrs. Cassell, Petter and Galpin of Ludgate Hill, London, who were printers, publishers and book binders, introduced a profit-sharing scheme early in 1878 but fifteen years later confessed that it had not helped to keep the younger members of staff with the firm, 'the contingent advantages not weighing with them when compared with an immediate advance of wages elsewhere'. The Cassell plan was not a particularly generous one. Between 1889-93 the ratio which the share in profits allocated to employees bore to the amount earned in wages was only two per cent. This compared with an average of just over six per cent obtained from a sample of forty-three firms reporting to Mr. Schloss.[135] In proportion to the number of industrial firms, profit-sharing was more extensively practiced in France. Its greater popularity with wage earners in that country than in Great Britain may have been due to the more substantial inducements offered. Rates of bonus were substantially higher. With the Maison Leclaire the ratio of bonus to annual wage ranged from thirteen to twenty-two per cent over the years 1870-82; with M. Bord the range was from over nine to twenty-two, while with the Paris and Orleans Railway there were eight years after 1857 when the bonus exceeded a fifth of the annual wages. However, the disproportion in benefits was nothing like as great as these figures suggest since the level of French wages was much below that of Britain. Nevertheless, the fact that the Frenchman participating in a profit-sharing scheme was able to earn substantially more than the customary rate of wages in his neighbourhood must have been a powerful inducement to co-operation with management.[136]

The influence of profit-sharing in Britain should not be gauged solely in terms of the numbers of firms practicing it or the numbers of work people involved. The projects which were successful served to demonstrate that, given an incentive and more congenial conditions of service, the labour of the wage earner would be more productive. 'The intelligent painstaking

134   T. W. Bushill, *Profit Sharing and the Labour Question*, p. 98.

135   *Report by Mr. D. F. Schloss on Profit Sharing, 1894*. p. 50. 1894 [C.7458] LXXX, 632. IUP Industrial Relations 22, p. 110. D. F. Schloss, *Methods of Industrial Remuneration*, p. 176.

136   S. Taylor, *Profit Sharing between Capital and Labour*, pp. 15, 31, 83.

employer', Schloss discovered, 'would find in this system a contrivance which would ultimately work, automatically, to continue and extend good relations between him and his workmen ... to materially increase his own profits and his people's well being'.[137]

10. Employers' liability

Under English common law a person is held to be liable not only for his own negligence but also for that of his servant, when acting under orders. Before the industrial revolution, when employment was usually on a small scale, the typical wage-earner was under the direct personal supervision of his employer who could therefore be held generally responsible for his safety when at work. But although the workman had the right to sue his master for negligence he did not in practice do so. Such an act would have been treated as insubordination and the workman who had the temerity to claim his rights would have had little prospect of future employment.

As the industrial revolution gathered momentum employment was increasingly concentrated in large establishments and the responsibility of the master for the safety of those he employed could not be so directly exercised. He was obliged to hire managers or deputies to be immediately responsible for groups of the work force. In the famous case *Priestly vs. Fowler,* in 1837, the court declared that Fowler was not liable for the injury caused by the overloading of his butcher's carts since the accident had been caused by the negligence of a fellow servant and not of the master. The presiding judge, Lord Abinger, admitted that the case was unprecedented but maintained that if the master was made liable in this case the acceptance of the principle would be bound to carry judges in similar cases in the future 'to an alarming extent':

> 'Where should we stop? We should have a master liable to his servant for the negligence of his chambermaid in putting him in a damp bed; for the negligence of the upholsterer in sending in a crazy bedstead, whereby he was made to fall while he was asleep; for the negligence of the cook in not properly cleaning the saucepans, for that of the butcher in sending in bad meat and for that of the builder who, by putting in bad foundations caused the house to fall, and bury master and servant together.'[138]

More importantly, the rapidly growing class of industrial entrepreneurs needed assurance that the value of investments in spinning mules, colliery

---

137 *Report to the Board of Trade on Profit Sharing, 1890-91,* p. 23. 1890-91 [C.6267] LXXVIII, 37. IUP Industrial Relations 22, p. 37.

138 David Gordon Hanes, *The First British Workmen's Compensation Act* (New Haven & London: Yale University Press, 1968), p. 11.

winding engines, etc, would not be reduced through the presentation of innumerable claims for compensation from injured work-people. It was essential that they should not be held liable for every case of injury arising from the working of the new machinery, otherwise continuing investment would be discouraged.

In 1850 the case *Hutchinson vs. York, Newcastle and Berwick Railway* made clear that the doctrine of common employment would also be applied to the rapidly expanding railway industry. Hutchinson, the servant of the railway, was injured in a collision when travelling in one of the company's trains. The company pleaded that the injury had been caused by a fellow servant in common employment with Hutchinson and that, by the precedent of *Priestly vs. Fowler* the company was not liable. The judge agreed that the two cases were 'indistinguishable' and that therefore there could be no compensation to the injured man. In *Wilson vs. Murray* (1868) the House of Lords decided that the doctrine of common employment extended to managers and supervisors of all kinds, thus making it possible for railway companies to plead that the injury or death of shunters, guards, drivers or other employees was due to the negligence of the superintendent of the line, traffic superintendent or locomotive super-intendent who were in 'common employment' with the injured man.[139]

One of the injustices arising from the doctrine of common employment was that although an employer was obliged to pay compensation for injury caused to a stranger, he often had no such obligation when injury was sustained by one of his own servants. If a builder's labourer and a passing stranger were both injured through the collapse of inadequately secured scaffolding, compensation would be paid to the stranger though not to the labourer. Similarly, the York, Newcastle and Berwick Railway, in the above-mentioned case, were liable to compensate passengers who were not its employees but who were injured in the collision, but not Hutchinson, one of the company's own staff.

The consequences of the application of the doctrine of common employment were far-reaching. The small employer who was in direct contact with his workmen was penalized in comparison with the large company which delegated responsibility through managers and super-intendents. He could be more easily convicted of negligence than could the directors of the large concern. Where it was possible to plead common employment, the owners and managers of a giant enterprise, such as a main line railway or a major iron foundry, had a reduced incentive to

139 *Report from the Select Committee on Employers' Liability for injury to their Servants, 1877.* p. iv. 1877 (285) X, 554. IUP Industrial Relations 19, p. 122. Geoffrey Alderman, *The Railway Interest* (Leicester: The University Press, 1973), p. 61.

install expensive safety devices for the protection of workmen. The small scale employer, whose resources were less adequate to meet additional overhead costs, was under the stronger necessity to incur the expense. The intrusion of this new doctrine in the middle years of the nineteenth century added still further to the risks and pitfalls confronting the injured workman seeking to obtain compensation from his employer. In any case he had the odious task of proving that his employer had been negligent and that he (the workman) had not been guilty of 'contributory negligence'. He had to plead his case correctly; or alternatively hire the expensive services of a lawyer. When to these obstacles was added the likelihood of a successful claim by the defendant that it was a case of 'common employment', it is not surprising that successful actions by injured workmen were rare.

Nor is it surprising that the agitation for full employers' liability and the abolition of the doctrine of common employment originated with coal miners, railwaymen and merchant seamen who suffered the worst effects of its application. In each of these cases the wage earner received his orders not from the owners of the mine, the railway or the ship, but from the colliery overman, the railway departmental head or the ship's captain. Thus the chances of obtaining compensation in the case of injury or death were more remote than in many other industries. However, the demand for the reform of the law was by no means confined to men employed in these trades. In the eight years 1868-75 inclusive, four trade unions, the Amalgamated Society of Engineers, the Ironfounders, the Boilermakers and the Amalgamated Society of Carpenters and Joiners paid a total of £24,117 for relief to families whose breadwinners had been injured. In the first twenty-five years of its existence the Engineers Society alone paid no less than £25,900 in compensation for accidents sustained by its members.[140] Understandably the leaders of these unions were quick to follow the lead of those organizations whose members were still more adversely affected by the law.

Agitation for the abolition of the doctrine of common employment began at least as early as 1858 when Alexander Macdonald spoke to a conference of miners' delegates on the subject at a meeting in Ashton under Lyne. Throughout a prolonged campaign there were two principal arguments used in support of a reform of the law. It was maintained that a more stringent enforcement of employers' liability and the removal of the alibi of 'common employment' would compel the masters to make more adequate provision for the safety of their workmen. In the second place it was argued that the abolition of the doctrine of common employment

140 *Report from the Select Committee on Employers' Liability for injuries to their Servants*, p. 4. 1876 (372) IX, 678. IUP Industrial Relations 19, p. 18.

would simply be the removal of an exceptional exclusion of large numbers of workmen from the ordinary protection of the law.[141] After the formation of the Amalgamated Society of Railway Servants in 1871-72, F. W. Evans, who was its general secretary for nine years after 1874, lent powerful support to Macdonald and W. P. Roberts 'the miners' advocate' in a campaign of parliamentary lobbying. It was possibly with the intention of forestalling the presentation of a more radical measure by friends of the railwaymen in parliament that the eminent railway director, Edward Watkin, introduced an Employers' Liability Bill in the Commons on 5 April 1875. Although it proposed to abolish the doctrine of common employment it limited the amount of compensation payable to one year's wages and was in many other ways narrow in scope and conservative in approach. The bill, and another similar to it presented in the following session, had no official backing from the Railway Companies' Association, an organization which had been founded (under a different name) in 1867 to protect the interests of the railway companies in parliament.

An Employers' Liability Bill sponsored by Alexander Macdonald, Michael Bass and other liberals in February 1876 attracted more support. But the opposition of the railway interest — there were 129 directors of major railway companies in the House of Commons at the time — and of the coal owners persuaded the government to set up a select committee

> 'to inquire whether it may be expedient to render masters liable for injuries occasioned by their servants by the negligent acts of ... those to whom the general control and superintendence of workshops and works is committed.'

Because they conceived the passage of the kind of bill envisaged would involve them in continuing heavy costs of litigation, the railway directors did their utmost to discredit the projected legislation. Mr George Findlay, Traffic Manager of the London and North Western Railway, told the committee that 'almost the entirety of the accidents was due to the negligence of the railwaymen'. Any alteration of the law would only serve to antagonize the railway companies and their servants. Railwaymen were quite happy under existing arrangements, he claimed, if only they were 'left alone by those agitators'. Hence the report of the committee included no revolutionary proposals. It recommended a modification of the doctrine of common employment rather than its abolition.

In the meantime the evidence submitted by Evans and other railway-men to the Royal Commission on Railway Accidents in 1876 probably did more to convince the liberal party that there was need for legislation than

141 S. and B. Webb, *Industrial Democracy*, p. 367. *Report of the Royal Commission on Railway Accidents, 1877*, p. 27. 1877 [C.1637] XLVIII, 27, IUP Transport and Communications: General 14, p. 35.

did the findings of the committee which had been specially briefed to deal with the problem. The report of the commission in 1877 noted that:

'the servants ... assert that in numerous cases they are sacrificed from causes and in circumstances which would clearly give a right to compensation, were it not that the law refuses to regard in any other light than as their fellow servants those to whom the companies delegate the masters' authority'.

It recommended that the railway companies should be made liable to their servants for the negligence of those to whom the masters' authority was delegated.[142]

When Alexander Macdonald re-introduced his Employers' Liability Bill in 1878 the Home Secretary, Sir R. A. Cross, promised the support of the government. But a confidential memorandum drafted by the Attorney General, Sir John Holder, may have dissuaded the majority of the cabinet from allowing time for the Bill's passage. Holder found the law which made an employer liable for the negligent acts of his servants 'indefensible', but he found that the exception by which the employer was exempt from liability due to the doctrine of common employment was also indefensible. The situation was thus of the existence of an unjust exception to a bad law. The solution recommended was that employers should 'not be liable to anybody for the negligent acts of their servants'. The defeat of the government in the Commons and the victory of the liberal party in the general election of 1880 prevented Holder from implementing the recommendations he had made to the cabinet.[143]

The Employers' Liability Act of 1880 marked a drawn battle between the Railway Companies' Association and its allies and the Amalgamated Society of Railway Servants. The companies scored a victory in that 'contracting out' of the Act was permitted where employers and workmen consented to a scheme of mutual insurance against accidents. Furthermore, the Act removed the doctrine of common employment in five specific cases only. These may be summarized as instances where a workman suffered injury through the negligence of foremen or superintendents. On the other hand the ASRS, through its spokesman in the Commons, Samuel Morley, succeeded in inserting a clause whereby employers were made liable 'by reason of the negligence of any person in the service of the employer who has charge or control of any signal points, locomotive engines, or trains upon a railway'.[144]

As soon as the legality of contracting out had been upheld in *Griffiths*

---

142 *Report of the Royal Commission on Railway Accidents, 1877*, p. 27. 1877 [C.1637] XLVII, p. 27. IUP Transport and Communications: General 14, p. 35.

143 D. G. Hanes, *The First British Workmen's Compensation Act, 1897*, p. 17.

144 G. Alderman, *The Railway Interest*, p. 75.

vs. the Earl of Dudley in the Queen's Bench division in 1881 there was a strong tendency amongst employers to establish mutual insurance schemes with their employees. Although many of such projects pre-dated the Employers' Liability Act of 1880, the new law directly led to a rapid growth in their number as employers were uncertain of their total annual financial liability where settlements were the result of litigation. On the other hand if the employees could be induced to participate in an insurance scheme the liability of the employer would be small and precisely predictable. After 1880 the Iron Trade Employers' Association covered the liability of firms employing 28,000 men in engineering and shipbuilding at an annual cost to the employers of between one shilling and threepence and two shillings and threepence per £100 paid in wages.[145] It was claimed by employers who contracted out of the Act that compensation was granted more speedily and more certainly under private insurance schemes than was possible under the Act because of the necessity for litigation in the latter case. The answer given by union leaders was that employers favoured insurance principally because it was cheaper. Although a workman might have to wait longer for an award under the Act he was often more generously compensated.

Nevertheless, there could be no mistaking the fact that it was 'notoriously difficult' for a claimant to succeed under the Employers' Liability Act of 1880. In 1890 there were 389 cases with claims amounting to £63,070. Of these only 208 were successful and the amount of compensation awarded was only £8,679, or just over £41 per successful case. In view of these disquieting statistics it is necessary to explain why the trade unions clung so doggedly to their demand for a new Employers' Liability Act which did away completely with contracting out.[146] So insistent were the unions that no government dared not to promise amending legislation. In 1890, on the occasion of the Queen's speech, *The Times* referred to a projected bill as 'a hardy annual which makes its appearance in the Queen's speech with the regularity of spring'.[147]

All but one of the representatives of the miners who gave evidence before the Select Committee on the Employers' Liability Act Amendment bill said that the men liked the 1880 Act because it tended 'to increase safety in mines'. W. H. Patterson, the financial secretary of the Durham Miners' Association reported that since the Act came into force many managers called their deputies and overmen together once a month and read over the special rules, the object being 'to keep them clear of the Liability Act'. Although merchant seamen were not covered under the

145   S. and B. Webb, *Industrial Democracy*, p. 376.
146   D. G. Hanes, *The First British Workmen's Compensation Act, 1897*, p. 68.
147   *The Times*, 5 April 1890.

Act, they wished to be included in any future legislation. J. Havelock Wilson, then president of the North of England seamen and Sea Going Firemen's Friendly Association, told the committee in June 1886 that it was the unanimous opinion of the 'thirty or forty' meetings he had attended that the protection of the Act ought to be extended to seamen 'to prevent accidents'. 'The seamen do not require the shipowner's money', he said, 'what we require is more security for life and limb at sea'. These witnesses were supported by A. H. Ruegg, a barrister, who maintained that the primary argument against allowing an employer to contract out was that if he had the 'liability of the Act over him' he would be 'much more likely to be careful about plant and about the superintendence'.[148]

Other witnesses before the committee did not agree that the Act had these salutary effects. Mr. L. A. A. Jones MP could see that there was 'a counterbalancing tendency . . . employers' liability insurance' which often made it unnecessary for employers to spend large sums on safety precautions. William Galt, an authority on railway accidents, though writing two years before the passage of the Employers' Liability Act could see that liability to pay compensation to injured workmen would not necessarily induce the directors to spend more money on safety precautions.

> 'Their gain by not adopting the most efficient means for maintaining their lines in good condition and managing their traffic in a proper manner, far exceeds the loss incurred by an occasional accident; they are therefore under the constant temptation to work their traffic badly and so run the risk of accidents . . . They calculate on having to pay a certain sum in compensation each year, and the saving they effect is the premium they receive for the risk incurred.'[149]

The Webbs came to a similar conclusion concerning the generality of employers. 'Insurance', they wrote, 'therefore stands in the way of the trade union plan of preventing accidents by making them costly. What has been discovered is, that in the majority of industries it costs less, whether in the form of an annual premium or in that of an occasional lump sum out of profits, to compensate for accidents rather than prevent them'.[150]

Since the more astute of the trade union leaders cannot have been blind to the fact that, even allowing for the limited range of industries it covered, the Employers' Liability Act of 1880 was not having the salutary

---

148   *Report from the Select Committee on the Employers' Liability Act Amendment Bill, 1886,* pp. 109, 401, 38. 1886 (192) VIII, 137, 419, 56. IUP Industrial Relations 19, pp. 551, 843, 480.

149   *Quarterly Review,* vol. 70 January, 1878, p. 80.

150   S. and B. Webb, *Industrial Democracy,* p. 375.

effect on accident prevention that had at one time been hoped, there were other more important reasons for their opposition to 'contracting out' and for their continuing support for a more stringent employers' liability bill. John Burns, speaking in the House of Commons on 13 February, 1894 got to the root of the matter when he asserted that 'the real object of the masters in promoting the mutual insurance schemes is to prejudice the workman to damage the friendly societies and injure the cause of trade unionism'.[151] Since contracting out was always linked with employer-sponsored accident insurance schemes it harmed trade unionism of the new model, friendly society, type. In so far as the workman paid contributions to the company scheme, his attachment, voluntary or involuntary, to his employers would be strengthened and his trade union's financial and moral hold over him weakened.

By the 1890s, however, both a new style of trade union leadership and a new philosophy of government had emerged. The new unionism placed greater emphasis on militant struggle and less on the provision of social security benefits as means of advancing the welfare of the membership. The younger generation of trade union leaders looked more to the state to legislate for an eight-hour day and more rigorous safety regulations in all places of employment rather than to unaided collective bargaining.

The conflict between the old and the new approach to accident compensation was seen in the debates on Asquith's Employers' Liability Bill of 1893. Asquith's policy was the traditional liberal one of abolishing special privileges and exceptions. The anomalies of the existing law were to be completely swept away by the complete abolition of the doctrine of common employment. There was to be no contracting out, since this created other anomalies. The proceedures for claiming compensation were to be simplified and speeded up. Joseph Chamberlain on the other hand maintained that while it was unjust to make employers liable to pay compensation in every case, it was also wrong for the workman to be uncertain of obtaining compensation when injured. The answer therefore was a workmen's compensation insurance scheme. Through the Lords' refusal to accept complete abolition of contracting out, Asquith's bill did not reach the statute book. The last and most thorough attempt to legislate on the principle of employers' liability to pay compensation for injury or death of their employees had ended in failure.

By the time Matthew White Ridley introduced Joseph Chamberlain's Workmen's Compensation Bill on 3 May 1897, MPs had ample oppor-tunity to consider political and social developments at home and abroad which had relevance to the problems Asquith had tried to resolve four years earlier. In industrial Germany the Industrial Accident Insurance Law

151 *Hansard,* 4th Ser. vol. 21, Cols. 439-40.

of 1884 was based on the belief that organized labour had to be placated and that it was worth the state's while to invest in the physical well being of the labour force by instituting a scheme of compulsory insurance against accidents. In the USA conservationist theories were being advanced. If it was in the interests of the nation to try to prevent the profligate wastage of natural resources, was it not equally important to prevent wastage of human resources? It was in response to arguments of this kind that state governments in the USA did more in respect of workmen's compensation laws before 1914 than for any other type of social security. Joseph Chamberlain shared these sentiments. But he also believed that property had to pay a 'ransom' to labour in exchange for the privileges it received. The obligation to pay compensation to those who suffered injury or death in industry was a part of this ransom. Since the great extension of the franchise in 1884 it was also imperative to pass radical measures to steal the thunder of the much feared militant unions of the unskilled labourers.[152]

It was tactically not practical politics in 1897 for the Conservatives to insist on the right of contracting out as they had done four years earlier when opposing Asquith's bill. Had they done so, there would have been a head-on collision with the unions and the Liberals, who were opposed to contracting out, would have gained much political capital. On the other hand the government could not very well ignore the views of leading businessmen who were prominent in the Conservative party and who were opposed to the general principle of employers' liability. A general workmen's compensation bill was the only alternative. By leaving seamen, agricultural workers and domestic servants out of the scope of the bill the government insured against opposition from the powerful shipping and landed interests. The bill therefore passed the Commons without a division. In the House of Lords the opposition of the Earl of Wemyss misfired. Completely deaf, he moved the third reading be postponed three months. It required much shouting from the Earl of Kimberley to explain to him that he was too late; the Bill was already on its way back to the Commons.[153]

The scope of the Workmen's Compensation Act, 1897, (60 and 61 Vict. c. 37) was confined to those employed in railways, factories, mines,

---

152   Gaston V. Reinlinger, 'Welfare Policy and Economic Development', *Journal of Economic History*, vol. XXVI No. 4, 1966, pp. 565-69. *Reports by H.M. Representatives Abroad on the Laws Regulating the liability of Employers in Foreign Countries, 1886*, p. 1. 1886 [C.4784] LXVII, 571 *et seq.* IUP Industrial Relations 19, p. 327 *et seq.*

153   William Cassell Mallalieu, 'Joseph Chamberlain and Workmen's Compensation', *Journal of Economic History*, vol. X No. 1. May 1950, pp. 54-55. D. G. Hanes, *The First British Workmen's Compensation Act, 1897*, p. 103.

quarries, engineering works and work in or about buildings more than thirty feet in height. Where there was personal injury by accident arising out of and in the course of employment in any of these trades the employer was liable to pay compensation. In the event of death the compensation payable was three years wages or £150, whichever was larger, to a maximum of £300. In the case of total incapacity resulting from an injury, there was a weekly payment of half the previous average weekly earnings. Correspondingly smaller sums were payable in cases where the injury resulted in partial incapacity. The Act had many defects. Because of the stipulation that compensation was not payable where the accident was caused by 'the gross carelessness of the worker' there was much litigation hingeing round the question of what constituted 'gross carelessness'. The compensation at death was related to previous earnings and was not varied according to the number of dependants of the deceased. Medical benefits were extremely limited. A wool sorter who contracted anthrax was compensated, a painter who suffered from lead poisoning was not. Whereas in Germany protection of the workers' rights was a state obligation, in Britain it was basically a private matter. No special apparatus was established to administer the law; it was up to the individual to pursue his case through the established courts. Above all the right to compensation was confined to about one third of the manual workers only. It gave no protection to white collar workers, agricultural workers, domestic servants and the self employed.[154]

On the other hand the Act marked a completely new departure in social policy. It was a very important beginning. The omission of agricultural workers was rectified in 1900 and of most other groups by further legislation in 1907, 1920 and 1923. Although the trade unions in 1897 opposed compulsory insurance as against the interest of friendly societies, and although the trade union leader Henry Broadhurst declared that the Act was 'an attempt to impose on the working people of this country the German system of compulsory insurance and to strike at the root of trade unionism', a new principle, that of the welfare state, had been embodied in legislation. At the TUC in 1898 James O'Grady emphasized some of the possible consequences of the legislation of the previous year. 'If', he said, 'the national prosperity depends on the well-being of the worker, the necessary corollary is that the state should care for him in sickness ... And if preference will be given (in employment) to young men with whom the risks of accidents are less ... pensions for old age will be advanced a considerable step nearer realization.'[155]

154   Henry Pelling, *Politics and Society in Late Victorian Britain* (London: Macmillan, 1968), p. 68. S. and B. Webb, *Industrial Democracy*, p. 388.
155   D. G. Hanes, *The First British Workmen's Compensation Act, 1897*, p. 56.

11. Unemployment

No enquiry was made by parliament into unemployment as a national problem until 1895. This might suggest that 'distress from want of employment' only assumed serious importance in the last decade of the nineteenth century. Nothing can have been further from the truth. In the aftermath of the Napoleonic Wars the march of the Blanketeers from Manchester in 1817 was intended to draw attention to unemployment and distress in the textile industry. Although the general trend of cotton-goods production was one of rapid expansion there were periods of severe recession in 1824-26, 1836-41, 1847 and 1854-57. When supplies of raw cotton from the USA were interrupted because of the Civil War in the early 1860s distress in Lancashire became acute. In the summer of 1862 a quarter of the population of Ashton-under-Lyne district was in receipt of poor relief.[156] Unemployment among the silk weavers of Coventry and Macclesfield was particularly severe after 1860 when greater quantities of French silks entered the British market under the terms of the Cobden Treaty. The heavy industries felt the impact of trade recession even more severely than did textiles. In the iron trade of north east England, 1858 was a year of very heavy unemployment.

It is impossible to give anything approaching a precise figure for the numbers of those out of work in Great Britain before the late 1880s when the Board of Trade began the collection of unemployment statistics, mainly from data provided by the trade unions. But estimates, based on the poor law returns, have been made from the late 1840s onwards. The calculations show that the unemployed formed at least eleven or twelve per cent of the work force in years of trade depression such as 1848 and 1858, but that they declined to under two per cent in boom years like 1872 and 1889-90.[157] Unemployment was certainly not just an occasional problem. The proportion of union members unemployed exceeded seven per cent in five of the years 1878-87.

One reason why there was no parliamentary investigation of unemployment as a national problem before the 1890s was that it was believed that disasters such as the Irish potato famine of 1845-46, the slump in the iron trade and in engineering of 1858, the plight of the silk weavers in 1860 and the Lancashire cotton famine of 1862-63 were essentially local or regional in character and therefore could be dealt with by legislation or administrative measures local, rather than national, in scope. Thus the

156   William Otto Henderson, *The Lancashire Cotton Famine, 1861-1865* (Manchester: Manchester University Press, 1934), p. 56.

157   M. Dessauer-Meinhardt, 'Unemployment Records, 1848-59', *Economic History Review*, vol. 10 No 1, February 1940, pp. 38-43; 'Monthly Unemployment Records, 1854-1892', *Economica*, New Ser. vol. VII, August 1940, pp. 322-26.

Public Works (Manufacturing Districts) Act of 1863 was intended to relieve distress in Lancashire by granting power to local authorities to borrow money cheaply from the Public Works Loan Commissioners to finance local improvements. This, and the earlier measures designed to alleviate the worst effects of the Irish famine in 1845-46, were totally inadequate to cope with the distress they were designed to alleviate, but fortunately for those in authority, the disasters were of limited duration. The prevalent attitude towards those who were unemployed, even in more normal times, was expressed by Charles Booth, the wealthy shipowner and pioneer social investigator, as late as June 1895. He was asked:

'Do you think that most of those who remain unemployed will be unemployed chiefly through some weakness of their own? He replied, "If you include weakness of character, I think so ... most of them have themselves to thank in some way for their irregular work." '[158]

Booth's statement was consistent with opinion in government circles where it was held that a workman should make provident provision during years of brisk trade for the inevitable hard times that intervened. It would not help those in straightened circumstances during years of trade depression to encourage them to rely on any kind of public assistance, for this would only discourage future thrift. Public works to provide employment were regarded as dangerous and futile; the money so 'squandered' would be at the expense of private investment. The resulting decline in employment in the private sector would simply offset any employment created by the increased outlay from public funds. Until his retirement in 1894 Gladstone lent the full weight of his authority in opposition to any extravagance in public expenditure. In 1886, faced with demands for public works schemes for road and house building, harbour construction and the erection of new prisons, he declared that such plans would be self-destructive. He thought it highly probable that they would lead to the dismissal of a number of those fortunate enough to be in employment in private industry.[159]

In the closing years of the nineteenth century, however, these views, at least in their extreme form, were becoming politically untenable. The unemployed, aided by the energetic activities of the Social Democratic Federation, were becoming more articulate. It was a fact fully appreciated by John Burns who warned:

'The unemployed labourer of today is not the replica of the out of work a few years back. With the restless and ever changing spirit of the

158 *Report from the Select Committee on Distress from Want of Employment, 1895*, p. 418. 1895 (111) IX, 438. IUP Industrial Relations 23, p. 452.

159 José Harris, *Unemployment and Politics: a Study in English Social Policy 1886-1914* (Oxford: Clarendon Press, 1972), p. 75.

times he has altered greatly. His predecessor was a patient long-suffering animal, accepting his position as beast of burden with a fatalistic taciturnity, looking upon his enforced idleness as inevitable and with blind submission enduring his lot ... Mute, inarticulate, unenfranchised, he escaped observation, he had no vote, no municipal influence.'[160]

Burns' statement is misleading in so far as it suggests that after the passing of the third Reform Bill in 1884 every unemployed man had a vote. Many of those casually employed were unregistered or ineligible for either the household or lodger vote. But his contrast between the attitude of the unemployed in the 1860s and 1870s, with the greater militancy of the last two decades of the century, is a valid one. The huge demonstration of the London unemployed on 8 February 1886 and other protests at the Lord Mayor's Show in November 1886, and in weekly meetings throughout the summer and autumn of 1887, greatly scared property owners in the capital. The size of the Lord Mayor's Mansion House Fund for the relief of unemployment suddenly shot up from £19,000 to £72,000 in the two days immediately following the demonstration of 8 February 1886. The enemployed were drawing attention to their predicament even though it was not through the medium of the ballot box.[161]

The problem of what to do with the unemployed was made more acute in consequence of the policy of the Local Government Board in the 1870s. Workhouse masters were instructed to detain all casual paupers and not to release those who had spent the night in a casual ward until after nine o'clock in the morning, thus greatly lessening any man's chances of finding employment. The frustrated masses then swelled the ranks of the demonstrators. The disturbances of 1886 and 1887 were directly linked with the success of the Charity Organization Society's 'No outdoor relief' campaign of the 1870s, though they sprang from a multitude of causes besides.

Joseph Chamberlain's famous circular of 15 March 1886 – issued only five weeks after the alarming demonstration of the unemployed in London and hailed as a major departure in policy – only touched the very fringes of the problem. Local authorities were urged to so phase their works programmes that more employment was provided in times of economic distress. The deserving unemployed were to be differently treated from the old lags : they were not to be classed as paupers. The circular was 'almost a complete failure' because some local authorities had already adopted the

160   John Burns, *The Unemployed* (Fabian Tract No. 47, 1893), p. 4.

161   Neal Blewett, 'The Franchise in the United Kingdom, 1885-1918', *Past and Present*, No. 32, December 1965, p. 31. Kenneth Douglas Brown, *Labour and Unemployment, 1900-1914* (Newton Abbot: David & Charles, 1971), p. 14.

policy of concentrating labour-intensive jobs in times of heavy unemployment, the kind of labour that was attracted was generally unskilled and sometimes virtually unemployable and such work as was carried out by a motley, untrained, labour force was expensive and inefficient. The amount of money that was made available was quite inadequate, and this was because of a lack of conviction that it was justifiable to spend it in creating employment, rather than from a real stringency. Joseph Chamberlain's successor at the Local Government Board, Mr. C. T. Ritchie, believed that the only real remedy was 'greater thrift, less drunkenness, more industry and fewer early marriages'. In 1892-93 when Chamberlain's circular was re-issued by Fowler, the Liberal President of the Local Government Board, employment was provided for 26,875 persons out of a total of at least 750,000 unemployed.[162]

Meanwhile other forces were operating to aggravate the problem of unemployment. New machinery was tending to supplant the skilled craft labour that had enjoyed a privileged position through the great boom of the third quarter of the nineteenth century. In the gas industry mechanical grabs were displacing the labour of sixteen men every time one of these new machines was employed to unload coal from barges. The endless chain system of bringing coal ashore was putting more men out of work. In 1897 the Annual Report of the Amalgamated Society of Engineers noted that the 'proportion of machine to hand work is an increasing one' and it urged that, unless they wished to become paupers, skilled craftsmen should 'follow the work to the machine' whilst retaining their differentials in pay.[163]

The decline in farm prices, particularly those of food grains, and the fall in profitability in this most labour-intensive sector of agriculture, aggravated the glut of labour in the rapidly growing cities as farmers dismissed their surplus labourers. The drift of labour to the cities was intensified by the improvement of communications as branch railway lines and tram networks reached out towards the rural areas. Sir John Gorst told the House of Commons, early in 1885, that of 10,000 men unemployed in West Ham, 5,000 had recently migrated from the countryside. However, two years earlier only one per cent of those who applied for Mansion House relief were ex-farm workers. It appears that employers preferred in the first instance to employ the healthier countrymen rather than the palefaced town bred labourers, though by the

162   J. Harris, *Unemployment and Politics,* pp. 75-78. Bentley B. Gilbert, *The Evolution of National Insurance in Britain* (London: Michael Joseph, 1966), pp. 237-8.

163   *Third Report, Select Committee on Distress from want of Employment, 1895,* p. 432. 1895 (365) IX, 452. IUP Industrial Relations 24, p. 466. H. A. Clegg, A. Fox and A. F. Thompson, *A History of British Trade Unions since 1889,* p. 141.

winter of 1894-95 they had not enough work even for those who had but lately arrived from the villages.[164]

The Select Committee on Distress from Want of Employment was set up in 1895 as a device to rescue the government from the dilemma of its own creation. Chamberlain's circular of 15 March 1886, for all its limitations, marked the first official recognition of a new attitude towards unemployment. It was the first nail in the coffin of the doctrine that the distressed man owed his condition to his own shortcomings. The circular accepted, if only by implication, that there were exceptional occasions when a man was deprived of work and impoverished through circumstances beyond his control. But after 1886 neither the cabinet nor the Local Government Board showed any eagerness to provide the necessary funds for the unemployed to be put to work. Local authorities were expected to finance employment projects. The great difficulty — one that remained through to the 1930s — was that those authorities with the greatest number of unemployed to relieve had the highest rates and the lowest rateable value per head of population. Furthermore, since the Local Government Board had issued instructions that the unemployed were to be given non-pauperizing employment, it was scarcely possible for the task of devising work schemes to be entrusted to the local Boards of Guardians.[165]

The committee represented a very wide cross-section of opinion. Some, like George Bartley, chairman of the Islington Charity Organization Society, were still adherents of the principles of deterrence and less eligibility; some, like John Burns and William Mather, a Shropshire ironmaster, were protagonists of the eight hour day. It was not to be expected that any great sense of purpose would be imparted by the chairman, Sir Henry Campbell Bannerman, who protested about being appointed 'chairman of this unemployed committee — a horrible thing'.

Despite its announced intention of considering schemes for immediate relief, the committee failed to reach a consensus view on this central question. They were agreed that the automatic disfranchisement of men who had been on any kind of poor relief should be discontinued. 'Deserving men' who sought relief in times of exceptional distress should still be allowed to exercise the vote. But as to recommending a scheme for immediate relief that would be likely to meet with the approval of parliament they had to admit that no plan had been submitted to them which fulfilled these conditions. They confessed that the whole question

164   *Third Report, Select Committee on Distress from Want of Employment, 1895,* p. 186. 1895 (365) IX, 206. IUP Industrial Relations 24, p. 220. J. Harris, *Unemployment and Politics,* p. 30.

165   J. Harris, *Unemployment and Politics,* p. 90.

of the best method of dealing with the unemployed was 'still in the experimental stages'.[166]

There was not even agreement as to the extent of the problem. Mr. H. Llewellyn Smith, who had been in charge of the Labour Department of the Board of Trade since the beginning of 1893, presented a table of the percentage of unemployed members in Trade Unions at the end of each month from January 1888; but he was obliged to confess that he could not give the total number of wage workers in the country.[167] In view of the very imperfect development of statistical services by the Board of Trade it was possible for Will Thorne to state that there 'were quite a million out of employment' and for Keir Hardie, who had conducted his own survey from reports of trades councils and trade unions, to assert that the unemployed numbered 'not far short of a million and three quarters'. No member of the committee disagreed when Mr. W. Hunter, the secretary of the Glasgow Trades Council, commented that 'it would be a very advantageous thing for everybody concerned were we able to lay our finger on the number of the unemployed, or to know it approximately'.[168]

In the event the committee's hearings proved a happy hunting ground for advocates of such a wide variety of panaceas as the creation of small holdings, emigration, the building of light railways with the aid of public funds and the eight hour day and work sharing. Contributions tended to be polemical rather than analytical. Charles Loch of the Charity Organization Society stressed the importance of thrift and advocated the continuation of the policy disfranchising the workman who applied for relief. George Lansbury protested about the imputation that a substantial proportion of the unemployed were loafers who were unwilling to work. 'If you are going to sort out loafers', he said 'clear out those at the West End first, and set those at the East End an example'.[169]

The one important exception was the evidence given by H. Llewellyn Smith, including as it did an important analysis of both seasonal and cyclical fluctuations in employment. His two-dimensional charts revealed

166 *Report from the Select Committee on Distress from want of Employment,* 1896, p. xv. 1896 (321) IX, 315. IUP Industrial Relations 24, pp. 104-5. J. Harris, *Unemployment and Politics,* p. 91.

167 *Third Report Select Committee on Distress from want of Employment, 1896,* p. 72. 1895 (365) IX, 92. IUP Industrial Relations 24, p. 106.

168 *Third Report, Select Committee on Distress from Want of Employment, 1895,* pp. 259, 430. 1895 (365) IX, 279, 450. IUP Industrial Relations 24, pp. 293, 464 and 1895 (111) p. 74 IUP Industrial Relations 23, p. 104.

169 *Report from the Select Committee on Distress from Want of Employment, 1895-96,* p. 404. 1896 (321) IX, 424. IUP Industrial Relations 24, p. 438. See also P. Ford, *Social Theory and Social Practice* (Shannon: Irish University Press, 1968) pp. 92-94.

that even in years of booming trade there was an 'irreducible minimum' of two per cent unemployment; that in the skilled trades, such as shipbuilding and engineering, unemployment sometimes exceeded eleven per cent during trade depressions and that after every four of five years of good trade there was a strong possibility of a period of business recession when unemployment was likely to increase rapidly. Smith's pioneering investigation into the pattern of unemployment and the development of the trade cycle was used by Beveridge and others for years to come as the standard framework of analysis of the problem of unemployment. One reason for the inconclusiveness of the reports of both committees was the lack of agreement among those who were closest to the unemployed — the socialists in the SDF and the ILP — on the right policy for reducing unemployment. The traditional remedy advocated by the trade unions for most of the nineteenth century was the shortening of the working day. The first campaign of the Amalgamated Society of Engineers after its foundation in 1851 was the abolition of compulsory overtime so that work could be more fairly distributed amongst the Union's membership. At the TUC in 1878 a fraternal delegate, the German Marxist, Adam Weiler, urged the reduction of working hours as a means of reducing unemployment. But opinion within the TUC was by this time divided between those who favoured the statutory limitation of hours and the craft unions which generally preferred the method of industrial bargaining. Tom Mann helped to swing opinion towards the statutory policy when he wrote his influential pamphlet *What a compulsory eight hour day means to the workers,* in 1886. In it he argued:

'We have something like seven million adult workers in the British Isles, working nominally under the nine hours system ... Let us see how many more hands would be put in employment if we struck one hour per day from those in work. It is roughly estimated that of the above mentioned workers there are about 900,000 now out of work ... Now strike off one hour per day from the six million in work. The result would be an immediate demand for 750,000 additional workers to keep up production at its present rates'.[170]

In fairness to the author it must be added that he conceded that the advantages of the reform 'would soon be swallowed up by fresh displacements of labour due to more efficient machinery', but that the change should nevertheless be carried out as it would give the workers more leisure, would allow them time to increase their understanding of society and would thus hasten 'the overthrow of capitalistic domination'.

170   Tom Mann, *What a compulsory eight hour day means to the workers* (London: Modern Press, 1886).

Three liberal industrialists: William Mather, William Allen and Mark Beaufoy, the first two engineers and the third a jam and vinegar manufacturer, thought there was good deal in what Tom Mann had written. Between 1889 and 1893 they introduced the eight hour day in their factories. The result was that the existing labour force produced as much in eight hours as had previously been produced in nine. No additional hands were needed. This experience brought about some change of direction of Socialist propaganda on the question of shorter hours. It is noticeable that when Tom Mann gave evidence before the Royal Commission on Labour he gave as the main reason for the eight hour day the improvement of the well being of the worker and his family. As a cure for unemployment he advocated the large scale extension of public ownership.[171]

Thus Will Thorne alone of the Socialist witnesses before the Select Committee in 1895 advocated the eight hour day as a contribution to the solution of the unemployment problem, while the remainder, apart from their proclamation of faith in public ownership, advocated a diversity of remedies, including the resettlement of labour on the land, the extension of labour exchanges and retraining schemes for industrial workers.

Thus the value of the reports of the select committees lies in what they reveal of the members' immaturity of economic analysis and lack of understanding of the causes of unemployment. The limited recommendations were virtually ignored by the government, by parliament and by the press. By the time the second report appeared, the influence of labour in parliament had declined as a result of the Conservative victory in the election of 1895. The new government was under less pressure to take action. The problem itself was greatly lessened by the improvement of trade in the later 1890s. A building boom took up most of the slack in the construction industry. Exports revived with the recovery of prices. It is significant that the TUC which had discussed unemployment through the eighties and early nineties did not debate the question between 1896-1903. A substantial revival of interest only came with the election of twenty-nine candidates of the Labour Representation Committee in the general election of 1906.

Whilst unemployment remained a prominent feature of the industrial scene there was little prospect of any impressive advance in the bargaining strength of labour in industrial relations. The 'reserve army' of labour put strict limits to hopes for any great advance in real wages. Not until the 1940s was there a dramatic change in the strengths of capital and labour. At the beginning of a long period of full employment a writer in *The*

171   J. Harris, *Unemployment and Politics*, p. 68.

Times saw the significance which unemployment had had for the relationship between masters and workmen up to that time:

> 'Unemployment is not a mere accidental blemish in a private-enterprise economy. On the contrary it is part of the essential mechanism of the system and has a definite function to fulfil. The first function of unemployment ... is that it maintains the authority of master over man. The master has normally been in the position to say: "If you don't want the job, there are plenty of others who do." '

There were very few years in the nineteenth century when this was not the situation.

12. The new unionism and the Royal Commission on Labour

On 21 February 1891, two days before Lord Salisbury's government announced the appointment of the Royal Commission on Labour, Lord Randolf Churchill delivered a major speech at a meeting organized by the Paddington Conservative Association. More than half his lengthy address was devoted to answering the question 'What are you going to do for the labouring classes?' This, he said, was the great issue of the day. It was the workers, he claimed, who 'had the power'. Without them the Conservative party could 'not entertain the great political objects it had in view'. The speaker went on to reveal why he had come to recognize the labour question as the great issue of the time. In recent months there had been 'a very remarkable development of strikes'. 1890 would go down in history as 'the great strike year'. The public were threatened with a great war between capital and labour in which capital was 'banded together on one side, never to yield' and confronted labour which was likewise 'banded together never to yield'. The results of the confrontation might be 'as disastrous, and even more disastrous, to the property of the country than civil war when armed force might be engaged'.[172]

The governing party's alarm at the labour situation in 1891 had some braodly similar features to the alarm which prompted that earlier major investigation, the Royal Commission on Trade Unions, in 1867. In both cases there was a remarkable upsurge of political activity of the working classes associated with an extension of the franchise; there was also, in both cases, a rapid and impressive increase of trade union membership accompanied by some manifestations of violence or, as in the later case, mass pressure through militant picketing. It is worth examining in somewhat more detail these two elements of political awakening and trade union upsurge in the context of the late 1880s and early 1890s.

172   *The Times*, 23 February, 1891.

The political revival of the 1860s was largely centred round the demand for the extension of the franchise; that of the 1880s and 1890s for the most part came after the extension of the franchise to many of the labouring classes under the third Reform Bill in 1884. The aims of the new movement were much wider than those of the trade unionists who had trampled down the railings of Hyde Park, London, in the great reform demonstration of 23 July 1866. The renewed political activity of the 1880s had a more collectivist emphasis.

The Socialist revival was heralded by the Democratic Federation, founded in 1881, and was given some popular appeal through the writings of its leader, H. M. Hyndman, especially through his *England for All* (published in 1881), which for the first time expressed the ideas of Karl Marx in everyday English. In 1884 the Democratic Federation was renamed the Social Democratic Federation and acquired a more distinctly socialist programme. Many of the most distinguished leaders of the new organization entered the socialist movement via the land reform agitation of the 1870s and 1880s. Perhaps the most notable of these recruits was H. H. Champion, secretary of the SDF, who had been educated at Marlborough and had served for a time as an army officer before using his independent income to support his career as a socialist propagandist.

Possibly even more important for the revival of working class political activity was the influence of Henry George whose *Progress and Poverty* was first published in America in 1879 but which went into many editions in England from 1881 onwards. George made three visits to Great Britain between 1881-1884, attracting huge audiences at the many meetings he addressed. His influence was great partly because his proposals for a single tax on the increment in land values and for the nationalization of the land were heard by many middle class and working class radicals who had been nurtured in similar ideas through Chartism, the Land Nationalization Society and the Land Reform Union. His emphasis that poverty is a product of man-made institutions 'helped to undermine the Victorian belief that social reform was impossible save through individual regeneration'. Along with the writings of Ruskin and Carlyle and the later works of J. S. Mill, *Progress and Poverty* did a great deal to undermine the hold which the classical economists, especially Malthus, had gained over the minds of the trade union leaders in the third quarter of the nineteenth century.[173]

Also influencing the spread of socialist ideas was the 'little band of

173   H. M. Pelling, *The Origins of the Labour Party, 1880-1900* (Oxford: Clarendon Press, 1965), Chap. II. John Saville, 'Henry George and the British Labour Movement' *Bulletin* of the Society for the Study of Labour History, No. 5, Autumn 1962, p. 19.

prophets' grouped into the Fabian Society from 1884 onwards. What they lacked in numbers they more than made up by outstanding ability and industry. Their collectivist views found expression in the famous Fabian Tracts and in statements made to innumerable select committees and other enquiries and public meetings. The Independent Labour Party was founded too late (1893) to mould the public opinion of the great awakening of 1889-92 which influenced Lord Salisbury's cabinet to set up the Royal Commission. By the turn of the century its influence was far more profound.

The socialist revival of the 1880s directly affected only a few thousand persons. The SDF was notoriously unsuccessful at winning both parliamentary and local elections. Although he had achieved a national reputation, and some wealth, as an artist and craftsman, William Morris was unable to recruit more than 230 members to the Socialist League (a breakaway from the SDF) during the first year of its existence, 1885. The significance of the creation of these small 'ginger groups', then, lay in their potential for organizing and indoctrinating a very much larger number of men and women when the economic conditions were ripe for a great upsurge in trade union activity.

In the two decades following the passage of the Trade Union Act in 1871 there was a remarkable change in the structure of the British labour force. Its most marked characteristic was the growth in numbers of the unskilled or semi-skilled persons employed in the service industries and in public administration. In gas, water and electricity undertakings the numbers employed rose from 18,000 to 38,000; in transport the increase was from 670,000 to 1,124,000 and in public administration it was from 113,000 to 163,000.[174] In a number of these rapidly growing occupations the total labour force employed on individual sites was often very large, as in the case of the great national dockyards and the larger gas plants. But although the job of union recruitment was to that extent made easier, the men employed were easily replaced, especially in times of trade recession, making collective bargaining far more difficult to achieve than was the case with the skilled trades.

The trade boom of 1889-91 provided the big opportunity for the organization of the large mass of semi-skilled and unskilled labourers in the gas, water, coal mining and transport industries — to mention only the most prominent examples — into trade unions of a new type. Membership of unions affiliated to the TUC grew very rapidly from 600,000 in 1888 to 1,516,000 in 1892. More significant was the rise in membership of general unions catering for the less skilled workers in transport, coal mining and

174   Brian Redman Mitchell and Phyllis Deane, *Abstract of British Historical Statistics* (Cambridge: Cambridge University Press, 1962), p. 60.

the gas industry. In the four years from 1888 to 1891 inclusive, membership of the Amalgamated Society of Railway Servants rose from 12,000 to 30,000 while the membership of the Miners' Federation of Great Britain shot up from 36,000 to 200,000. J. Havelock Wilson told the commission that enrolments in his union, the National Amalgamated Sailors' and Firemen's Union, had jumped from 8,000 in 1888 to 130,000 in 1892. 20,000 members joined Will Thorne's Gas Workers' and General Labourers Union within six months in 1889.[175]

The beginnings of the late nineteenth century development of general unionism can be traced back at least to the formation of the National Labour Federation on Tyneside in 1886. While the trustees of this new organization included well known 'old' trade unionists of the cautious kind, like Thomas Burt and Charles Fenwick, other leaders such as the chairman, E. R. Pease, were socialists, and membership was open to men of all trades. The period of very rapid expansion of general unionism, however, was between 1888-1891.

Since it was a common characteristic of employment in these rapidly expanding occupations that the place of the gasworker, tramwayman, carter or dock labourer could easily be filled from the reserve army of labour, the only chance of successful industrial action was 'to recruit into one gigantic union all those who could possibly blackleg' on those striking for better working conditions.[176] The ideal — far from being realized at any time — would have been the recruitment of every unskilled worker into one general union. Valiant attempts were made to achieve something approaching this ideal, at least on a regional level, and the names of the new organizations set up during the boom years reflect the nature of the attempt that was being made. Some of the better known unions then formed included the National Union of Gasworkers and General Labourers; the Dock, Wharf, and Riverside Labourers' Union and the Leeds Amalgamated Association of Builders' Labourers, all established in 1889, and the General Railway Workers' Union and the Navvies', Bricklayers' Labourers, and General Labourers' Union, both founded in the following year.

The new unions were strongest in the largest works, particularly where these were municipally owned, as Labour or 'progressive' local councilors could press for union recognition and the payment of standard rates of wages to employees, and even, in some few instances, establish the

175 *Royal Commission on Labour, Minutes of Evidence, Group 'B', 1892*, p. 469. 1892 [C.6708-V] XXXV, 477. IUP Industrial Relations 26, p. 583. Will Thorne, *My Life's Battles* (London: George Newnes Ltd., 1924), pp. 76-77.

176 E. J. Hobsbawm, 'General Labour Unions in Britain, 1889-1914', *Labouring Men'*, p. 181.

union shop. Although the essential precondition for success was strong union organization, as the case of the Hull dock workers amply demonstrated, it helped greatly to have a sympathetic local authority as employer.[177]

Industrial relations in the old craft occupations were genteel by comparison with the situation in the public utility industries. Ben Tillett described from first hand experience how it was in the London docks.

'To obtain employment we are driven into a shed, iron barred from end to end, outside of which a forman or contractor walks up and down with the air of a dealer in a cattle market, picking and choosing from a crowd of men, who in their eagerness to obtain employment trample each other underfoot, and where, like beasts, they fight for a days work.'[178]

The only hope of a strike succeeding where such were the customary methods of labour recruitment was for mass picketing to be conducted, if not with violence, then at least without the wearing of kid gloves.

With the labour supply sharply fluctuating and undependable it is not difficult to understand why the leaders of the new unionism should have favoured the method of legislation rather than that of industrial bargaining to obtain the eight hour day. At the first meeting of the Second International in 1889 the representatives of labour from twenty-two nations recommended that the first of May should be set aside as labour day when the workers would demand of the authorities 'the legal reduction of the working day to eight hours'. The Gas Workers' and General Labourers' Union gave prompt support to this resolution by organizing a demonstration in Hyde Park in favour of a legal eight hour working day.[179]

It was simply not feasible to expect the unskilled and casually employed labourers to pay large weekly contributions to friendly society type trade unions; the contents of their weekly pay packets were neither large enough nor sufficiently stable to make such savings possible. Will Thorne wrote in the Annual Report of the Gas Workers and General Labourers in November 1889 that he did not believe in having 'sick pay,

177   Raymond Brown, *Waterfront Organisation in Hull, 1870-1900* (University of Hull Occasional Papers in Economic and Social History, No. 5, 1972). A. E. P. Duffy, 'New Unionism in Britain, 1889-90: A Reappraisal', *Economic History Review,* 2nd Ser., vol. XIV (1961).

178   Ben Tillett, *Memories and Reflections* (London: John Long Ltd., 1931), pp. 75-76.

179   Report to the Delegates of the Brussels International Congress, 1891 cited in *Labour's Turning Point, 1880-1900,* E. J. Hobsbawm (ed.) (London: Lawrence and Wishart, 1948), p. 110.

out of work pays and a number of other pays' since the whole aim of the union was 'to reduce the hours of labour and reduce Sunday work' which were the primary causes of sickness and unemployment among gas workers.

It was all very well for the leaders of the older craft unions to accept the situation of the labour market and to depend mainly on collective bargaining to shorten working hours and improve rates of pay. They were in a position to influence the market for labour. The younger generation of trade unionists, organizing men in the public utilities, knew full well that the acceptance of the 'market rate' would make life quite intolerable for their members. At the end of the century the Webbs recognized the distinct change in standpoint of leaders of the new unionism. It was that 'considerations of market price or business profit ought, in the interests of the community, to be strictly subordinated to the fundamental question of, 'Can a man live by the trade?'[180]

Such considerations had particular relevance to the growing numbers of female wage earners who were frequently amongst the worst exploited in a whole range of industries. Compared with the very large numbers of them that were employed in the textile industry, in the manufacture of all types of clothing and, at least in the earlier part of the nineteenth century, in coal mining and in agriculture, very few women were involved in the trade union movement until the 1870s. Women were allowed as members of the Manchester Cotton Spinners Society as early as 1795; but such an enlightened policy of union leadership was very exceptional. All too frequently the principal unions excluded women from membership on the grounds that women workers undercut men's rates of wages. Women sometimes got round this difficulty by forming separate unions, as in the case of the West of Scotland Power Loom Female Weavers Society of 1833. Generally they remained completely unorganized.

The pioneer of womens' trade unionism in the 1870s and 1880s was Mrs. Emma Paterson, the daughter of a London schoolmaster who founded the Women's Protective and Provident League (later the Women's Trade Union League) in 1874 'to improve the industrial and social position of women'. Initially membership was largely confined to middle class ladies and gentlemen anxious to help exploited women workers in the clothing and other sweated trades. Nevertheless, it did inspire the formation of a number of unions for women employed in cigar making, tailoring and other occupations. In 1875 Mrs. Paterson was the first woman to be elected as a delegate to the TUC, a position she held continuously until 1884. From 1882 onwards women trade unionists in

180   S. and B. Webb, *Industrial Democracy*, p. 230.

the metropolis had their own federal organization, the London Women's Trades Council.[181]

The organization of women made the most rapid advances during the upsurge of new unionism after 1888. The successful strike of the women and girls employed in Bryant and May's Match Factory in East London, following Mrs. Annie Besant's exposure of their working conditions in the May 1888 number of *The Link*, has rightly been regarded as an important turning point in the history of women's emancipation.[182] The general labour unions which sprang up at this time, in contrast with the older craft unions, opened their ranks to women members. The Dock, Wharf, Riverside and General Labourers' Union opened up women's branches and appointed women organizers. In its foundation year 1889, the National Union of Gasworkers and General Labourers opened a branch for women members at Singleton. At the same time increasing numbers of women clerical workers and telegraphists were becoming organized. Those employed in the Post Office enrolled in the United Kingdom Postal Clerks Association which was formed in 1887. In 1889 more than 2,000 tailoresses employed in the Leeds district struck work for an improvement in their rates of pay. Although they were defeated, they attracted a great deal of support in the area.

The policy of the TUC towards the organization of women vacillated. Although in 1874 it resolved 'to promote the self-relying trade union movement among women', the Parliamentary Committee, three years later, issued a statement completely contradictory in spirit to the earlier resolution. 'It was the duty of men and husbands', so the all-male committee pronounced, 'to bring about a condition of things when their wives should be in their proper sphere at home instead of being dragged into competition for livelihood with the great and strong men of the world'. Nevertheless 'the great and strong men' of the 1885 TUC yielded to the growing feminist movement and resolved that 'where women do the same work as men they shall receive equal pay'.[183]

No doubt the change in the composition, appearance and outlook of the TUC from 1890 helps to explain the disquiet of the Salisbury government about the labour question. Hitherto the Parliamentary Committee of the TUC was regarded as a moderating influence over the labour movement. The main preoccupation of leaders of the calibre of Henry Broadhurst and George Howell seemed to be to keep in the good

181   Trades Union Congress, *Women in the Trade Union Movement* (London: TUC, 1955), pp. 45-47.

182   The story has been told in Ann Stafford, *Match to Fire the Thames* (London: Hodder & Stoughton, 1961).

183   Trades Union Congress, *Women in the Trade Union Movement*, pp. 51-52.

books of the Liberal party. John Burns, who attended the 1890 TUC, noticed the difference from earlier years:—

'Physically the "old" unionists were much bigger than the new . . . A great number of them looked like respectable city gentlemen; wore very good coats, large watch chains, and high hats, and in many cases were of such splendid build and proportions that they presented an aldermanic, not to say magisterial form and dignity. Amongst the new delegates not a single one wore a tall hat. They looked workmen: they were workmen.'[184]

Thus it was the intrusion of trade unionism into industries and social classes hitherto largely untouched by its influence; the defiant rather than compromising attitude of the new leaders, the organization of women workers and the demand for a much greater degree of state intervention to help the less fortunately placed members of society which alarmed the government of the day. It was all the more alarming that these startling changes came just at the time when Britain was beginning to feel the pinch of the competition of German and American goods in her overseas and domestic markets.

In his Paddington speech, Lord Randolf Churchill, beating the gun of the official announcement of a Labour Commission by two days, suggested how its appointment might help to stave off a possible catastrophe:

'If a Royal Commission could be appointed to enquire into such subjects . . . it would give not only the greatest possible satisfaction to the labouring classes (who would feel that we were really anxiously considering their position), but would probably be the means of eliciting the most valuable and useful information which would be of greatest value to the working classes themselves when digested.'[185]

The Times also shared the hope that the findings of the Commission would sober down the extremism of the leaders of the new unionism. It trusted that 'a searching enquiry' would 'knock finally on the head a good many nostrums at present bandied about, with a confidence entirely unwarranted by knowledge, among well meaning people'. With the new unionists' demand for the eight hour day very much in mind, it was hoped that 'the working man could learn that the complex and delicate fabric of our industry and commerce ought not to be delivered over to legislative experiments'.[186]

It was not until 10 April 1891 that the names of the twenty-seven

184 Cited in Keith Dawson and Peter Wall, *Trade Unions* (Oxford: Oxford University Press, 1968), p. 37.

185 *The Times,* 23 February 1891.

186 *The Times,* 24 February 1891.

commissioners were announced. There could be no questioning the
outstanding talents of many of those who agreed to serve. Professor Alfred
Marshall was the leading economist of his day, Samuel Plimsoll had an
unrivalled knowledge of maritime labour and Jessie Collins was the
foremost exponent of land reforms. But for a commission whose task was
to examine industrial relations the representation of working men was
inadequate. Only six members: Messrs. T. Burt, W. Abraham, J. Mawdsley,
M. Austin, H. Tait and T. Mann, directly represented the wage earners,
though others, including A. J. Mundella and Samuel Plimsoll, were
sympathetic to labour. More glaring was the complete exclusion of
women. In the House of Commons on 6 March 1891 Mr. Summers pointed
out that 656,549 of the 1,084,361 persons employed in the mills and
factories of the U.K. were women, and pleaded with W. H. Smith, the First
Lord of the Treasury, to nominate at least one woman commissioner. The
minister promised he would 'carefully consider all suggestions'. However,
ten days later he informed another member of the House that the
government had come to the conclusion that on the whole 'it was not
advisable that women should be placed on the commission'.[187] Presum-
ably because it was imagined that some women would feel extremely
nervous appearing before such a distinguished all-male assembly, the
commission decided not to summon female witnesses. But since it could
not fail to take evidence from such a large element in the labour force, it
decided to appoint four 'lady assistant commissioners' to conduct local
enquiries into the conditions of the employment of women in various
occupations. From the seventeen reports the four ladies presented, the
commission was able to present its own observations and recommendations in its fifth and final report.[188]

The most striking characteristic of the whole enquiry is the contrast
between the enormous mass of evidence about working conditions in the
three major industrial groupings – 'A': mining, iron and steel, engineering,
shipbuilding and cognate trades; 'B': transport and agriculture and 'C':
textiles, clothing, chemicals building and miscellaneous – and the very
modest scale of the recommendations in the final report. Hence the
outstanding value of the Labour Commission is in what the minutes of
evidence and reports of special commissioners reveal about industrial
relations, the rates of wages and conditions of employment of all the
major occupations of the kingdom. As a key to government thinking,
future plans and legislation, it is far less significant.

187   *Hansard*, 3rd Ser. vol. 351, Cols. 437 and 1065-66. For the general criticisms
made by Mrs. Webb and the controversy over the value of the Commission, see P.
Ford, *Social Theory and Social Practice*, pp. 69, 70, 74, 152.

188   *Fifth and Final Report, Royal Commission on Labour, 1894,* p. 90. 1894
[C.7421] XXXV, 98. IUP Industrial Relations 44, p. 98.

The minutes of evidence are most valuable for those occupations where union organization was either very weak or non existent. Agricultural trade unionism was at a very low ebb in the early 1890s. The assistant commissioners whose task it was to visit the farming districts found only six — Hillingbourn, Langport, Maldon Stratford on Avon, Swaffham and Thingo — where branches of the National Agricultural Labourers Union, or other smaller organizations, had achieved some success in recruitment. Thus the sixty page report on *The Agricultural Labourer*, written by William C. Little, is of enhanced value because of the paucity of detailed trade union records of these years. For the same reasons the reports of the four lady assistant commissioners are invaluable as disclosing the multifarious reasons for the inferior industrial position of women workers. In one of its most outspoken paragraphs, the Majority Report expressed the opinion that 'in cases where they (i.e. women) receive less than men for work, which taking everything into account is of equal value to the employer, it is clear that they would gain much even from a little organization'.[189]

The Commission showed considerable insight in explaining why trade unionism was strong in some sectors of the economy and weak in others. In coal mining the bargaining strength of the Miners Federation of Great Britain, founded in 1888, was greatly enhanced by the safety clauses of the Coal Mines Regulation Act of 1887, particularly by Rule 39, which stated that 'no person now employed as a coal or ironstone getter shall be allowed to work alone . . . in the face of the workings until he has had two years experience'. Though this was a provision initially designed to secure greater safety in the mines, the Commission noted that it also made it impossible 'to bring in new men in case of a strike to take the place of the strikers'.[190]

The expansion of the occupations requiring mainly unskilled labour was seen to bring about a change in the methods of industrial bargaining. Where labour had no 'natural monopoly' through the possession of specialized skills there was a tendency towards the use of more or less violent methods of action to prevent the introduction of non unionist or 'free' labourers. The other tendency was towards the spread of general unionism which the Report described as an attempt to bring the various sections not, strictly speaking, engaged in the same occupation, to the assistance of each other in industrial conflicts'.[191]

189   *Fifth and Final Report, Royal Commission on Labour, 1894*, p. 96. 1894 [C.7421] XXXV, 104. IUP Industrial Relations 44, p. 104.

190   *Fifth and Final Report, Royal Commission on Labour, 1894*, p. 30. 1894 [C.7421] XXXV, 38 IUP Industrial Relations 44, p. 38.

191   *Fifth and Final Report, Royal Commission on Labour, 1894*, p. 31. 1894 [C.7421] XXXV, 39. IUP Industrial Relations 44, p. 39.

Unlike the Royal Commission on Trade Unions in 1867, the Labour Commission viewed with a degree of equanimity the consolidation of organizations of both employers and of workers. It found that 'powerful trades unions on the one side and powerful associations of employers on the other had been the means of bringing together in conference the representatives of both classes, enabling each to appreciate the position of the other'.

The Webbs considered that these tendencies led inevitably to compulsory trade union membership and an equally strong collective organization of the employers. They supported the proposal of the Duke of Devonshire and four other employer members of the Commission that collective agreements should be legally binding. Trade unions, they considered, should be given legal personality for this limited purpose: 'the trade union should be liable to be sued only in respect of collective agreements made with the Employers' Association, and then only for definite penalties specified in such agreements'.[192] The trade unions as members of the Commission, however, were completely against all proposals of this kind. In the light of subsequent controversies over the role of the Industrial Relations Court under the Industrial Relations Act of 1971, the views expressed by the trade union leaders of 1894 in their Minority Report are worth recalling:

'To expose the large amalgamated societies of the country with their accumulated funds sometimes reaching a quarter of a million sterling, to be sued for damages by any employer in any part of the country, or by any discontented member or non-unionist, for the action of some branch secretary or delegate would be a great injustice. If every trade union was liable to be perpetually harassed by actions at law on account of the doings of individual members; if trade union funds were to be depleted by lawyers fees and costs, if not even by damages or fines, it would go far to make trade unionism impossible for any but the most prosperous and experienced artisans. The present freedom of trade unions from any interference from the courts of law – anomalous as it may appear to lawyers – was, after prolonged struggle and parliamentary agitation, conceded in 1871, and finally became law in 1875. Any attempts to revoke this hardly won charter of trade union freedom, or in any way to tamper with the purely voluntary character of their associations, would, in our opinion, provoke the most embittered resistance from the whole body of trade unionists, and would, we think, be undesirable from every point of view.'[193]

192   S. and B. Webb, *Industrial Democracy*, p. 534.

193   *Fifth and Final Report, Royal Commission on Labour, 1894*, p. 54, 146. 1894 [C.7421] XXXV, 62, 154. IUP Industrial Relations 44, p. 62, 154.

In 1894 the majority commissioners refrained from making any decisive recommendation about the legal status of trade unions. They deemed it politic to let well alone.

Having dodged this and other major issues, such as the whole question of public ownership and the respective merits of free enterprise and socialist economies, the Commission confined itself to recommendations of a relatively minor character. The recommendation that the Board of Trade should assume a greater initiative in providing arrangements for the conciliation of industrial disputes was perhaps the most important of these. It was the one proposal of the Commission that was followed, fairly speedily, by legislation – the Conciliation Act of 1896.

In 1894, when the final report of the Labour Commission was published, neither the .government nor the employers were so alarmed about the labour situation as they had been when the Commission was appointed three years earlier. Labour's strong bargaining position of 1889-90 had disappeared by 1894. During the many months in which the Commision was sitting, the level of unemployment as recorded by the trade unions had practically doubled – from 3.5 per cent to 6.9 per cent. At the high tide of union expansion in 1891 approximately 1,500,000 persons were enrolled in trade unions of all kinds. But from 1892 overall membership declined slightly and it did not start to rise again until 1897. Those who saw the meteoric rise of trade unionism to 1892 as a threat to the economy and to society had their fears allayed in the years which followed. The new unionists' dominance of the TUC also proved to be short lived. By 1894 their foothold had weakened: by 1895 the 'old guard' had regained control.[194]

At the same time the employers met the challenge of the new unionism by a closure of their ranks. Particularly in shipping, in engineering and in railway transport, employers' federations had great success in holding trade unionism at bay. Most successful were the shipowners. In September 1890 the Shipping Federation was founded 'as a fighting machine to counter the strike weapon'.[195] By establishing Free Labour Bureaux in the major ports and giving employment only to those men who had been issued with the Federation's 'ticket' the influence of the trade unions both in shipping and in the dock yards was greatly reduced. By the end of 1891 Havelock Wilson's National Amalgamated Sailors' and Firemen's Union had lost over half the 60,000 members it had recruited in the boom. At the same time the membership of Ben Tillett's Dock, Wharf Riverside and

194 B. R. Mitchell and P. Deane, *Abstract of British Historical Statistics,* p. 64. S. and B. Webb, *History of Trade Unionism,* p. 423.

195 Leslie Hughes Powell, *The Shipping Federation* (London: The Shipping Federation, 1950), p. 5.

General Labourers' Union fell from 57,000 in 1890 to 30,000 in 1891. The workers at Hull resisted the employers' counter offensive longer than elsewhere, partly because of the pro-union attitude of one of the largest shipowners in the port, Thomas Wilson Sons and Co. However, matters came to a head in 1893 when, under pressure from marine insurance companies and other shipowners, Wilsons rejoined the Shipping Federation. With the employers now presenting a united front, the Hull Dockers Union was defeated in a prolonged strike. National dockyard organization had largely collapsed through the combined effects of trade depression and the operation of the Free Labour Bureaux.[196]

The railway companies were slower in developing united resistance to the demands of labour than were the shipowners. Until the later 1890s they had proved able to deal with their labour problems on a company basis. But when the membership of the Amalgamated Society of Railway Servants began to grow rapidly, under the stimulus of competition from the General Railway Workers Union after 1890, the railway companies began to think more seriously of co-operation. In November 1897, faced with the unions' demands embodied in an 'All Grades Programme', the leading companies agreed not to concede increases in wages or reduction in hours of work.[197] Employers in engineering were also slower in combining to defend their interests than were the shipowners. However, when the Amalgamated Society of Engineers led a strike for the eight hour day in 1897 the recently formed Engineering Employers' Federation, under the energetic leadership of Col. Dyer, retaliated with a most efficient lock-out of the men. The employers announced their determination 'to manage their own affairs' without interference from the union. After a prolonged struggle the men were obliged to return to work virtually on the employers' terms.[198]

It was the growing political awareness of labour as well as its rapidly increasing industrial strength which aroused concern in government circles at the time of the appointment of the Labour Commission. The results of the general election of 1892 seemed to confirm the seriousness of the situation. For the first time in history, two independent socialist leaders, J. Kier Hardie and R. B. Cunninghame Graham, were elected to the House of Commons. And yet in the political sphere also there seemed to be less cause for concern in the later 1890s than there had been earlier in the decade. Both of the socialist victors of 1892 were defeated in the general election of 1895. At the end of the 1890s the only working-class MPs were 'Lib-Labs' safely within the fold of the Liberal party.

196   R. Brown, *Waterfront Organisation in Hull 1870-1900*, pp. 52, 68.

197   G. Alderman, *The Railway Interest*, p. 166.

198   Richard Hyman, *The Workers' Union* (Oxford: Clarendon Press, 1971), p. 3.

Even the legal standing of the trade unions was coming increasingly into question as the century drew to its close. The trade unionists on the Labour Commission through the forcefulness of their Minority Report on the question, succeeded in persuading the majority of the members that it would be unwise to tamper with the existing legal position of the unions. But if the Commission was satisfied that it was best to 'let well alone', many employers were not. Led by *The Times* and other newspapers, they conducted a sustained campaign to curtail the power of trade unionists to conduct boycotts and to picket establishments where strikes were in progress. Reflecting the fear of the employing classes, the judicial bench, in a series of judgements passed between 1893 and 1901, gradually eroded the trade unions' right to strike. When a local committee of building unions in Hull tried to dissuade an employer, Temperton, from supplying with building materials a fellow employer whose workmen were on strike, the court in the case *Temperton vs. Russell* declared that the union had acted illegally. In the case *Trollope vs. the London Building Trades Federation* two years later the publication of a black list of either workmen or employers was held to be illegal. When Mr. Wilkins, the secretary of the Amalgamated Trades Society of Fancy Leather Workers organized the picketing of the firm of J. Lyons and Sons, leather goods manufacturers, Mr. Justice North in the case of *Lyons vs. Wilkins* in 1896 gave an order restraining the union from picketing.[199]

The industrial, political and legal successes of the employing classes brought an inevitable reaction from organized labour. In 1895, before the experience of the engineers' defeat, the TUC rejected a proposal for a general federation of trades. The proposal was raised again in September 1897, only a few weeks after the engineers' attempt to obtain the eight hour day had been crushed, and this time it was carried with only one dissentient. The General Federation of Trade Unions then came into being. The adverse legal judgements and the inability of the Lib-Lab MPs to effect their reversal were influences helping to persuade the TUC to opt for independent labour representation in parliament. At the meeting of the Trades Union Congress on 5 September 1899 the Parliamentary Committee reported that 'it was almost impossible to get any useful Bill through the House unless the government allowed it to pass by withdrawing its opposition'. The Committee was of the opinion that if any remedy was to be effected it would have to be done by the working classes at the polls. Two days later Mr. W. Holmes of the Amalgamated Society of

199   B. C. Roberts, *The Trades Union Congress 1868-1921*, p. 164. John Saville 'Trade Unions and Free Labour; the background to the Taff Vale Decision', in *Essays in Labour History*, vol. 1, Asa Briggs and John Saville (eds.) (London: Macmillan, 1960) pp. 317-50.

Railway Servants moved that the Parliamentary Committee should be instructed 'to invite the co-operation of all the co-operative, socialistic, trade union, and other working class organizations to jointly co-operate . . . in convening a special congress of representation, from such of the above-named organizations as may be willing to take part, to devise ways and means for securing the return of an increased number of Labour members to the next Parliament'. From the conference of the following year the Labour Representation Committee, forerunner of the Labour Party, was born. As the new century dawned the trade unions began the process of creating their own political instrument. Particularly after 1906, when twenty-nine candidates of the LRC were returned to parliament, the complexion of twentieth century industrial relations was changed. The scales now began to be more evenly balanced between capital and labour.

The Documents

INDUSTRIAL RELATIONS

The industrial manufacturing and working classes were products of the tremendous forces of change which affected Britain and the world in the late eighteenth century. The interests of these two classes were diametrically opposed and the conflict between them was to become one of the greatest threats to national and international peace. Britain was the first country to undergo industrialization; she was also one of the few European countries to escape any form of socialist revolution and this despite the fact that Karl Marx wrote his *Das Kapital* in London, then head and heart of the capitalist world. In praising the British machinery of social and economic inquiry in the preface to *Das Kapital* Marx, the apostle of class war, put his finger on the principal reason why class war was avoided in England: other countries, he wrote, 'would be appalled at the state of things' if their governments appointed periodic commissions of inquiry into economic conditions.

There is no doubt but that the unique system of royal commission and select committee inquiries played an important role in containing the class war in Britain and, more importantly, in bringing a measure of justice and harmony to relations between employers and employed.

In its Industrial Relations set of British Parliamentary Papers Irish University Press has brought together in one unit the major papers which document the development of every facet of Britain's system of labour relations: trade unionism, the truck and sweating systems, master and servant law, empolyers' liability, wages statistics, unemployment. The social, economic and political content of these papers is simply enormous. From the 1824 inquiry which, on *laissez faire* principles, recommended repeal of the Combination Act to the gigantic Labour Commission inquiry in the nineties, the material on trade unions is as inexhaustible as it is indispensable: the aims, constitutions and regulations of hundreds of unions; their legal status; minute analyses of the circumstances of strikes and lock-outs, violence and intimidation, and the growth of socialist doctrine. In each of the areas mentioned the parliamentary inquiries were the seeds from which grew laws and social institutions unknown to and unnecessary for pre-industrial man, e.g. courts of arbitration and conciliation, labour exchanges and unemployment insurance. The paths to such institutions were in most cases long and tortuous. Information was often inaccurate and inadequate – the modern statistical techniques used by the Board of Trade in compiling the census of labour (IUP volumes Industrial Relations 21 and 22) were an important advance in this field. Social and economic theory too was wanting as is indicated by the difficulties which befell the Labour Commission and the Select Committee on unemployment. But out of these muddles and entanglements of data and theory there evolved the modern welfare state, in a piecemeal manner at first but always fast enough to prevent cataclysmic upheaval.

Original references

The system of identification gives the sessional year followed by the number of the paper in brackets and the number of the volume in which the paper was bound in the original series. The number of a sessional paper appears in round brackets and that of a command paper in square brackets.

Industrial Relations 1   Reports of minutes of evidence from the select committee on artisans and machinery, 1824. (652 pp.)

This select committee, chaired by the radical MP Joseph Hume, was appointed to examine the state of the British laws on the export of machinery, the emigration of artisans and workmen's combinations. All the reports contain oral evidence, and the sixth includes a summary of conclusions and recommendations.

In view of the extreme scarcity of trade union records at this early date, the evidence given by working spinners, printers, shoemakers, hatters, shipwrights, engineers and others on the functioning of their trade societies during the period of operation of the Combination Laws is of unique value. The committee also heard much evidence of the existence of combinations of masters to keep down the rate of wages, though such combinations were as illegal as those of the men they employed.

Some of the leading employers of the day, including the engineers T. C. Herves and M. Maudslay, the cotton master T. Ashton and the flax spinner, John Marshall, gave valuable evidence on trade practices and the state of the labour market in Britain and France.

There is detailed evidence of industrial disputes in Glasgow, London, Liverpool, Dublin and Manchester during the first quarter of the nineteenth century. The witnesses, whose evidence had been carefully vetted by Francis Place before they were interviewed by the committee, gave detailed instances of the arbitrary and capricious operation of the Combination Laws.

Original reference
1824   (51) V   Artisans, machinery and combination laws, Sel. Cttee.
                                   Rep., mins. of ev.

Industrial Relations 2 Report from the select committee on the Combination Laws with minutes of evidence, 1825. (500 pp.)

The repeal of the anti-combination legislation in 1824, coming as it did at a time of booming trade, led to a rapid increase in workers' organizations, particularly on Tyneside. Since trade combinations were now no longer illegal, industrial disputes achieved a greater prominence. MPs gained the impression of a flood tide of industrial unrest and, in some alarm, appointed a select committee to re-examine the Combination Laws. The committee's report and evidence are in an excellent guide to the early history of trade unions, providing extensive material on working conditions, wages, grievances and the extent of combination in such trades as shipbuilding, weaving, coopering, papermaking, coach building and mining. The committee sought especially to discover the extent to which trade unions condoned violence and intimidation – over a period of a few months there had been more than sixty cases of industrial violence in Dublin.

The report summarized the main findings from the evidence and recommended legislation to control unions: combinations of workmen should be permitted but should not be allowed to interfere with the rights of property; the unions should be regulated according to the principles of the common law and the freedom of the individual – employer or worker – should be protected in every respect.

The secrecy surrounding many unions made it difficult to obtain accurate information on their real aims and methods. Wherever such information was available the committee recorded and analysed it – the appendix has valuable materials on the constitutions, regulations and funds of fourteen unions.

Original references

1825	(437) IV	The effect of the Act. 5 Geo. IV c. 95, Sel. Cttee. Rep., appendix.
	(417)	The effect of the Act. 5 Geo. IV c. 95, Sel. Cttee. Rep., mins of ev.

Industrial Relations 3 First and second reports from the select committee on combinations of workmen, with minutes of evidence, appendix and index, 1837-38. (648 pp.)

The trade recession of 1837, which was felt most severely in the then dominant textile industry, sharpened class conflict in the main producing areas of Manchester, Glasgow, Dublin and Belfast. The factory workers' unions fought a long and bitter struggle to resist wage reductions. The select committee of 1837, including such prominent members as Daniel O'Connell and Lord Ashley, examined the working of the Combination Act of 1824 in relation to the recent conflicts, but extended its investigations into the printing and timber trades. John Doherty's account of the Friendly Association of Cotton Spinners of Manchester and Neighbourhood and Angus Campbell's evidence on the activities of the Glasgow Association of Cotton Spinners provide a first hand record of the influence of these two important organizations. Also of special note are the long statements of Archibald Alison, Scottish lawyer and historian, who supplements Campbell's account of trade union activity in Glasgow and the evidence of Michael Staunton, Dublin newspaper proprietor, on labour relations in the printing trades.

The investigation of instances of violence and intimidation takes up a large part of the volume which is a repository of detail, much of which is unavailable elsewhere, on the aims, policies, constitutions and methods of the first trade unions.

Original references

1837-38 (488) VIII	Combinations of workmen, Sel. Cttee. 1st Rep., mins. of ev., appendix.
(646)	Combinations of workmen, Sel. Cttee. 2nd Rep., mins. of ev., appendix, index.

Industrial Relations 4   Reports from select committees on the operation of the Truck Acts and on railway labourers, with minutes of evidence, appendices and indexes, 1842-46. (502 pp.)

Legislation designed to prevent the payment of wages in truck, i.e. in any other form than the coin of the realm unconditionally given, had existed since 1465. Repeated enactments had failed to stop the evil. In the 1840s the evidence suggests that the evil was spreading rather than declining. The 'Tommy Shop', or company store, in which workers received inferior and exorbitantly priced articles, was still a major means of exploitation. The committee of 1842 presented no formal report, but the worst abuses of the system were fully documented. The committee was primarily concerned to examine the effectiveness of the Truck Act of 1831 and the evidence collected throws a flood of light on conditions of employment in such industries as iron-founding, nail-making, coal-mining, stone-quarrying and cloth-making. The exposure of this seamy side of British industrial practice failed to stir parliament into action. It was not until 1887 that another general truck act was passed.

Railway navvies, whose working conditions were examined by the committee in 1846, were exempt from the provisions of the 1831 Act. The railway companies' 'Tommy Shops', frequented by some 200,000 men at the time of the railway mania, were perfectly legal, though none the less an imposition on the men. The committee heard evidence of deplorable living conditions, an alarmingly high incidence of accidents and the absence of education. It commended the work of chaplains and scripture readers but also urged the provision of facilities for secular teaching. Largely on the basis of Chadwick's evidence of French railway building practice, it recommended the provision of 'prefab' houses to accommodate the labour force and urged the government to make the railway companies liable to pay compensation in all cases of accident. Although the committee's recommendations were ignored by the government, the 200 pages of evidence are a unique source of information on the conditions of employment of the men who built British railways.

Original references

| 1842 | (471) IX | Truck Acts, Sel. Cttee. Rep., mins. of ev., appendix, index. |
| 1846 | (530) XIII | Railway labourers, Sel. Cttee. Rep., mins., of ev., index. |

Industrial Relations 5   Report from the select committee on the Payment of Wages Bill and on the Payment of Wages (Hosiery) Bill, with minutes of evidence and index, 1854. (468 pp.)

This select committee was appointed to consider two bills, presented to parliament in 1854, designed to strengthen the laws against the truck system. Extensive evidence was heard on wage-payment practices particularly in the truck areas of Staffordshire, South Wales and Scotland. The witnesses included workmen, money paying and truck paying employers, lawyers, magistrates and government officials. Sir Archibald Alison, the Scotish lawyer and historian, and Hugh Tremenheere, who for the previous ten years had been employed by the government to examine the workings of the truck system, were important witnesses. Tremenheer's wide experience of the coal mining industry was particularly valuable.

The evidence falls under three main heads: the truck system; the validity and feasibility of legislative interference on the matter of payment of wages; the Payment of Wages Bills of 1854. The material on truck describes its extent, its social effects and its advantages and disadvantages as an economic system. There was wide variation of opinion on the value of laws against truck. Old guard adherents of *laissez faire* considered that as the employment contract was free, state interference was unjustifiable. Other witnesses recommended state intervention to prevent the exploitation of the workers. The objectives of the 1854 Payment of Wages Bills were described, some clauses were analysed and amendments were suggested.

The evidence reveals that where the truck system was prevalent trade unionism was weak or non-existent. Hence the trade union movement's involvement in campaigns against truck paying masters. Important information about the rates of profit in industry and the role of magistrates in enforcing wages legislation is also to be found in this volume.

Original reference
1854   (382) XVI   Payment of Wages Bill and Payment of Wages (Hosiery) Bill, Sel. Cttee. Rep., mins of ev., index.

Industrial Relations 6 Report from the select committee on the stoppage of wages in hosiery manufacture, with proceedings, minutes of evidence, appendix and index, 1854-55. (736 pp.)

In the 1850s most of the work in the hosiery industry was still carried out on traditional lines in the homes of the workers. Knitting frames and raw materials were supplied by the manufacturers and distributed by middlemen. The workers were paid for what they produced but were required in turn to pay frame rents and middlemen's charges. Exorbitant frame rents, rather than profit from the sale of produce, often provided the largest source of income for the manufacturer, particularly in times of trade recession. In some areas rents were exacted even when workers were inoperative through illness.

The 1854-55 committee examined the matter of rents and charges in the hosiery industry, taking evidence from large numbers of manufacturers, middlemen and workers. The evidence highlights the inefficiency of the traditionalist system and the gross exploitation of the workers. Low wages were a deterrent to technical innovation. The adoption of the factory system with modern machinery meant huge capital investment, redeployment of labour and the threat of redundancy: witness, even from the workers, were reluctant to accept too-sweeping changes. The committee while recommending the introduction of an act similar to the Truck Act to prohibit deductions from wages was not in favour of excessive state intervention. It urged that exorbitant deductions from wages should be prevented by law but that the rationalization of the industry should not be forced from outside.

This volume provides a preview of some of the conditions which were later to give rise to the sweating system.

Original reference
1854-55 (421) XIV   Stoppage of wages (Hosiery), Sel. Cttee. Rep., mins. of
                           ev., appendices, index.

Industrial Relations 7   Reports from select committees on the settlement of disputes between masters and operatives, 1856-60. (504 pp.)

Experiences such as the prolonged dispute in the Preston textile industry in the winter of 1853-54 led in 1856 to the appointment of the committee to examine 'the expediency of establishing equitable tribunals for the amicable settlement of disputes between masters and operatives'. Several attempts had already been made to establish machinery of arbitration. An Act of the reign of George IV specified that in certain circumstances industrial disputes could be settled either by having recourse to the justice of the peace or by some other agreed procedure. This Act was largely inoperative because employers and workers were reluctant to air their disputes in the law courts. The Councils of the Prud'Hommes, recently established in France, had some influence on the development of arbitration and conciliation in England.

By 1856 both workers and employers saw the expediency of reasonable settlement of disputes but there were many difficult issues – should arbitration and conciliation courts be statutory or voluntary; should their findings be legally binding; what rights had the legislature to intervene in the contract of employment? The committee took evidence under three main headings (a) the traditional relations between employers and workers (b) the working of the Councils of the Prud'Hommes in France (c) desirable alterations in British labour law. Much of the evidence deals with the hosiery, pottery and silk industries. It has extensive discussion of the causes and effects of strikes and detailed accounts of recent strikes. The committee reported in favour of courts of conciliation and arbitration whose findings would not be legally binding.

The 1860 Select Committee re-examined the question of settling labour disputes. They took further evidence on several aspects of industrial relations and again reported in favour of statutory arbitration and conciliation machinery.

Original references
1856   (343) XIII   Masters and operatives (equitable councils of
                          conciliation), Sel. Cttee. Rep., mins of ev., appendix,
                          index.
1860   (307) XXII   The best means of settling disputes between masters and
                          operatives, Sel. Cttee. Rep., mins. of ev., appendix and
                          index.

Industrial Relations 8   First to fourth reports from the royal
  commission on trade unions and other organizations and a
  report on the Sheffield outrages, with minutes of evidence
  and appendix, 1867. (880 pp.)

Although Chartism was the dominant movement in the later 1830s and
early 1840s there were often close links between Chartists and trade
unionists, especially in the coal mining industry. In the more prosperous
1850s and 1860s trade unionism, especially among the skilled workers,
gathered strength. From the middle 1860s its leaders became much more
politically active than they had been in the previous decade.

The immediate occasion for the appointment of the Royal Commission
was the publicity given to the Sheffield outrages – the acts of violence and
intimidation carried out against blacklegs in the cutlery and ancillary
trades. However, MPs were apprehensive of the growing economic and
political power of the unions and therefore widened the terms of reference
of the commission to include the organization and rules of trade unions
and other associations of employers and workers.

The commission members were Sir William Erle (chairman), Thomas
George (Earl of Lichfield), Francis Chateris, Sir Edmund Walker Head, Sir
Daniel Gooch, Herman Marivale, James Booth, John A. Roebuck, William
Matthews, Thoms Hughes and Frederic Harrison. Before the appointment
of the commission there had been serious differences between the trade
union leaders, but believing that the very existence of the unions was being
challenged, they gradually sank their differences and came together (from
1868) in the Trades Union Congress.

The commission submitted eleven reports (nine of them minutes of
evidence only) and these with the reports and evidence of sworn inquiries
into the Sheffield and Manchester outrages are contained in IUP volumes
Industrial Relations 8–10.

This volume contains the first four reports of minutes of evidence
together with the report and evidence on the Sheffield outrages. The main
body of the evidence in the former concerns the constitution, rules, aims
and methods of unions. The witnesses included several members of the
'Junta' including Richard Applegarth (carpenters and joiners), William
Allan (engineers) and Edwin Coulson (London bricklayers). The carefully
prepared and reasoned answers of these men helped create a new public
image of their movement.

The Sheffield outrages inquiry was carried out by a special group of
three appointed by Act of Parliament. The report and 450 pages of
evidence describe many of the worst examples of trade union violence and
intimidation. The evidence provides a vast body of information on unions

in Sheffield and shows that there was little sympathy among the unions with the recent barbaric methods.

Original references

1867	[3873] XXXII	Organization and rules of trade unions and other associations, R. Com. 1st Rep., mins. of ev.
	[3893]	Organization and rules of trade unions and other association, R. Com. 2nd Rep., mins., of ev.
	[3910]	Organization and rules of trade unions and other associations, R. Com. 3rd Rep., mins. of ev.
	[3952]	Organization and rules of trade unions and other associations, R. Com. 4th Rep., mins. of ev.
	[3952-I]	Organization and rules of trade unions and other associations, Sheffield outrages inquiry, Rep., mins. of ev., Vols. I and II.

Industrial Relations 9   Fifth to tenth reports from the royal commission on trade unions and other organizations and the report on the Manchester outrages, with minutes of evidence and appendix, 1867-68. (920 pp.)

The evidence submitted by the commission here is similar in content to that in the earlier reports. The basic concern was to assess the orthodoxy of trade union aims and methods and the extent to which they could be given legal sanction. Industries extensively covered were engineering and shipbuilding in both England and Scotland, the iron and coal trades, glass manufacture, printing and tailoring; these industries figure prominently in labour inquiries throughout the century. Representatives of both employers' and employees' organizations were examined. These included many prominent people; Allan, MacDonald, John Kane, President of the National Association of Malleable Iron Workers, Daniel Guile, Secretary of the Friendly Society of Iron Founders, and Anthony Mundella the hosiery manufacturer. Throughout the evidence copious information was provided on the constitutions and regulations of unions, and the circumstances surrounding recent strikes and disputes were described and analysed. The Manchester outrages inquiry presents a similar picture to that of the Sheffield inquiry. The more notorious cases were investigated in detail — this was possible only because witnesses were given protection from criminal proceedings.

Original references

1867-68	[3980-I] XXXIX	Organization and rules of trade unions and other associations, R. Com. 5th Rep., mins. of ev.
	[3980-II]	Organization and rules of trade unions and other associations, R. Com. 6th Rep., mins. of ev.
	[3980-III]	Organization and rules of trade unions and other associations, R. Com. 7th Rep., mins. of ev.

[3980-IV]   Organization and rules of trade unions and other
                   associations, R. Com. 8th Rep., mins. of ev.
[3980-V]   Organization and rules of trade unions and other
                   associations, R. Com. 9th Rep., mins. of ev.
[3980-VI]   Organization and rules of trade unions and other
                   associations, R. Com. 10th Rep., mins. of ev.
[3980]   Organization and rules of trade unions and other
                   associations, Manchester outrages inquiry, Vol. I Rep.,
                   Vol. II mins. of ev.

Industrial Relations 10   Eleventh and final report from the royal commission on trade unions and the first and second reports from the Board of Trade of proceedings under the Conciliation (Trade Disputes) Act 1896, with appendices and index, 1868-99. (584 pp.)

After an inquiry spread over two years, in which trade unionists sought to depict themselves as responsible persons rather than as hot-headed revolutionaries, the commission submitted findings which established trade unionism as an accepted part of British industrial and economic life. The final report reviewed the evidence on the aims and methods of unions, their influence on the character of workmen, their effects on the trade and industry of the country, their legal position, the machinery of arbitration and conciliation and the nature and extent of the co-operative movement. The commission justified trade unionism, pointing out that it was impossible to indict the movement because of isolated sectional outrages. They accepted that unions were necessary to protect the interests of workers but refused to condone interference with the rights of individuals to dispose of their labour as they wished. For this reason they condemned picketing.

A minority report signed by Harrison, the Positivist, and Hughes, the Christian Socialist, on the commission, recommended explicit legalization of unions and protection for their funds in all cases where their aims and methods were within the law. The outcome of the report was the 1871 Trade Union and Criminal Law Amendment Acts, the former protecting the unions, the latter declaring picketing, etc. illegal. The removal of the Criminal Law Amendment Act became a strong priority with the labour movement in subsequent years.

Volume II of the report contains a digest of the evidence, correspondence with diplomatic representatives abroad on industrial relations questions, answers to questionnaires from trade union secretaries and others, and statistics on unions.

The inquiry, taking place in the years immediately after the 1867 Reform Act, marks an important stage in the rise of the working classes but a difficult road lay ahead before the whole labour question was re-examined by the Labour Commission in 1891. The remaining two papers in this volume date from the period after the Labour Commission. They are reports by the Board of Trade on the cases dealt with by the Board as mediator in trade disputes.

Original references

1868-69	[4123] XXXI	Organization and rules of trade unions and other associations, R. Com. 11th and final Rep., Vol. I.
	[4123-I]	Organization and rules of trade unions and other associations, R. Comm. 11th and final Rep., Vol. II, mins. of ev., appendix.
1897	[C.8533] LXXXIII	Proceedings under the Conciliation (Trade Disputes) Act 1896; Board of Trade 1st Rep.
1899	(275) LXXXVIII	Proceedings under the Conciliation (Trade Disputes) Act 1896; Board of Trade 2nd Rep.

Industrial Relations 11 Report from the commissioners on the truck system, with minutes of evidence and appendices, 1871. (1,208 pp.)

Despite earlier legislation and parliamentary inquiries (IUP Industrial Relations 4 and 5) the truck system continued to be widespread in the second half of the century. In 1870 C. S. Bowen and A. C. Sellar were appointed by Act of Parliament to inquire into the operation of truck legislation and to report generally on the system. The commissioners heard evidence from over 500 witnesses on industries including coal and iron, hosiery, hardware and watch manufacture in centres throughout England, Scotland and Wales. The evidence details the effects of truck and provides much incidental information on the industries examined. The appendix contains returns of truck shops known to the police throughout Britain, balance sheets and store inventories from the shops and sample lists of purchases, detailing quality and cost. The witnesses included workmen and their wives, proprietors and clerks of truck shops, government inspectors, sheriffs, county auditors and clergymen. The report is divided into two parts: part one outlines the general nature, extent and effects of truck while part two describes the system as operated by particular firms, e.g. the Ebbw Vale Coal, Iron and Steel Company, one of the largest in South Wales and employing 12,500 people. In South Wales truck was more widespread than elsewhere. Many workers never handled cash and in some areas tobacco was used as a currency medium. On 'turnbook day' in many Welsh industries, liberal credit was given at the company shop in lieu of the following month's expected earnings, thus effectively forcing workers to remain in the company's employment. The evidence showed that women and children queued in frost and snow on the eve of 'turnbook day' in competition for choice goods.

Valuable information on the labour forces and total wage payments of a number of large firms is presented in the second part of the report. The commissioners concluded that the greatest evils of truck were perpetrated by 'small extortionists' rather than large companies. They recommended measures to combat exploitation, that workers should be paid weekly in cash, that inspectors be appointed to enforce legislation, that existing laws be clarified and amended where necessary and that penalties for breach of the law be more severe.

Original references
1871   [C.326] XXXVI   The truck system, Com. Vol. I, Rep., schedules, supplement.
        [C.327]   The truck system, Com. Vol. II, mins. of ev.

Industrial Relations 12   Second report from the commissioners and other papers on the truck system, with minutes of evidence, appendices and index, 1872-97. (680 pp., 1 folding coloured map)

In their second report the Truck Commissioners concentrated their inquiry on the system as practised in the Shetland Islands. Because barter and payment in kind were necessary elements in the underdeveloped economies of the Shetlands rather than instruments of exploitation, the inquiry entailed a scrutiny of the whole social and economic life of the islands. The islands' main industry was fishing. Other industries and occupations dealt with in evidence were kelp gathering, homespinning, hosiery and lace manufacture and mixed farming.

The small class of merchant importers and exporters in the Shetlands, who were also frequently the principal landowners, were at the centre of the social and economic life. Their monopoly of trade and commerce extended from determining the price of fish to controlling the retail shops. In many cases islanders were inextricably tied to particular merchants because of credit situations. This was part and parcel of a system very different from that prevailing in the industrial areas of Britain and was not necessarily evil in its effects. It was by mutual understanding rather than by firm contract that the islanders confined their custom to the merchant's shop, and the annual settlement of accounts suited both. The report is a valuable guide to the social and economic life of the Shetlands and similar outlying areas of the United Kingdom in the nineteenth century. It ranges from descriptions of Shetland cottages to statistics on the prices and quality of goods sold in the island shops.

The remaining papers in the volume are a review of the truck system in Scotland compiled by Alexander Redgrave, the chief inspector of factories (1887); a memorandum on the principal provisions of the Truck Acts with an abstract of the more important court cases and decisions interpreting them (1896); a memorandum briefing factory inspectors on their duties in enforcing the Truck laws (1897).

Original references

1872	[C.555] XXXV	The truck system, Com. 2nd Rep., Vol. I, appendix, Shetland.
	[C.555-I]	The truck system, Com. 2nd Rep., Vol. II, mins. of ev.
1887	[C.4982] LXVI	The truck system in Scotland, Chief Inspector of Factories, Rep.
1896	[C.8048] LXXVI	Truck Acts and Checkweighing Clause in the Coal Mines Regulation Acts, memorandum.
1897	[C.8330] LXXX	Truck Acts, memorandum for use of H.M. Inspectors of mines and factories.

Industrial Relations 13 First report from the select committee of the House of Lords and reports to the Board of Trade on the sweating system, with minutes of evidence and appendix, 1887-88. (1,096 pp.)

In the 1880s the large influx of Russian and German Jews, driven by starvation and persecution from the continent, was concentrated in a few urban areas, notably the East End of London. Their arrival led some contemporary observers to blame them for the survival and intensification of inhuman working condtions. However, the primary reason for the survival of sweating — a system of manufacture in which middlemen contracted to do work for manufacturers and sublet it to workers at very low wages — was the continuance of outwork. Sweated workers toiled long hours in hundreds of small garrets and basements where they were not subject to the provisions of the many Factory and Workshop Acts passed since the 1830s.

IUP Industrial Relations 13-17 contain detailed documentation of the sweating system in the form of reports submitted to the Board of Trade (1887-88) and reports from the Select Committee of the House of Lords 1888-90. The Board of Trade reports described the operation of the system in London and Leeds. The Select Committee dealt with sweating in the East End of London in its first report and requested an extension of its scope of inquiry to cover the other cities and towns of Britain. Over a hundred witnesses gave evidence, including Charles Booth and Beatrice Potter the social researchers, Arnold Henry White, author of *Problems of a Great City,* John Maple and Samuel Montagu, members of parliament, and several clergymen. The resultant thousand-page documentary describes conditions in the sweat shops, the demoralizing of the workers, the influences of trade unionism, the operation of the Factory Acts and many other facets of the system. The causes of the Jewish immigration and its extent, the activities of the Jewish Board of Guardians and the work Jews engaged in were examined. The volume is a valuable source for social historians of London and for the history of the Jews in Britain.

Original references
1887	(331) LXXXIX	Sweating system in the East End of London, labour correspondent of the Board of Trade, Rep.
1888	[C.5513] LXXXVI	Sweating system in Leeds, labour correspondent of the Board of Trade, Rep.
1888	(361) XX	Sweating system, Sel. Cttee. HL. 1st Rep., mins. of ev., appendix.

Industrial Relations 14   Second report from the select committee of the House of Lords on the sweating system, with proceedings, minutes of evidence and appendix, 1888. (616 pp.)

The committee's scope of inquiry was extended at their request to the country generally. In their second report they submitted further evidence on the sweating system in London dealing specifically with dock work, boot and shoe manufacture, army clothing and accoutrements manufacture and government contracts. Registration of workshops, the wages and conditions of sweated workers, the effects of the co-operative movement on sweated trades, the apprenticeship system, Jewish immigration and prostitution among sweated workers are a selection of topics extensively discussed. The witnesses comprised representatives of docks and factory management, masters of sweat shops, sweated workers and trade unionists. Ben Tillett, the trade-union leader, provided in his evidence a thorough account of dock labour. Tillett described the system of hiring, working and payment and outlined the difference between dock and wharf work. Du Plat Taylor of the East and West India Dock Company and Arnold White were other well-known witnesses, and the Salvation Army was among the charitable organizations represented.

Original reference
1888	(448) XXI	Sweating system, Sel. Cttee. HL. 2nd Rep., mins. of ev., appendix.

Industrial Relations 15   Third report from the select committee of the House of Lords on the sweating system, with
minutes of evidence and appendices, 1889. (728 pp.)

The third report included further evidence on sweating in London, mainly
from physicians and dealing with the effects of overcrowded and
insanitary conditions in sweat shops, and with accidents in the docks. The
main body of the evidence, however, dealt with hardware manufactur
(nails, chains, etc.) in the midland counties. It painted a dingy inhuman
picture of the working conditions of women and children, and described
how the manufacturer (the head of the contracting and sub-contracting
structure) pitted middlemen and workers one against another to reduce
costs and how foremen were bribed to get the work done as cheaply as
possible.

The evidence provides much statistical and other information on the
industries involved covering the nature of the work, the renting of places
in workshops, prices paid for work, and sanitary conditions. Witnesses
from all levels of the industries were interviewed; some outlined the
economic reasons for sweating and put forward proposals for improvement.

The volume includes further material on contracts for army accoutrements and the appendix contains replies from factory inspectors and a
scheme for reorganizing the nail and chain-making industries.

Original reference
1889   (165) XIII   Sweating system, Sel. Cttee. HL. 3rd Rep., mins. of ev.,
                             appendix.

Industrial Relations 16   Fourth and fifth reports from the
select committee of the House of Lords on the sweating
system, with proceedings, minutes of evidence and
appendices, 1889-90. (800 pp.)

The industries dealt with in the fourth report were similar to those in the
earlier reports: tailoring, boot and shoe and upholstery manufacture.
Among the regions covered were Manchester, Birmingham, Leeds,
Liverpool, Glasgow, Edinburgh and Newcastle. The witnesses included
clergymen, physicians, statisticians, factory and sanitary inspectors,
journalists, industrialists, factory managers, factory and sweated workers
and representatives of trade, co-operative and charitable organizations.

The fifth report summarized the committee's findings from what
Professor P. Ford numbers among the great social inquiries (*Social Theory*

and Social Practice, p. 68). The committee had been brought face to face with 'the suffering victims of a grim industrial underworld' and forced to see the sweating system in human terms. They regarded as its chief cause the gathering together in towns of helpless communities – ghettoes in modern terms. Prohibition of sub-contracting, prohibition of alien immigration, prohibition of outwork and 'well considered' trade unions were examined as means of alleviating the evils of sweating, but no clearcut legislative solution was regarded possible – in the final reckoning only changes in social and moral attitudes could bring real improvement. The committee put forward several suggestions for immediate action such as stricter enforcement of sanitary legislation. They urged especially that sweating in connection with government contracts be eradicated and this resulted in the House of Commons' Fair Wages Resolution (see IUP Industrial Relations 22).

The weakness of the report was that undue emphasis was placed on the practice of sub-contracting, especially by small masters, and not enough importance was attached to outwork employment, for which large wholesale firms, as well as small scale middlemen, were responsible.

Original references
1889	(331) XIV Pt. I	Sweating system, Sel. Cttee. HL. 4th Rep., mins. of ev., appendix.
1890	(169) XVII	Sweating system, Sel. Cttee. HL. 5th Rep., appendix.

Industrial Relations 17   Indices parts I, II and III to the evidence before the select committee of the House of Lords on the sweating system, 1889. (1,036 pp.)

The indexes are divided into three parts: Part I covers (a) the contents of the first and second reports, omitting the evidence on military accoutrements, and (b) the contents of the third and fourth reports on the tailoring trade and on dock accidents; Part II covers the remainder of the evidence; Part III is an analysis of the evidence from the third and fourth reports.

Original references
1889	(331-I) XIV Pt. II	Sweating system, Sel. Cttee. HL., index part I.
	(331-II)	Sweating system, Sel. Cttee. HL., index part II.
	(331-III) Pt. III	Sweating system, Sel. Cttee. HL., index part III, analysis of ev. 3rd and 4th Reps.

Industrial Relations 18   Select Committee and royal commission reports on Master and Servant Law, with minutes of evidence, appendices and index, 1865-75. (560 pp.)

Evidence in IUP Industrial Relations 2 indicates that as early as 1825 workers in Dublin were objecting to the terms 'master and servant'. The interpretation and administration of the Master and Servant laws weighed heavily against the employee who could be convicted and imprisoned for the most trifling breaches of contract. The first concerted opposition by workers to these laws took the form of legal actions taken by William Prowting Roberts in the forties. Largely as a result of agitation initiated by the Glasgow Trades Council, a select committee was appointed in 1865 to examine the laws and the expediency of amending them. The committee included Cobbett, Roebuck, Forster and Algernon Egerton. Among the witnesses were Alexander Macdonald, Alfred Mault (Secretary of the General Builders Association), representatives of the legal profession and of employers and employees in the printing, pottery, coal and iron industries. The provisions of the law and its administration were minutely examined under such headings as: breach of contract as a criminal offence; court procedure in breach of contract cases; frequency of prosecutions, etc. The committee submitted an eight-point report stating that the existing law was objectionable and suggesting a basis for reform which resulted in the 1867 Master and Servant Act. When the 1867 Act was passed the trade union movement was on trial before a royal commission (IUP Industrial Relations 8-10). The Criminal Law Amendment Act (1871) which resulted from this trial helped bring about the downfall of the Liberals at the 1874 general election. The Tories appointed a royal commission to examine the operation of both the 1867 and 1871 Acts. The trade unions boycotted the commission but Macdonald, the miners' leader, and Hughes, the Christian Socialist, agreed to be members. Macdonald submitted a minority report. The commission submitted a majority report recommending that the Master and Servant Act be divested of everything of a criminal or penal nature but that the Criminal Law Amendment Act should remain largely as it was. The government, however, replaced this Act by the Conspiracy and Protection of Property Act, and replaced the Master and Servant Act by the Employers and Workmen Act. Picketing was legalized and the employment contract became a civil agreement between legally equal partners. The appendix to the Royal Commission Report has valuable notes on cases dealt with under the two Acts. The remaining paper in the volume contains interesting information on the employment contract in several European countries.

Original references

1865	(370) VIII	Contracts of service between master and servant, Sel. Cttee. Rep., mins. of ev.
1866	(449) XIII	Contracts of service between master and servant, Sel. Cttee. Rep., mins. of ev., appendix.
1874	[C.1094] XXIV	Master and Servant Act, 1867, Criminal Law Amendment Act 1871, 34 and 35 Vict. c. 32 (Labour Laws Commission), R. Com. 1st Rep., mins. of ev.

1875   [C.1157] XXX   Master and Servant Act 1867, Criminal Law Amendment
                          Act 1871, 34 and 35 Vict. c. 32 (Labour Laws Commis-
                          sion), R. Com. 2nd and final Rep.
         [C.1157-I]   Master and Servant Act 1867, Criminal Law Amendment
                          Act 1871, 34 and 35 Vict. c. 32 (Labour Laws Commis-
                          sion), R. Com. 2nd and final Rep., mins. of ev., appendix.
1875   (171) LXII   Master and servant (law of foreign countries), Reps.

Industrial Relations 19   Reports from select committees and other reports on employers' liability for injuries to their servants, and the insurance of persons employed in mines, with proceedings, minutes of evidence, appendices and indices, 1876-86. (1,096 pp.)

A Select Committee was appointed in 1876 to inquire whether employers should be made responsible for accidents caused by the negligence of managerial staff and also whether the definition of 'common employment' could be clarified. The existing common law principle was that an employer was liable for accidents caused by his own fault or by that of his servants working under his instructions. By the 'common employment' doctrine the employer was not liable for accidents caused to a workman by the fault of a fellow workman of the same grade.

The committee took evidence from witnesses who had special experience of the legal and practical problems involved: Howell, parliamentary secretary on trade union matters; Courtenay Peregrine Ilbert, a legal expert in the field; Henry Broadhurst, the secretary of the Trades Union Congress Parliamentary Committee. Several important issues in the philosophy and history of law were dealt with in the evidence. Joseph Brown Q.C. described the understanding of the employer-employee relationship which formed the basis of the existing law and commented on its justice and on its relationship to Roman law. He described the views of French and American courts on employers' liability. A fundamental issue in the law was whether the workman should have to take the risks incidental to his trade. Other topics discussed were the ambiguities of the existing law and its interpretation. The meaning of 'common employment' was the subject of a large section of evidence. The report itself is a valuable summary of legal thinking on employers' liability at the time.

The Employers' Liability Act of 1880 which resulted from the investigations of the committee, removed the doctrine of common employment in a good many cases where a workman suffered injury through the negligence of his foreman or his immediate superintendent. But since it permitted 'contracting out' in cases where mutual insurance schemes were agreed between masters and men, the agitation for a more comprehensive measure continued.

In 1886 another committee considered two Bills both of which were more far reaching than the Act of 1880. The evidence taken by this committee contains a wealth of information on every aspect of employers' liability, but it was a further eleven years before a new act was passed.

Original references

1876	(372) IX	Employers' liability for injuries to their servants, Sel. Cttee. Rep., mins. of ev., index.
1877	(285) X	Employers' liability for injuries to their servants, Sel. Cttee. Rep., mins. of ev., appendix, index.
1880	[C.2607] LIX	Employers' liability (foreign countries), Reps.
	[C.2631]	Employers' liability (foreign countries), translation of documents.
1886	[C.4784] LXVII	Employers' liability (foreign countries), Reps. of H.M. representatives abroad.
1886	(192) VIII	Employers' Liability Act (1880) Amendment Bill, Sel. Cttee. Rep., mins. of ev., appendix and index.

Industrial Relations 20   Returns of labour statistics from the Board of Trade with reports and appendices, 1887-92). (1,024 pp.)

Industrial Relations 20-22 contain returns and reports on wages compiled by the Commercial Department of the Board of Trade as a result of a House of Commons' resolution in 1886 requesting a census of labour statistics. The first return in this volume covers the period from 1830 to 1886 and is based on (a) the 'Tables of Revenue, Population and Commerce' issued prior to 1853 by the original Statistical Department of the Board of Trade, (b) the series of miscellaneous statistics of the United Kingdom which began in 1857 and (c) some previously unprinted statistics. Prior to 1853 the majority of the statistics refer to the textile iron, boot and shoe, and building industries but after 1857 the glass, sugar, paper and chemical industries are well represented.

The main series of returns are for 1886 and were the result of the first attempt to apply modern statistical techniques to British labour data. They were submitted in instalments, each accompanied by an introduction describing the methods used, explaining the various computations made and analysing the overall meaning of the data. These four returns deal with: the principal and minor textile trades; mines and quarries; and police, road workers and workers in gasworks and waterworks.

The aims which the Board of Trade set itself were to estimate the condition of workers in each industry and the condition of different categories of workers in a given industry, and to calculate the total income of the working classes and break it down into per capita averages. For the modern macro-economist, the Board of Trade returns are an important milestone. They give the numbers employed and the weekly wages and hours of work for each category of work in a number of major industrial regions. Male, female and juvenile workers are dealt with separately. Such figures as the number of samples on which the average was based the number of samples within ten per cent of the average, and average maxima and minima are included in the tables. For the historian, the returns are the hard facts with which he can support his conclusions as in no previous period. For the economic planner and researcher, they are the stuff of his trade.

Original references

1887	[C.5172] LXXXIX	Wage rates, 1830-86, returns.
1889	[C.5807] LXX	Wages in the principal textile trades, return.
1890	[C.6161] LXVIII	Wages in the minor textile trades, return with rep.
1890-91	[C.6455] LXXVIII	Wages in mines and quarries, return with rep.
1892	[C.6715] LXVIII	Wages paid by local authorities and private companies to police and to work people employed on the roads, etc. and at gas and waterworks, return with rep.

Industrial Relations 21 Reports on the wages of manual labourers and domestic servants and on wages and the cost of production, with appendices, index and tables, 1890-99. (800 pp.)

The appointment of the Labour Commission in 1891 made the need for reliable labour statistics more urgent and accelerated the work of the Board of Trade in providing them. The final instalment of the census of wages and a report on the whole project were submitted in 1893. The report summarized and analysed the returns and described some of the plans which the Commercial Department proposed to adopt in developing a system of labour statistics. It recognized the importance of such statistics in the discussion of labour questions, particularly if regular collection was established so that overall trends could be observed. The returns dealt with a wide range of industries not covered previously: iron and steel, shipbuilding, railways, chemicals, printing, brewing and distilling. A report submitted in 1899 on the wages of domestic servants covering England. Wales, Scotland and Ireland is also included in the volume.

The report on wages and cost of production was based on information in parliamentary papers and on the accounts of leading joint stock companies. It provided and interpreted data on the proportion between cost of raw materials, wages, profits and other production expenses in the selling price of the products of leading industries: agriculture, mining, shipbuilding, iron and steel, engineering, textiles, transport, gas manufacture and brewing and distilling. The utility of this information was by no means confined to wage fixing — it is on such data that modern economic analysis is based.

Original references

1893-94 [C.6889]	LXXXIII Pt.II	Wages of the manual labour classes in the United Kingdom, rep., returns.
1899	[C.9346] XCII	Money wages of indoor domestic servants, Miss Collet, rep.
1890-91 [C.6535]	LXXVIII	The relation of wages in certain industries to the cost of production, T. H. Elliot, Board of Trade, rep.

Industrial Relations 22   Reports from the select committees and other reports on wages (government contracts) and on profit sharing, with proceedings, minutes of evidence, appendices and indices, 1890-97. (1,088 pp.)

The workman in 1846, the year of free trade, was still a pawn in the economic system. By 1890 the range of accepted ideas had changed so much that wages could be thought of in terms of the profitability of the industry. Furthermore, ideas derived from the co-operative and collectivist movements were appearing in forms compatible with the principle of free enterprise — gain sharing and production bonuses. Such ideas and practices were by no means widespread in British industry but the fact that they were there at all was a significant pointer for the future.

The three reports on various forms of profit sharing in this volume are valuable reviews of the influence of co-operative and collectivist ideas during the century. These reports described the development of co-operation and profit sharing and the extent to which they were practised in the eighteen-nineties. The material on co-operative enterprises is particularly interesting as is a discussion of Webster's definitions of profit and gain. The reports also deal with profit sharing in American industry.

The select committee reports on wages paid in connection with government contracts are important because they instance changes in parliament's policy on wage control. The committees sought to discover how far the House of Commons 'Fair Wages Resolution' of 1891 was being implemented. The resolution stated that it was the duty of the government in all contracts to prevent the evils disclosed by the sweating committee and to insert clauses preventing subletting and make every effort to secure currently accepted 'fair' wages in the trade for workmen employed on government contracts. Parliament had shown its support for fair wages but was ruling by example rather than by legislation. The sweating committee had refrained from recommending the fixing of wages and this made parliament's initiative all the more significant. The report and evidence of the 1895 committee described the nature and extent of current contracts in printing and binding with special emphasis on sweating and subcontracting. The 1896 and 1897 select committees provided the same kind of information on government contracts generally.

Original references

1890-91	[C.6267] LXXVIII	Profit sharing, rep. to Board of Trade, appendices.
1894	[C.7458] LXXX	Profit sharing, rep. to Board of Trade, appendices and index.
1895	[C.7848] LXXX	Profit sharing, rep. to Board of Trade, appendices.
1895	(362) XIII	Stationery Contracts (Fair Wages Resolution), Sel. Cttee. Rep., mins. of ev., etc.
1896	(230) XIII	Stationery Contracts (Fair Wages Resolution), Sel. Cttee. Rep., mins. of ev., etc.
1896	(277) X	Government Contracts (Fair Wages Resolution), Sel. Cttee. Rep., mins. of ev., etc.
1897	(334) X	Government Contracts (Fair Wages Resolution), Sel. Cttee. Rep., mins. of ev., appendix, index.

Industrial Relations 23   First and second reports from the select committee on distress from want of employment, with proceedings, minutes of evidence and appendix, 1895. (736 pp.)

Unemployment, a term which is so central in the language of sociologists and economists today, was not nearly so well defined in 1895 This was not because unemployment did not exist but because there was little understanding of why or to what extent it existed. Unemployment analysis as we know it was still in its infancy. The select committee on distress from want of employment appointed in 1895 was confronted with the same lack of data and theoretical principles which hampered so many of the great parliamentary inquiries between 1880 and 1895 (see Ford, *Social Theory and Social Practice*, pp. 96-102).

The immediate reason for the inquiry was the high level of unemployment during the harsh winter of 1894-95. The committee's terms of reference covered: the extent of distress from unemployment; the relevant powers of local and central authorities and the steps which should be taken to deal with the problem. In view of the high level of distress at the time an interim report on immediate practical measures was requested. A circular was dispatched to the mayors of towns and the chairmen of district councils seeking information on (a) distress in the district and its causes (b) relieving measures taken (c) whether an unemployment register was kept (d) suggestions for relief. A tubular analysis of the replies is contained in the appendix to the second report. Some 1,200 districts and almost twenty million people were represented.

Witnesses whose evidence was submitted with the first report included James Keir Hardie and Sir Hugh Owen (secretary of the Local Government Board). The evidence deals with the general questions mentioned in the terms of reference and more particularly with the measures which were immediately necessary. The district of West Ham was subjected to special examination as typifying the general distress. The committee detailed the schemes put forward by Keir Hardie and others. These incorporated such proposals as the issue of food, public relief works and establishment of a common fund to augment existing funds in poorer unions.

Original references
1895	(111) VIII	Distress from want of employment, Sel. Cttee. Rep., mins. of ev.
	(253)	Distress from want of employment, Sel. Cttee. 2nd Rep., appendix.

Industrial Relations 24   Reports from the select committee on distress from want of employment, with minutes of evidence, appendices and index, 1895-96. (1,200 pp.)

The appendix to the third report has further tables of information abstracted from replies to the circular (these refer mainly to Scotland) and several other reports and tables of statistics on distress, unemployment and pauperism and on the machinery for dealing with them. The evidence with the report was taken from poor law officials of unions in the London area, the representatives of charitable organizations (the Salvation Army, the Church Army, the Charity Organization Society and the Mansion House Unemployed Committee) and noted sociologists and economists including Charles Booth, and Llewellyn Smith. It includes a great deal of factual material on the extent and effects of distress, the powers of the Boards of Guardians in dealing with it and the work of the charitable organizations. Evidence analysing facts shows important advances in technique. This was especially instanced in Llewellyn Smith's use of charts and plans to reduce the total recorded volume of unemployment in recent years to that resulting from trade cycles and that resulting from seasonal variations. The committee paid special attention to the tin plate and building industries in order to discover how the various factors causing unemployment combined. They examined Dutch and Belgian labour colonies in search of a means for dealing with unemployment. In their third report they discussed many of the possible avenues of approach and the problems which curtailed them. The Poor Law Guardians, for example, had statutory powers to set paupers to work for wages but the loss of the franchise occasioned by accepting poor law assistance was a serious obstacle. This problem was examined in the 1896 report.

With the improvement of trade and the increase in job opportunities in the later 1890s the government rapidly lost interest in the problem of unemployment and took no further action on the very limited recommendations of the committees' reports. Even the TUC largely ignored the question between 1896-1903.

Original references

| 1895 | (365) IX | Distress from want of employment, Sel. Cttee. 3rd Rep., mins. of ev., appendix. |
| 1896 | (321) IX | Distress from want of employment, Sel. Cttee. Rep., mins. of ev., appendix, index. |

THE LABOUR COMMISSION

Membership of trade unions affiliated to the TUC rose rapidly from 600,000 in 1888 to 1,576,000 in 1892. This remarkable increase was largely concentrated in the organizations of unskilled and general workers whose industrial policies were generally more aggressive than were those of the 'new Model' unions of the previous generation. A wave of industrial unrest swept the country in 1889-90. At the same time there was a new political awakening of the working class with a growing acceptance of socialist ideology. These were the developments which persuaded the government of Lord Salisbury to set on foot a major enquiry into labour relations.

Judged by the quality of its members and the volume of its reports the Labour Commission appointed in 1891 was one of the most high powered and productive inquiries of the entire century. But that organized inquiry however well imbued with genius, could have provided new and more profound answers to the social question seems contrary to the essentially sporadic nature of advances in human affairs. Furthermore, the commission having among its members both capitalists and left wing socialists was too much predetermined in dissent to have been likely to agree even on workable compromises to say nothing of providing new and deeper insights. For these and other reasons the undramatic conclusions, especially of the majority report, neither fulfilled the expectations of contemporaries nor were in keeping with the vastness and thoroughness of the investigations.

The difficulties commenced with the interpretation of the terms of reference — questions affecting the relations between employers and employees and the conditions of labour which had been raised in recent disputes, and whether any evils could be remedied by legislation. The majority chose a narrow and precise interpretation excluding consideration of the fundamental nature of society and the causes of wealth and poverty. But in an age deeply stirred by revolutionary social theories and new utopian ideas and better informed of the real conditions of sections of the working classes, fundamental social questions could never be very far from the surface, and in the tomes of evidence this is abundantly clear.

We are still too much involved in the capitalist-socialist conflict to have a clear idea of its eventual outcome or even to judge with any certainty the conclusions of the Labour Commission; but this takes not one jot from the value of the commission's voluminous reports as a gigantic historical record of the labour scene in Britain and throughout the world at the end of the nineteenth century. Few commissions could point among their members to such a range and expertise of knowledge and experience: Balfour, Hicks-Beach, Alfred Marshall, F. Pollock, Samuel Plimsoll, Jesse

Collings, Tom Mann and Thomas Burt. The commission interviewed 600 witnesses and asked nearly 100,000 questions besides collecting extensive replies to questionnaires and compiling copious reports on the labour question in every area of the world. Professor Ford in *Social Theory and Social Practice* (p. 68) says: 'Embedded in its sixty-seven separately numbered papers is a mass of information on labour conditions and organization, some of it to be found nowhere else in such detail.' The large number of papers and the order in which they were submitted made the total report of the commission disorganized and Irish University Press editors have rearranged the papers so as to bring sections of the report on the same subject matter together and present a much more workable research unit. For the purpose of collecting evidence the commission was divided into three committees and the industries to be examined were similarly divided into groups:— A: iron, engineering, hardware, shipbuilding, and cognate trades; B: transport and agriculture; C: textiles, clothing, chemical, building and miscellaneous trades. On general questions pertaining to labour, the commission took evidence sitting as a whole while in the case of agriculture the inquiry was conducted through the medium of assistant commissioners. To Geoffrey Drage, the commission's secretary and his office fell the onerous task of providing digests, summaries and indexes of the entire evidence and also of compiling a review of the literature on the labour question throughout the world.

Industrial Relations 25   First report from the royal commission on labour, with the minutes of evidence (group A volume I), appendices, and the digest of evidence (group A volume I), 1892. (624 pp.)

In their first four reports the Labour Commission submitted without comment, evidence, oral and written, already collected. The first report comprises volumes of oral evidence from the sub-committees on Groups A, B and C industries together with their digests (IUP Industrial Relations 25-27). Volume I of the evidence on group A industries deals with iron, coal and slate mining. The majority of the witnesses were representatives of employers' and employees' organizations – trade unions, miners' friendly societies and coal owners' associations, e.g. the Quarrymen's Union of North Wales and the National Association of Colliery Managers. The evidence covered most of the major mining areas in England, Scotland and Wales: Northumberland, Durham, Cleveland, Derbyshire, Staffordshire, Yorkshire, Lancashire, Nottinghamshire, Fife and Kinross, and mining districts in North and South Wales.

Topics on which there is extensive evidence in this volume include the mining industry itself, trade unions and employers' associations (number of members, rules and regulations and activities); working conditions (types of work, hours and wages, fluctuations in wages and employment, contracting and subcontracting, piece work, labour saving machinery and safety regulations); the causes and results of disputes; relations between union executives and men; and the co-operative movements and their effects.

The main purpose of the oral evidence was to elucidate the causes and circumstances of industrial disputes and to discover how they could best be prevented and settled. In doing this, detailed statistical and other information was sought on every aspect of labour matters. Such information was all the more necessary because there was no central fund of labour statistics available. For the researcher the evidence has manifold values: it provides some of the most detailed labour and trade union statistics of the period; it gives very thorough and realistic descriptions of working conditions in almost every industry; it documents the labour mood of the period by detailing the views, prejudices and grievances of employers and workers at first hand and by giving hundreds of on-the-spot accounts of strikes and disputes — overall it is a mammoth guide to the influence of the labour and trade union movements.

As in the other volumes of oral evidence, the digests contain (a) a précis of the evidence of each witness (b) abstracts of evidence on strikes and lock-outs, the eight-hour day, arbitration and conciliation and Acts of Parliament (c) an anlysis of evidence and (d) a glossary of technical terms.

Original references
1892   [C.6708] XXXIV Labour, R. Com. 1st Rep.
        [C.6708-IV]   Labour, R. Com. 1st Rep., mins. of ev., appendices, Group A, Vol. I.
        [C.6708-I]   Labour, R. Com. 1st Rep., digest of ev., Group A, Vol. I.

Industrial Relations 26   Royal commission on labour, minutes of evidence (group B volume I) with appendices and digest of evidence (group B volume I), 1892. (816 pp. 2 folding maps, 1 coloured)

Volume I of the evidence on Group B industries deals with shipping and dockland labour. Witnesses, representing the Amalgamated Society of Stevedores, the Shipping Federation, the London and India Docks Company, the Amalgamated Society of Watermen and Lightermen of the Thames and other similar organizations provided a vast compendium of information particularly on trade unionism and industrial disputes. Apart from the general topics already referred to in connection with volume 25 there is wide-ranging evidence on problems specific to dock and shipping labour: the method of hiring, unemployment, conflicts between unionists and non-unionists, municipalization of docks, women's employment, dockers' and seamen's homes and lodgings and the seaworthiness of ships.

Among the witnesses were several trade union leaders, notably Ben Tillett whose evidence, though representing the socialist viewpoint, exemplifies the material in the volume. Tillett described the structure of dock labour, discussing the extent of seasonal variation in employment and explaining why the large tonnage handled at the port of London provided so little work. He condemned the system of selecting and hiring labour and the indiscriminate employment of boys. He emphasized that the conditions of dockers were merely exemplary of workers' conditions generally and urged the reorganization of society on socialist lines as the only lasting solution. The appendix includes much supplementary material on the topics covered: statistics on the tonnage handled in the port of London and on fluctuations in unemployment there; accounts of speeches made by trade union leaders and of other addresses and manifestoes relating to the labour movement.

Original references

| 1892 | [C.6708-V] XXXV | Labour, R. Com. 1st Rep., mins. of ev., appendices, Group B, Vol. I. |
| 1892 | [C.6708-II] XXXIV | Labour, R. Com. 1st Rep., digest of ev., Group B, Vol. I. |

Industrial Relations 27   Royal commission on labour, minutes of evidence (group C volume I) with appendices and the digest of evidence (group C volume I), 1892. (632 pp.)

This volume deals largely with the textile and confectionery industries and with public house employees. Most of the witnesses were representatives of trade unions and employers' associations but non-union workers and chambers of commerce in the textile towns were also represented. As many textile workers were female, Committee B appointed lady sub-commissioners to enquire into the employment of women (see IUP Industrial Relations 34). No female witnesses appeared directly before the commission. A notable point about the textile industry was the number of 'half-timers' employed and factory inspectors and teachers were interviewed on this aspect of the subject. The volume has the same breadth and detail of information and opinion as the previous two. The cotton, woollem and jute industries of Leeds, Bradford, Halifax, Manchester and Dundee are particularly well represented. There is a wealth of material on recent disputes both general and local: the causes, organization and conduct of strikes, their cost to the workers and to the industry, their outcome and the machinery established in the several districts for conciliation and arbitration. The rules and regulations and funds of trade unions and employers' organizations are detailed both in the evidence and appendices and the effects of trade unionism are assesed. Much evidence is devoted to the operation of the Factory and Workshop Acts, the Employers' Liability Act, the Truck Acts and the Limited Liability and Joint Stock Company Acts.

Original references

1892	[C.6708-VI] XXXV	Labour, R. Com. 1st Rep., mins. of ev., appendices, Group C, Vol. I.
1892	[C.6708-III] XXXIV	Labour, R. Com. 1st Rep., 1st Rep., digest of ev., Group C, Vol. I.

Industrial Relations 28   Second report from the royal commission on labour, with minutes of evidence (group A volume II), 1892. (816 pp. 1 folding table)

The second report comprises further oral evidence (IUP 28-30), replies to questionnaires (IUP 35 and 36), the first two volumes of reports on labour conditions in foreign countries (IUP 42), and a series of memoranda on the rules of employers' and employees' associations (IUP 37).

Volume II of Group A evidence has further material on mining, but deals mainly with the iron, engineering and hardware industries. Much of the mining evidence relates to the Rhondda, Aberdare and Merthyr valleys and to Staffordshire. The main body of evidence, taken from trade union and employers' organization representatives, provides an extensive and detailed account of working conditions, relations between employers and employees, and the causes and results of strikes. Members of conciliation and arbitration councils and committees were among those examined. Some of the trade union leaders, among them James Keir Hardie, founder of the British Labour Party, urged that only in a socialistic context could lasting industrial peace be found. These witnesses explained their particular versions of socialist doctrine and applied them to their own industries. One witness, for example, testified that industry must eventually develop so that profits, wages and prices would be planned and arranged jointly by workers and employers.

Appendices in this volume range from copies of sliding scale wage agreements and cases and questions considered by the Wages Board of the South Wales Iron and Steel Workers' Association to a diagram illustrating variations in the price of pig iron from 1879-91. Blast furnace workers, engineers and engineering workers, nut and bolt makers, and lock and key smiths are among the categories of workers dealt with in the appendices.

Original references

1892	[C.6795] XXXVI Pt. I	Labour, R. Com. 2nd Rep.
	[6795-IV] XXXVI	Labour, R. Com. 2nd Rep., mins. of ev., appendices Group A, Vol. II.
1892	[6795-I] XXXVI Pt. III	Labour, R. Com. 2nd Rep., digest of ev., Group A, Vol. II.

Industrial Relations 29   Royal commission on labour, minutes of evidence (group B volume II) with appendices and digest of evidence (group B volume II), 1892. (624 pp.)

In their second volume of evidence committee B presented further material on dock and waterside labour and more extensive material on water transport and on the tram, omnibus and cab sections of land transport. The witnesses included Samuel Plimsoll, union officials and employers' representatives. The Shipping Federation, the National Independent Seamen and Firemen's Association, the United Bargemen and Watermen's Protection Society, the Liverpool Cotton and General Warehouse Porters' Society were some of the organizations represented. The working conditions of shipriggers, dockers, warehouse workers, canal boatmen, cabmen, omnibus drivers and other were described and discussed. Evidence was taken in many cases from both union and non-union delegates. The evidence on land transport was confined to London but on the other subjects covered many of the major ports and inland waterways of Britain.

One section of evidence was devoted to a conflict between Joseph Havelock Wilson's National Amalgamated Sailors' and Firemen's Union and the Shipping Federation (Wilson's evidence is contained in IUP 26). In another section Charles Booth gave an account of his inquiry into dock labour in London, reviewing minutely changes in employment and wage levels over a year. Plimsoll's evidence dealt with the conditions of merchant seamen and with loss of life due to overloading of ships. Topics in the evidence on inland water transport include the poor quality of boats, the navigability of rivers and canals and the 'short hours' movement.

The long appendix contains a wide variety of interesting and valuable material: rules of unions; newspaper reports on labour topics; tables of rates of wages; accounts of insurance and accident funds; arbitrator's verdicts on disputes in Hull; a list of assaults made on non-union workers; tables of ships registered in Britain and the merchandise carried by them; extensive material on shipwrecks and schemes for municipalization of bus and tram transport.

Original references
1892   [C.6795-V] XXXVI Pt. II Labour, R. Com. 2nd Rep., mins. of ev.,
                                 appendices, Group B, Vol. II.
1892   [C.6795-II] XXXVI Pt. III Labour, R. Com. 2nd Rep., digest of ev.,
                                  Group B, Vol. II.

Industrial Relations 30 Royal commission on labour, minutes of evidence (group C volume II) with appendices and digest of evidence (group C volume II), 1892. (656 pp.)

A representative selection of interests covered in this second volume of Group C evidence is as follows: framework knitters; individual hosiery firms; the Midland Counties Hosiery Federation; the jute, boot and shoe and carpet industries; carpenters, plasterers, joiners, plumbers, bricklayers, coopers and coachmakers; building trade societies, licensed victuallers; chemical industry workers. Conditions of labour, wages and hours, recent disputes and strikes, the rules and finances of trade unions, and the state of the industries and trades themselves are covered with the same comprehensive detail and discussion of specific cases as in previous volumes. There is a good deal of evidence on sanitary conditions and safety regulations and on the operation of the Employers' Liability Act. The appendix includes returns of average earnings of weavers, accounts of arbitration and conciliation systems, a résumé on the finances of co-operative industries, newspaper comments on disputes and controversies and details of insurance schemes for relieving employers of their responsibilities under the Employers' Liability Act. A noteworthy point is the difficulty with which the committee confined witnesses to the narrower interpretation of the terms of reference of the commission and steered them away from the more general questions which were to be considered by the commission sitting as a whole.

Original references
1892   [C.6795-VI] XXXVI Pt. II Labour, R. Com. 2nd Rep., mins. of ev.,
                                  appendices, Group C, Vol. II.
1892   [C.6795-III] XXXVI Pt. III Labour, R. Com. 2nd Rep., digest of ev.,
                                   Group C, Vol. II.

Industrial Relations 31 Third report from the royal commission on labour, with the minutes of evidence (group A volume III), appendices and digest of evidence (group A volume III), 1893-94. (728 pp.)

In their third report the commissioners submitted oral evidence from 218 witnesses taken by the three committees (IUP 31-33), and the assistant commissioners reports on the agricultural labourers (IUP 38-41) and on the employment of women (IUP 34).

Volume III of Group A evidence was taken from over fifty witnesses representing trade unions, employers' associations and conciliation and arbitration boards in a wide range of industries and trades: engineering, shipbuilding, edgetools manufacture, nail and chainmaking, iron and brass foundries, boilermakers, blacksmiths, ordnance store labourers and labourers in government dockyards. Engineering, shipbuilding and associated iron trades are the most widely covered. The subjects of evidence are mainly the same as in earlier volumes of evidence. Evidence from chambers of commerce places the more detailed information in context and gives a general picture of developments in labour relations. A section of evidence on mines and quarries has a memorandum on a dispute in Durham Coalmines in 1892, and also contains tables comparing miners' wages in Britain, the United States and continental Europe. Another memorandum includes statistics on the iron ore deposits of Britain and the United States and on the numbers employed in British iron industries. The appendix has many valuable items including ground and elevation plans illustrating the condition of miners' houses, lists of prices paid for piece work and accounts of actions instituted by the Boilermakers' Society under the Employers' Liability Act. The digest contains an index to all three volumes of Group A evidence.

Original references
1893-94 [C.6894] XXXII Labour, R. Com. 3rd Rep.
          [C.6894-VII]   Labour, R. Com. 3rd Rep., mins. of ev., appendices,
                           Group A, Vol. III.
          [C.6894-X]   Labour, R. Com. 3rd Rep., digest of ev., Group A,
                           Vol. III.

Industrial Relations 32 Royal commission on labour, minutes of evidence (group B volume III) with appendices and digest of evidence (group B volume III), 1893-94. (888 pp. 17 folding coloured charts)

The majority of the third volume of Group B evidence was on railway, water and city transport. In addition further material was presented on docks, wharves and warehouses, especially in Dublin where labour disputes were reaching a peak during this period. In the water transport section officials of the various organizations described the industry and its labour problems. Apart from giving extensive information on labour relations in inland waterways transport, this section of evidence is a valuable survey of a way of life which has now virtually disappeared.

The evidence on city transport is mainly concerned with London but also extends to other major cities. Witnesses represented omnibus, tram and cab companies in London and elsewhere, public transport companies in Huddersfield and Glasgow, and workers, both union and non-union. Muncipalization of city transport was discussed extensively and there is considerable material on the relative efficiency of private and public enterprises. Another much discussed issue was legislative regulation of workers' wages and conditions.

Original references

1893-94 [C.6894-VIII] XXXIII   Labour, R. Com. 3rd Rep., mins. of ev., appendices, Group B, Vol. III.

      [C.6894-XI]   Labour, R. Com. 3rd Rep., digest of ev., Group B, Vol. III.

Industrial Relations 33   Royal commission on labour, minutes of evidence (group C volume III) with appendices and digest of evidence (group C volume III) 1893-94. (1,080 pp.)

This evidence from about ninety witnesses deals further with sections of the textile, clothing and building trades, and more thoroughly with the coal and gas, chemical and printing trades. It also covers miscellaneous categories of workers such as footware makers, bakers, butchers, shop assistants and domestic servants. Information and comment on labour relations and conditions in the printing trade in England, Scotland and Ireland, were provided by officials of the Amalgamated Society of Lithographic Printers and the Typographical Association. Other parties represented were the National Union of Gas Workers and General Labourers, chemical workers' unions, the National Union of Shop Assistants, firms in the printing and bottlemaking industries and the Metropolitan Grocers' and Provision Dealers' Association.

    The volume is another rich source of information and discussion on conditions of labour and industrial relations in specific industries as well as on more general labour and social questions. The material ranges over such topics as strikes, victimization, the role of parliament in labour negotiations, the value of profit-sharing and the co-operative movement.

Original references

1893-94 [C.6894-IX] XXXIV   Labour, R. Com. 3rd Rep., mins. of ev., appendices, Group C, Vol. III.

      [C.6894-XII]   Labour, R. Com. 3rd Rep., digest of ev., Group C, Vol. III.

Industrial Relations 34   Royal commission on labour, the indices volumes I-III to the evidence (groups A, B and C) with an appendix and reports on the employment of women, 1893-94. (888 pp.)

The six reports on the employment of women compiled by Eliza Orme,

Clara Collet, Mary Abraham and Margaret Irwin were based on existing information in parliamentary papers, personal investigation of work-places and evidence taken from employers and workers. They present and interpret a wide range of statistical and factual information. The oral evidence is arranged in tabular format providing easy reference to facts and opinions. The reports cover England, Wales, Scotland and Ireland and include extensive material on the main industrial centres including London, Bristol, Birmingham, Liverpool, Manchester, Glasgow and Dublin. Points examined with particular attention throughout were: (a) differences in the rates of wages for male and female workers; (b) special grievances of women workers; (c) the effects of industrial employment on the health, morality and home life of women; (d) the exclusion of women from suitable employment. The reports throw valuable light on the general socio-economic conditions of working-class women.

There are three different indices to the oral evidence taken by the committees: a witness index which refers from the witness's name to the analysis of his evidence in the digest volumes; a subject index which is intended as a supplementary guide to the digest by allowing ready access to the original evidence; a trades index which provides a complete picture of the labour question in each trade investigated. The index also includes a glossary of all the technical terms used by witnesses, presented so as to minmize errors in interpreting evidence due to local and personal usage of terms. The glossary has numerous illustrations.

Original References

1893-94 [C.6894-XXIII] XXXVII Pt. I	Labour, R. Com. 3rd Rep., employment of women, assistant commissioners Reps.
1893-94 [C.7063-IV] XXXVIII	Labour, R. Com. 4th Rep., index to ev. Vol. I, Groups A, B and C, subjects.
[C.7063-V]	Labour, R. Com. 4th Rep., index to ev. Vol. II, Part I, trades, Group A.
[C.7063-V-A]	Labour, R. Com. 4th Rep., index to ev. Vol. II, Part II, trades, Group B.
[C.7063-V-B]	Labour, R. Com. 4th Rep., index to ev. Vol. II, Part III, trades, Group C.
[C.7063-V-C]	Labour, R. Com. 4th Rep., index Vol. III, technical glossaries with introduction, indexes, appendices.

Industrial Relations 35   Royal Commission on labour, answers to schedules of questions issued by groups A and B of the commission, 1892. (664 pp.)

The questionnaires sent to trade unions, employers, employers' associations and related bodies sought concise information on numbers of workmen, conditions of employment, strikes and lock-outs and other labour questions. The replies were arranged and tabulated and a summary introduction for each group of industries drawn up by Geoffrey Drage, the secretary of the commission. These introductions are useful comparative guides to the overall picture of wages and conditions in many industries. A breakdown of some of the topics dealt with is as follows: (a) *hours* – normal, variations in particular trades, the demand for an eight-hour day, overtime and holidays; (b) *conditions of employment* – regularity, fluctuations and their causes, safety, sanitary conditions, distribution of jobs among male and female workers, apprenticeship and technical education, work done by machinery, conditions in public authority employment; (c) *strikes and lock-outs* – frequency, causes, attitude of trade unions, outcome, modes of negotiation; (d) *the introduction of sliding scale wages* and (e) *profit sharing and co-operation*. In both Groups A and B answers there is material on employment agencies which were becoming important at the time.

In the introduction to the Group B answers a number of particularly noteworthy points were discussed – the employment of foreigners, the possibility of introducing a system of certificates or licences to distinguish competent from incompetent workmen, and a proposal that employed workers should voluntarily restrict their work in order to reduce unemployment.

Original references

| 1892 | [C.6795-VII] XXXVI Pt. III | Labour, R. Com. 2nd Rep., answers to schedules of questions, Group A. |
| | [C.6795-VIII] | Labour, R. Com. 2nd Rep., answers to schedules of questions, Group B. |

Industrial Relations 36   Royal commission on labour, answers to schedules of questions issued by group C of the commission, 1892. (984 pp.)

The answers on Group C industries are arranged and tabulated and provided with an introduction as those for Groups A and B. They came from trades councils, chambers of commerce and associations of female workers in addition to trade unions, employers, and employers' organizations. Out of the 781 unions circularized, 281 replied and out of 847 employers and employers' associations, 392 replied. Nevertheless, the replies gave fairly comprehensive information on wages and conditions and with the oral evidence helped to supply the commission with badly needed labour statistics.

The introduction commented on the difficulty of getting accurate statistics and gave a collated account of the different types of work in

Group C under a wide range of headings all of which are statistically documented in the tables of replies: the sweating system; the effects of importation of foreign goods; sub-contracting; sickness and accident schemes; housing schemes; competition between machine and handmade goods, etc. Group C covered many classes of female occupations especially in the textile industry and clothing trades. Statistics on strikes and disputes form a large section of the replies and many ideas for preventing and settling them and for improving labour relations generally are delineated and evaluated. In this section also suggestions are made on the official collection and publication of labout statistics.

Original reference
1892   [C.6795-IX] XXXVI Pt. IV   Labour, R. Com. 2nd Rep., answers to
                                       schedules of questions, Group C.

Industrial Relations 37   Royal commission on labour, rules of associations of employers and of employed, with introductory memoranda, 1892. (568 pp.)

These tables and the memoranda were also compiled under the dirction of Geoffrey Drage. They present a comprehensive and concise picture of employers' and workers' combinations. There are introductory memoranda on (a) associations of employers (b) associations of workers (c) trades councils (d) chambers of commerce (e) boards of arbitration and conciliation, and joint committees of workers and employers. Each memorandum summarized such information as number of associations, distribution among the trades, constitutions and objectives, forms of government, conditions of membership, activities, benefit funds, attitudes to employers or employees, etc. The memoranda describe and comment on the overall picture. The tables provide specific details on nearly 600 organizations including a summary of the rules and regulations of each. The appendix has a selection of complete lists of rules and regulations of a number of different types of association giving an idea of the volume and complexity of the material dealt with in the tables. One of the motives behind the compilation of this volume was to analyse the problems involved in co-ordinating and centralizing employers' and employees' organizations so as to prevent chaotic and useless disputes.

Original reference
1892   [C.6795-XII] XXXVI Pt. V   Labour, R. Com. 2nd Rep., rules of associa-
                                       tions of employers and employed, intro-
                                       ductory memoranda.

Industrial Relations 38 Royal commission on labour, reports
from the assistant agricultural commissioners (volume I
England parts I-VI) with indices, 1893-94. (946 pp.)

A plan proposed by William C. Little was adopted by the Labour
Commission in its inquiry into the condition of agricultural labourers
(agriculture was one of the industries in Group B). Little suggested that
assistant commissioners be appointed to report on districts chosen so as to
represent a wide variety of agricultural conditions, population density and
competing industries. For the purposes of contrast and comparison each
individual commissioner was allotted a number of districts displaying
varying conditions of farming and affluence. Instructions delineating the
main fields of inquiry were given to each and these constitute the main
headings in the reports: general features of the area; the supply of labour;
conditions of employment; wages and other earnings; housing and
accommodation; land and gardens owned or rented by labourers; trade
unions and benefit societies; conclusions on the general condition of
agricultural labourers and suggestions for improvement. The selected areas
followed the boundaries of the poor law unions except in Scotland where
these did not exist. The assistant commissioners compiled separate reports
on each district allotted to them and a general report covering all the
districts. Little was appointed senior assistant commissioner and instructed
to draw up a report summarizing the overall condition of agricultural
labourers in Great Britain and Ireland (IUP Industrial Relations 42). This
volume contains all the agricultural labourer reports for England. The six
main reports with their sub-reports, covering poor law unions in nearly
every county, are not only invaluable sources for the condition of the
agricultural labourer but are veritable mines of socio-economic information on England's rural community at the end of the century. In the
introduction to each report the general geological, geographical and
climatic features of each area are summarized and related to the types of
agriculture carried on. This is followed by an outline of the population
density of each union, and by agricultural statistics covering area of arable
land, size of holdings, methods of cultivation, crops, livestock, etc. In
many cases this section also covers such topics as congested districts,
overall condition of the population and the extent of poor law relief.

Original references

1893-94 [C.6894-I] XXXV	Labour, R. Com. 3rd Rep., agricultural labourer, England Vol. I Part I, W. E. Bear, Reps., appendices.
[C.6894-II]	Labour, R. Com. 3rd Rep., agricultural labourer, England Vol. I Part II, C. M. Chapman, Reps., appendices.

[C.6894-III]	Labour, R. Com. 3rd Rep., agricultural labourer, England Vol. I Part III, A. Wilson Fox, Reps., appendices.
[C.6894-IV]	Labour, R. Com. 3rd Rep., agricultural labourer, England Vol. I Part IV, R. C. Richards, Reps., appendices.
[C.6894-V]	Labour, R. Com. 3rd Rep., agricultural labourer, England Vol. I Part V, A. J. Spencer, Reps., appendices.
[C.6894-VI]	Labour, R. Com. 3rd Rep., agricultural labourer, England Vol. I Part VI, E. Wilkinson, Reps., appendices.
[C.6894-XIII]	Labour, R. Com. 3rd Rep., agricultural labourer, England Vol. I Parts I-VI, indexes, analytical and general.

Industrial Relations 39   Royal commission on labour, reports from the assistant agricultural commissioners (volume II Wales) and (volume III Scotland parts I and II) with indices, 1893-94. (632 pp.)

The Welsh and Scottish reports have the same detailed economic and social information as those for England (volume 38) and in addition contain a wealth of observations and impressions which catch the atmosphere as well as the bare statistics of rural life. The Welsh reports, compiled by C. M. Chapman and D. Thomas, dealt with districts in many parts of the principality. They concluded that the conditions of the agricultural labourer, especially in the south, were better than ever before but stressed that, in assessing these conditions, account should be taken of variation in the availability and cost of essential commodities. Agricultural education was described and discussed, and put forward as one of the chief needs of the farm labourer. The absence of recreation and entertainment facilities was also stressed – village coffee houses and reading rooms were extremely rare and refreshment businesses usually failed. On the positive side, the commissioners pointed to the Eistedfod and the Sunday school movement as the major intellectual agencies reaching the masses in Wales and moulding their character.

The commissioners commented on the moral as well as the material well-being of the workers and on the relationship between the two. The illegitimacy rates were high and the references to clandestine love affairs and to the method of courtship known as 'bundling' vividly depict the lustiness as well as the hardships of nineteenth-century rural life.

Because of the absence of poor law unions the Scottish reports examined the counties in groups, embracing a wide range of conditions from the highlands and barren north to the more hospitable lowlands. The

main headings are similar to those of the other reports and there are
detailed statistics for each district: ratios of barren to arable land, crops
and yields, extent of land reclamation, the mechanization of labour, wage
increases, illegitimacy rates, rural depopulation, farm economics, etc. The
main purpose of the reports, to examine the condition of the agricultural
labourer, is thoroughly achieved but, in addition, all the reports depict
social conditions generally. Indexes to both series of reports are included.

Original references
1893-94 [C.6894-XIV] XXXVI   Labour, R. Com. 3rd Rep., agricultural labourer,
                                 Wales, Vol. II, D. Ll. Thomas, C. M. Chapman,
                                 Reps., appendices and indexes.

       [C.6894-XV]   Labour, R. Com. 3rd Rep., agricultural labourer,
                                 Scotland, Vol. III Part I, H. Rutherffurd, G. R.
                                 Gillespie, Reps.

       [C.6894-XVI]   Labour, R. Com. 3rd Rep., agricultural labourer,
                                 Scotland, Vol. III Part II, R. Hunter Pringle, E.
                                 Wilkinson, Reps., appendices.

       [C.6894-XVII]   Labour, R. Com. 3rd Rep., agricultural labourer,
                                 Scotland, Vol. III, Part III, indexes to reps. in
                                 Vol. III.

Industrial Relations 40   Royal commission on labour, reports from the assistant agricultural commissioners (volume IV Ireland parts I-IV) with indices, 1893-94. (552 pp.)

Rural Ireland not having experienced the relieving influences of the
Industrial Revolution and still within living memory of the Great Famine
presented a very different picture from the English or even the Scottish
countryside. The very appearance of the land reflected the extreme
poverty and social decay which the commissioners' deeper inspection
thoroughly documented.

The assistant commissioners' reports provide comprehensive, factual
and statistical information on all aspects of Irish rural working conditions
and society covering: nature and fertility of soils; systems of cultivation;
employment resources outside agriculture (including fishing, kelp gathering, turf cutting and illicit distilling); detailed descriptions of houses; the
character and habits of the population; the size of families and the effects
of early marriages; the diets of labourers and small farmers; statistics on
wages and conditions of employment, etc.

This volume is invaluable for students of socio-economic conditions in
Ireland in the late nineteenth century.

Original references
1893-94 [C.6894-XVII] XXXVII Pt. I   Labour, R. Com. 3rd Rep., agricultural
                                        labourer, Ireland, Vol. IV Part I, R. R. McCrea,
                                        Reps., appendices.

[C.6894-XIX]   Labour, R. Com. 3rd Rep., agricultural
                      labourer, Ireland, Vol. IV Part II, W. P.
                      O'Brien, Reps., appendices.

[C.6894-XX]   Labour, R. Com. 3rd Rep. agricultural
                      labourer, Ireland, Vol. IV Part III, R. C.
                      Richards, Reps., appendices.

[C.6894-XXI]   Labour, R. Com. 3rd Rep., agricultural
                      labourer, Ireland, Vol. IV Part IV, A. Wilson
                      Fox, Reps., appendices.

[C.6894-XXII]   Labour, R. Com. 3rd Rep., agricultural
                      labourer, Ireland, Vol. IV Part V, index to
                      Irish Reps. Parts I-IV.

Industrial Relations 41   Royal commission on labour, general report from the senior assistant agricultural commissioner, Mr. William C. Little, with miscellaneous memoranda, abstracts and statistical tables, 1893-94. (672 pp. 3 folding coloured maps)

The sources for William C. Little's summary report on the agricultural labourer included both the assistant commissioners' reports on selected districts and the reports of earlier relevant parliamentary inquiries. Little took 1867 as his starting year because the Royal Commission Report of that year on the employment of children and young people in agriculture gave a very complete picture of the circumstances of the agricultural labourer and because 1867 marked the end of distinct epoch in the social and economic history of the rural population. From then on, Little claimed, there had been a quiet revolution in rural economics (up to one-third of farm profits had been transferred from farmers to labourers). In the earlier section of his report he documented this revolution examining the census ratio of agriculturalists to total population, the ration of labourers to farmers, the number of adult male, female and child wage-earners, etc.

The main headings of the report were those suggested by the instructions to assistant commissioners (*see* Industrial Relations volume 38). The section of the report on England gives summary statistics for the whole country under each head. Notable topics covered include: causes of decreased employment; advantages of yearly hiring; harvest work; industrial and supplementary employment; cottage accommodation (construction, tenure, etc.) and the extent of labour unrest. Little stated that the general consensus of opinion was that agricultural labourers' conditions had greatly improved during the previous twenty years though this improvement was not evenly distributed. He used both current books on the subject and the assistant commissioners' reports to demonstrate this improvement. From statistics in an article by Gustav F. Steffen in a recent issue of *Nineteenth Century Magazine* he deduced that never before would 'the agricultural labourer have been able to supply the family requirements of meat and wheat and have such a surplus' as in the period 1881-90. Little disagreed with Steffen's contentions that supplementary sources of income had been eroded away and that the labourer suffered from curtailment of luxuries and leisure, and damage to health from long irregular hours. In his concluding remarks he isolated housing as needing the greatest improvements.

The lengthy second part of the report has extensive memoranda summarizing the findings of relevant earlier inquiries for England, Wales, Scotland and Ireland and statistics including Board of Agricultural and census returns.

Original references

1893-94 [C.6894-XXV] XXXVII Pt. II	Labour, R. Com. 3rd Rep., agricultural labourer, Vol. V Part I, W. C. Little, General Rep.
[C.6894-XXIV]	Labour, R. Com. 3rd Rep., agricultural labourer, Vol. V Part II, W. C. Little, miscellaneous memoranda, abstracts and statistical tables; England and Wales, Scotland, Ireland.

Industrial Relations 42   Royal commission on labour, foreign reports volumes I-XI with an appendix on the migration of labour, 1892-94. (1,192 pp. 10 maps [9 coloured, 7 folding])

The provision of résumés on labour conditions and the state of industrial relations all over the world was the most difficult task which fell to Geoffrey Drage the commission secretary. His eleven reports ranging from those on the United States and European countries to those on remote parts of the East Indies are a vast reservoir of information , ethnic and cultural as well as social and economic. The reports were based on a wide range of sources both official and private: reports from the United States Department of Labour, private correspondence with Indian government officials, state correspondence with labour ministries in European countries and hundreds of books and articles. Each report has a list of sources appended. All the reports follow the same broad outline: a general introduction to the area and its geography, enthnology, and modes of industry; an account of labour relations (strikes and disputes, arbitration and conciliation machinery, conditions of labour in Groups A, B and C industries), and a final section on special topics such as diamond mining in Kimberley, co-operative industries in Holland, and the condition of the peasantry in Russia and the Balkan states. The German report, for example, has a section on the origins and development of German socialism, mentioning the influence of Marx, the aims of the Social Democrats and internationalist, anarchist and communist tendencies. There is similar material on the development of syndicates in France, and on the social condition of Russia and the development of nihilism there from Turgenev's time up to 1890. The reports on the Austro-Hungarian empire have ethnographical and geographical surveys complete with maps. All the reports have extensive labour and industrial statistics and the appendices contain a wide variety of documents on all aspects of the inquiry. An appendix to the reports on the colonies and Indian Empire provides an extensive review of migration of labour throughout the world.

The volume is the result of the first attempt to deal with the whole literature of the world, official and unofficial, on the labour question.

Original references

1892	[C.6795-X] XXXVI Pt. V	Labour, R. Com. 2nd Rep., foreign reps., Vol. I, appendices, United States.
	[C.6795-XI]	Labour, R. Com. 2nd Rep., foreign reps., Vol. II, appendices, colonies, Indian empire, appendix on migration of labour.
1893-94	[C.7063-VI] XXXIX Pt. II	Labour, R. Com. 4th Rep., foreign reps., Vol. III, appendices, Holland.
	[C.7063-VII]	Labour, R. Com. 4th Rep., foreign reps., Vol. V, appendices, Germany.
	[C.7063-VIII]	Labour, R. Com. 4th Rep., foreign reps., Vol. IV, Belgium.
	[C.7063-IX]	Labour, R. Com. 4th Rep., foreign reps., Vol. VI, appendices, France.
	[C.7063-X]	Labour, R. Com. 4th Rep., foreign reps., Vol. VII, appendices, Switzerland.
	[C.7063-XII]	Labour, R. Com. 4th Rep., foreign reps., Vol. VIII, appendices, Italy.
	[C.7063-XIII]	Labour, R. Com. 4th Rep., foreign reps., Vol. IX, appendices, Denmark, Sweden and Norway, Spain and Portugal.
	[C.7063-XIV]	Labour, R. Com. 4th Rep., foreign reps., Vol. X, appendices, Russia.
	[C.7063-XI]	Labour, R. Com. 4th Rep., foreign reps., Vol. XI, appendices Austria-Hungary and the Balkan States.

Industrial Relations 43   Fourth report from the royal commission on labour with minutes and digest of evidence before the commission sitting as a whole, appendix and indices, 1893-94. (1,192 pp. 4 diagrams [1 folding])

The Royal Commission sitting as a whole took evidence on more general aspects of the labour question. John T. Mitchell, chairman of the

Co-operative Wholesale Society and several managers of similar under-takings gave evidence on co-operative production and distribution. Edward W. Brabrook, chief registrar of friendly societies, supplied general statistics on co-operative, building and friendly societies and trade unions. William Ogle, superintendent of statistics in the General Registrar Office, described the vital statistics of the industrial classes detailing mortality rates in different industries and from various diseases. Other notable sections of evidence were: Tom Mann on state and municipal control of industry, unemployment, the formation of a labour department and the eight-hour day; Sydney Webb on the industrial organization of society; Dr Elgin Gould on the United States government offices and departments of labour; Robert Giffen on the collection of labour statistics by the Board of Trade and the bearing of these statistics on remedies proposed in the evidence: Henry Hyndman's evidence on class antagonism and socialist doctrine; and criticisms of the evidence tendered by Webb and Mann.

The appendix has a wide range of documents illustrating many sections of the evidence: names, addresses and other details of registered trade unions, rules and finances of co-operative enterprises, etc. The digest is similar in format to those for the committee evidence; witness, subject and trade indexes are also included.

Original references

1893-94 [C.7063] XXXIX Pt. I	Labour, R. Com. 4th Rep.
[C.7063-I]	Labour, R. Com. 4th Rep., mins. of ev. sitting as a whole.
[C.7063-II]	Labour, R. Com. 4th Rep., digest of ev. sitting as a whole.
[C.7063-III]	Labour, R. Com. 4th Rep., index Vol. IV (witness, subject, trade), to ev. sitting as a whole.
[C.7063-III-A]	Labour, R. Com. 4th Rep., appendix to mins. of ev. sitting as a whole.

Industrial Relations 44 Fifth and final report from the royal commission on labour with report from the secretary on the work of the office, summaries of evidence, appendices and index, 1894. (864 pp. 3 folding tables)

After a marathon inquiry, the final report of the Labour Commission was received with little welcome and was even condemned outrightly in some quarters. It was of course unlikely from the outset, that the whole commission could have agreed to a single report unless socialist doctrines were at least partially incorporated. In the event, a majority and several minority reports were submitted. The majority document attempted to review and analyse the huge compendium of facts, opinions and arguments brought to the commission's notice and to deduce conclusions and recommendations to fit a narrow interpretation of the terms of reference. Recommendations where they emerged at all were pallid and sometimes not clearly borne out by the evidence. The minority on the other hand dispensed with the evidence and drew up a more forceful document based on *a priori* principles and intended more as a labour manifesto than as the reasoned outcome of the inquiry.

Some headings in the majority report are: conditions of employment; associations and organizations of employers and employed; relations between employers and workers; conciliation and arbitration; limitation of hours of work by legislation; a labour department and labour statistics; the employment of women and the health of workers. The majority did not attempt to discuss the fundamental reasons for wealth and poverty of the 'social question'. In their conclusions they ruled out statutory tribunals to settle labour disputes but recommended a central department to promote industrial peace through voluntary effort. On public takeover of industry they suggested that the worker's condition might be much less amenable to improvement if he had to negotiate with a powerful public body. For the historian of industrial relations the Labour Commission's final report is not less valuable because it failed to find solutions for one of the most fundamental problems of our times. It is a record of the attempts, however inadequate, of the most gifted and experienced minds of the time to understand the implications of the labour question and to come to terms with trade unionism, collective socialism and the co-operative and profit sharing movements. Its attempts to understand the economic factors affecting labour are particularly significant. In one sense the majority report marked an important stage in British thinking on labour relations for it helped to gain acceptance of the principle of negotiation between well-organized voluntary associations with a minimum of state interference.

Part II of the report has masterly summaries of the evidence bearing on the terms of reference, compiled by Drage, together with appendices on many topics e.g. Acts of Parliament, state and municipal employment and employment of women.

Original references

1894	[C.7421] XXXV	Labour, R. Com. 5th and final Rep., Part I.
	[C.7421-I]	Labour, R. Com. 5th and final Rep., Part II, secretary's rep. on the work of the office, summaries of ev. with index, appendices.

Contents

BIBLIOGRAPHY

Collections of Documents
Bibliographies
General Histories of Trade Unions and Industrial Relations
Trade Unionism before the Repeal of the Combination Laws
Industrial Relations in the Second Quarter of the Nineteenth
   Century
The New Model
The Development of Arbitration and Conciliation
The Royal Commission and the Labour Laws
The Trades Union Congress and Trades Councils
Trades Unions in Different Industries
The Truck System
The Sweating System
Co-operation and Profit Sharing
Employers' Liability
Unemployment
The New Unionism and the Royal Commission on Labour
Biographies

Bibliography

Collections of Documents
The best source book for the period it covers is G. D. H. Cole and A. W. Filson, *British Working Class Movements: Select Documents, 1789-1875* (London: Macmillan, 1951). The three volumes in the *History in the Making* Series, Max Morris, *From Cobbett to the Chartists,* James B. Jefferys, *Labour's Formative Years, 1849-79* and E. J. Hobsbawm's *Labour's Turning Point, 1880-1900,* published in London by Lawrence & Wishart in 1948, all have the merit of including documents representing the employers' standpoint as well as that of the wage earners. Arthur Aspinall, *Early English Trade Unions* (London: Batchworth Press, 1949), is an ably-edited compilation of documents from the Public Record Office. For the printing trade there is Ellic Howe (ed.) *The London Compositor; documents relating to wages, working conditions and customs in the London printing trade, 1785-1900* (London: Bibliographical Society, 1947). For the first TUC, as seen from contemporary sources, there is Edmund Frow and Michael Katanka (ed.), 1868, *Year of the Unions* (London: Michael Katanka, 1968).

Bibliographies
Indispensable for up to date references on industrial relations are the issues of the *Bulletin* of the Society for the Study of Labour History (1960 to the present). No. 3 (Autumn 1961). contains a list of publications which appeared 1945-54 and No. 1 (Autumn 1960), a list for 1955-60. Subsequent issues have kept the record up to date. No. 11 (Autumn 1965), contains a bibliography on White Collar Unionism compiled by George S. Bains and Harold Pollins. No. 25 (Autumn 1972), includes Chimen Abramsky's 'Checklist of Labour Periodicals'. Vol. 1 of *Llafur* (1 May 1972), the publication of the Society for the Study of Welsh Labour History, contains a list of works on Welsh labour history. Indispensable for Scotland is Ian MacDougall, *An Interim bibliography of the Scottish Working Class Movement and of other labour records held in Scotland* (Edinburgh: Society for the Study of Labour History, Scottish Committee, 1965). See also the Scottish Labour History Journal for more up to date references. Ruth and Edmund Frow and Michael Katanka, *The History of British Trade Unionism: A Select Bibliography* (London: Historical Association pamphlet H 76, 1969), lists 549 published items of general labour history, the histories of individual trade unions, biographies and autobiographies of trade union leaders, journals, documents and trials and also includes an incomplete list of locations of important collections of books and documents relating to the trade union movement. (For a more detailed survey of these depositories and their contents the student should refer to the various issues of the *Bulletin* of the Society for the Study of Labour History). Andrew William Gottschalk, T. G. Wittingham and N. Williams, *British Industrial Relations, an annotated Bibliography* (Nottingham: University of Nottingham, Department of Adult Education, 1969) is principally concerned with developments in the 1950s and 1960s, but is none the less valuable for comparative and theoretical purposes. The bibliography compiled by R. A. Peddie for Sidney and Beatrice Webb,

History of Trade Unionism, 1894 edn. (London: Longmans, 1894), though including many pamphlets only known to be available in the Webb Collection of the British Library of Political and Economic Science (London: London School of Economics), includes many other items not listed elsewhere. Also of great value is the bibliography included in Sydney and Beatrice Webb, *Industrial Democracy,* one vol. edn. (London: Longmans Green & Co., 1902).

General Histories of Trade Unions and Industrial Relations
The best recent short introduction to the development of British trade unionism and collective bargaining is Henry M. Pelling, *A History of British Trade Unionism,* 2nd edn. (London: Macmillan 1972). Albert E. Masson *British Trade Unions 1870-75* (London: Macmillan, 1872), is much briefer, is more controversial, and covers only a part of the century, but it has a useful bibliography. Still indispensable, though originally published over seventy years ago, is Sidney and Beatrice Webb, *History of Trade Unionism,* 2nd edn. (London: Longmans Green & Co., 1920) and the same authors' *Industrial Democracy,* one vol. edn. (London: Longmans Green & Co., 1902), the former chronological in treatment, the latter thematic. Also of very great value is G. D. H. Cole, *A Short History of the British Working Class Movement, 1789-1947* (London: Allen & Unwin, 1948). Hugh A. Clegg, Alan Fox and Arthur F. Thompson, *A History of British Trade Unions since 1889, vol. 1 1889-1910* (Oxford: Clarendon Press, 1964) contains a lengthy first chapter on developments before 1889. A Marxist approach is given in A. L. Morton and George Tate, *The British Labour Movement, 1770-1920* (London: Lawrence & Wishart, 1956). Important collections of essays include Eric J. Hobsbawm, *Labouring Men* (London: Weidenfeld & Nicolson, 1964) and Asa Briggs and John Saville (ed.) *Essays in Labour History,* vols. 1 and 2 (London: Macmillan 1960 and 1971).

Trade Unionism before the Repeal of the Combination Laws
The outstanding work in this period is E. P. Thompson, *The Making of the English Working Class* (London: Gollancz, 1963). Still of value are M. D. George, 'The Combination Laws Reconsidered', *Economic History,* i (1927) and 'The Combination Laws', *The Economic History Review* vol. vi (1936). For Scotland, J. L. Gray, 'The Law of Combination in Scotland', *Economica* vii (1928) is important. The role of Francis Place in effecting the repeal of the Acts is considered in Graham Wallas, *The Life of Francis Place, 1771-1954,* rev. ed. (London: Allen & Unwin, 1918). Recent additions to our knowledge of this subject are Mary Thale (ed.) *The Autobiography of Francis Place* (Cambridge: Cambridge University Press, 1972) and Roy Anthony Church and Stanley David Chapmen, 'Gravener Henson and the Making of the English Working Class' in Eric Lionel Jones and Gordon Edmund Mingay (ed.) *Land, Labour and Population in the Industrial Revolution* (London: Edward Arnold, 1967). See also W. E. S. Thomas, 'Francis Place and Working Class History', *Historical Journal,* v (1962). P. H. J. H. Gosden, *Friendly Societies in England 1815-71* (Manchester: Manchester University Press, 1961) is still the only book on this subject. A very valuable recent work on machine wrecking is Malcolm Ian Thomis, *The Luddites* (Newton Abbot: David & Charles, 1970). Also

of value are E. J. Hobsbawm 'The Machine Breakers', *Labouring Men* (London: Weidenfeld & Nicolson, 1964) and the older works by J. L. and Barbara Hammond *The Skilled Labourer 1760-1832* (London: Longmans, Green & Co., 1919) and F. O. Darvall, *Popular Disturbances and Public Order in Regency England* (London: Oxford University Press, 1934). For early nineteenth-century agrarian disturbances there are two distinguished works: A. J. Peacock, *Bread or Blood, the agrarian riots in East Anglia, 1816* (London: Gollancz, 1965) and E. J. Hobsbawm and George Rudé, *Captain Swing* (rev. ed.) (London: Penguin Books, 1973).

Industrial Relations in the Second Quarter of the Nineteenth Century
The ambitious attempts at forming comprehensive trades unions are considered in G. D. H. Cole, *Attempts at General Union* (London: Macmillan, 1953). A recent account of the best known episode in British trade union history is J. Marlow, *The Tolpuddle Martyrs* (London: André Deutsch, 1971). The centenary publication of the TUC, *The Martyrs of Tolpuddle* (1934), is a worthy tribute to the occasion. The part played by these and other Methodists in the trade union movement is the theme of R. F. Wearmouth, *Methodism and the Trade Unions* (London: Epworth Press, 1959). The influence of Robert Owen on the labour movement has been the subject of many books. A brilliant recent example is John F. C. Harrison, *Robert Owen and Owenism in Britain and America* (London: Routledge and Kegan Paul, 1969). Of many other studies Margaret I. Cole, *Robert Owen of New Lanark* (London: Batchworth Press, 1953); G. D. H. Cole, *The Life of Robert Owen,* 3rd ed. (London: Frank Cass, 1965) and S. Pollard and J. Salt, *Robert Owen, Prophet of the Poor* (London: Macmillan, 1971) are all worthy of mention. The link between Chartism and the trade unions was stronger than was at one time imagined. Raymond Challinor and Brian Ripley, *The Miners Association: a trade union in the age of the Chartists* (London: Lawrence & Wishart, 1968) makes this link clear in the case of a major industry. See also Arthur J. Taylor 'The Miners Association of Great Britain and Ireland, 1842-48', *Economica,* Vol. XXII, 1955. Other works which deal with the links between trade unionism and Chartism are Asa Briggs (ed.) *Chartist Studies* (London: Macmillan, 1959). F. C. Mather, *Public Order in the Age of the Chartists* (Manchester: Manchester University Press, 1960) and Ioerwerth Prothero, 'London Chartism, and the Trades', *Economic History Review,* 2nd Ser. vol. XXIV No. 2 (May 1971). The conflicts over the curriculum in the mechanics institutes as well as many other aspects of the education of the working classes are examined in Brian Simon, *Studies in the History of Education 1770-1870* (London: Lawrence and Wishart, 1960). Much insight into the ideological background to the labour movement in the first half of the nineteenth century many be obtained from G. D. H. Cole *A History of Socialist Thought: The Forerunners, 1789-1850* (London: Macmillan, 1953). A pioneering work on the much neglected aspect of the role and status of women workers is Ivy Pinchbeck, *Women workers in the Industrial Revolution* (London: Frank Cass reprint, 1969). In the absence of state supported labour exchanges the early unions helped their members to find work. This feature of their activity is considered by E. J. Hobsbawm in 'The Tramping Artisan', *Labouring Men* (London: Weidenfeld & Nicolson, 1964). The Victorian middle class image of trade

unionism is revealed in P. Brantlinger, 'The Case against Trade Unions in early Victorian fiction', *Victorian Studies*, vol. 13, 1969-70, pp. 37-52.

The New Model
For an authoritative survey of trade union trends in the 1850s and 1860s there is G. D. H. Cole, 'Some notes on British Trade Unionism in the Thrid Quarter of the Nineteenth Century', in E. M. Carus-Wilson (ed.), *Essays in Economic History*, vol. III (London: Arnold, 1962). The economic basis for the development of the 'New Model' type of trade unionism is explained in E. J. Hobsbawm, 'The Labour Aristocracy', *Labouring Men* (London: Weidenfeld and Nicolson, 1964) though this interpretation is challenged in H. M. Pelling *Popular Politics and Society in Late Victorian Britain* (London: Macmillan, 1968).

The influence of the teachings of the classical economists on union leaders in this period is examined in R. V. Clements, 'British Trade Unions and Popular Political Economy 1850-75', *Economic History Review*, 2nd Ser. XIV (1961). C. Erickson, 'The encouragement of Emigration by British Trade Unions, 1850-1900', *Population Studies*, vol. III (1949-50) W. S. Shepperson, 'Industrial Emigration in Early Victorian Britain', *Journal of Economic History*, vol. XIII (1953) and R. V. Clements, 'Trade Unions and Emigration, 1840-80'. *Population Studies*, vol. IX (1955), all consider the efforts of the trade unions to improve their bargaining position by reducing labour surpluses. New insight into the foundation of the Amalgamated Society of Engineers (the 'New Model') is given in K. Burgess, 'Technological Change and the 1852 Lock out in the British Engineering Industry', *International Review of Social History*, vol. XIV (1969).

The Development of Arbitration and Conciliation
The best general account is Ian Gordon Sharp, *Industrial Conciliation and Arbitration in Great Britain* (London: Allen and Unwin, 1950). The beginnings of the movement are dealt with in Victor Leonard Allen 'The Origins of Industrial Conciliation and Arbitration', *International Review of Social History*, vol. IX, 1964, John Richard Hicks, 'The Early History of Industrial Conciliation in England', *Economica*, vol. X, 1930 and A. J. Odber, 'The Origins of Industrial Peace: the Manufactured Iron Trade of the North of England', *Oxford Economic Papers*, n.s., vol. III, 1951. For a work written by a leading exponent of arbitration see Rupert Kettle, *Strikes and Arbitrations* (Wolverhampton: Simpkin, 1868), and for the reactions of a moderate trade union leader there is George Howell, *The Conflicts of Capital and Labour Historically and Economically Considered*, 2nd Rev. edn. (London: Macmillan, 1890). The union leader collaborated with the successful hosiery manufacturer in a jubilee tribute to the co-operation of capital and labour, Anthony John Mundella and George Howell, 'Industrial Association 1837-87', in Thomas Humphry Ward *The Reign of Victoria*, vol. II (London: Smith & Elder, 1887). Another late Victorian authority is James Stephen Jeans, *Conciliation and Arbitration in Labour Disputes* (London: Crosby, Lockwood & Son, 1894). The work of A. J. Mundella for conciliation in the Hosiery trade may be evaluated in Roy Anthony Church, 'Technological Change and the Hosiery Board of Conciliation and Arbitration, 1860-84', *Yorkshire Bulletin of Economic*

and Social Research, vol. XV. (1963). An excellent recent article is J. H. Porter, 'Wage Bargaining under Conciliation Agreements', *Economic History Review,* n.s. vol. XXIII No. 3 (December 1970) while another valuable study by the same author is 'David Dale and Conciliation in the Northern Manufactured Iron Trade, 1860-1914', *Northern History,* vol. 5 (1970).

The Royal Commission and the Labour Laws

The appointment of the Royal Commission was immediately occasioned by the events in Sheffield. A valuable exposition of the traditions in the Sheffield trades is given in Sidney Pollard's Introduction to *The Sheffield Outrages* (Bath: Adams and Dart, 1967). Invaluable for the political background of the 1860s is Royden Harrison, *Before the Socialists: Studies in Labour and Politics, 1861-81* (London: Routledge & Kegan Paul, 1965). An earlier work, Frances Elma Gillespie, *Labour and Politics in England, 1850-67* (Durham N.C.: Duke University Press, 1928) is still worth reading. The unions as a pressure group are the subject of two articles by H. W. McCready, 'British Labour and the Royal Commission, on Trade Unions', *University of Toronto Quarterly,* vol. XXIV (1955) and 'British Labour's Lobby 1867-75', *Canadian Journal of Economics and Political Science,* xxii (1956). For the part played by the leader of the carpenters' and joiners' union there is Asa Briggs' 'Robert Applegarth and the Trade Unions' in his *Victorian People* (London: Odhams Press, 1954). The part played by an ambitious trade union politician of the first generation is examined in Fred Marc Leventhal, *Respectable Radical: George Howell and Victorian Working Class Politics* (London: Weidenfeld and Nicolson, 1971). Important as revealing the strength of trade unionism at the time is, *United Kingdom, First Annual Trade Union Directory, 1861* (Republished, London: Gregg Press, 1968). With the repeal of the last of the 'taxes on knowledge' in 1861, newspapers played an increasingly important part in the activities of the labour movement. The influence of the leading trade union newspaper of the time is the subject of Stephen Coltham, 'The Bee-Hive Newspaper: its origin and early struggles', in Asa Briggs and John Saville (ed.) *Essays in Labour History,* vol. 1 (London: Macmillan, 1960). The same author has a useful survey 'English Working class Newspapers in 1867' in *Victorian Studies* vol. 13 (1969-70). Covering a wider span of time is Chimen Abramsky's 'Checklist of Labour Periodicals, 1794-1920', *Bulletin* of the Society for the Study of Labour History, No. 25 (Autumn 1972).

The conflicts over the Labour Laws can be followed in Robert Yorke Hedges and Allan Winterbottom, *Legal History of Trade Unionism* (London: Longmans, 1930) Norman Arthur Citrine, *Trade Union Law* (London: Stevens & Sons, 1950) and Kenneth William Wedderburn, *The Worker and the Law* (London: MacGibbon & Kee, 1966). For the crucial legal cases Edward William Cox, *Criminal Law Cases,* vol. X pt. VI and vol. XII (London: W. Cox, 1864-67, 1875), are indispensable reading. The left-wing interpretation is given in Denis Nowell Pritt and Richard Freeman, *The Law versus the Ttade Unions* (London: Lawrence & Wishart, 1958) and in D. N. Pritt's *Employers, Workers and Trade Unions* (London: Lawrence and Wishart, 1970).

These were the years of the foundation and activity of the First

International. Different aspects of these events are examined in Henry Joseph Collins and Chimen Abramsky, *Karl Marx and the British Labour Movement: Years of the First International* (London: Macmillan, 1965) and in Henry J. Collins, 'The English Branches of the First International', in Asa Briggs and John Saville (ed.), *Essays in Labour History* vol. 1 (London: Macmillan, 1960) and in the same author's 'The International and the British Labour Movement', *Bulletin* of the Society for the Study of Labour History, No. 9 (Autumn 1964).

The Trades Union Congress and Trades Councils

The standard account of the TUC is Benjamin Charles Roberts, *The Trades Union Congress, 1868-1921* (London: Allen and Unwin, 1958). There is a much shorter general account in John Lovell and Benjamin Charles Roberts, *Short History of the TUC* (London: Macmillan, 1968). The steps leading to the foundation of the TUC are traced in Albert Edward Musson, *The Congress of 1868: The Origins and Establishment of the Trades Union Congress* (London: TUC, 1955), (rev. ed. 1968). There is a stimulating re-appraisal of the role of the TUC after its first hundred years in Victor W. L. Allen 'The Centenary of the British Trade Union Congress' in Ralph Milliband and John Saville (eds.), *The Socialist Register, 1968* (London: Merlin Press, 1968).

For a short introductory survey on the growth of trades councils there is Betty Grant 'Trades Councils, 1860-1914', *Amateur Historian*, vol. III, 1957. An early and not very adequate general account is Cicely Richards, *A History of Trades Councils 1860-75,* with an introduction by G. D. H. Cole (London: Labour Research Department and Allen & Unwin, 1920). The best histories of individual trades councils are Kenneth Donald Buckley, *Trade Unionism in Aberdeen, 1878-1900* (Edinburgh: Oliver & Boyd, 1955) and John Corbett, *The Birmingham Trades Council, 1866-1966* (London: Lawrence & Wishart, 1966). The story of the most influential of this genre has been told with disappointing sketchiness in George Tate *The London Trades Council, 1860-1950* (London: Lawrence & Wishart, 1950). Other brief accounts include William Hamling, *A Short History of the Liverpool Trades' Council, 1848-1948* (Liverpool: Trades Council, 1948); George Barnsby, *The origins of Wolverhampton Trades Council* (Wolverhampton: Trades Council, 1965) and Sidney Pollard, J. Mendelson, V. Thornes and W. Owen, *The Sheffield Trades and Labour Council, 1858-1958* (Sheffield: Trades and Labour Council, 1958). Important, because of the crucial years covered, is Ian MacDougall, *The Minutes of Edinburgh Trades Council, 1859-1873* (Edinburgh: Scottish History Society, 1968).

Few regional histories of the labour movement have been written. An early example is Thomas Johnston, *The History of the Working Classes in Scotland* (Glasgow: Forward Publishing Co. 1922). A shorter recent account is William Hutton Marwick, *A Short History of Labour in Scotland* (Edinburgh: Chambers, 1967). In a class by itself as a major contribution to urban labour history is Sidney Pollard, *A History of Labour in Sheffield* (Liverpool, University Press, 1959).

A recent work of importance for the labour movement of the North-West is Harold Hikins (ed.), *Building the Union: Essays in the growth of the Workers' Movement, Merseyside 1756-1967* (Liverpool: Toulouse Press, for the Liverpool Trades Council, 1973).

Trade Unions in Different Industries

An early work on the organization of farm labourers which scarcely did justice to the subject was Ernest Selley, *Village Trade Unions in Two Centuries* (London: Allen & Unwin, 1919), Reginald Goves *'Sharpen the Sickle!': The History of the Farm Workers Union* (London: Porcupine Press, 1949) is the most useful and readable general account. It has been followed by a number of more specialized studies including J. P. D. Dunbabin, 'The Revolt in the Field: The Agricultural Labourers' Movement in the 1870s', *Past and Present*, No. 26 (1963); Alan J. Peacock, 'The Revolt of the Field in East Anglia', in Lionel Maxwell Mumby (ed.), *The Luddites and Other Essays* (London: Michael Katanka Books, 1971); Reginald Charles Russell, *'The Revolt of the Field in Lincolnshire'* (Boston Lincs: Lincolnshire County Committee, National Union of Agricultural Workers, 1956) and David W. Howell, 'The Agricultural Labourer in 19th century Wales', *Bulletin of the Society for the Study of Labour History*, No. 23, Autumn 1971.

Two books which record the organization of the bookbinders and paper workers are Ellic Howe and J. Child, *Society of London Bookbinders* (London: Sylvan Press, 1952) and C. J. Bundock, *National Union of Printing, Bookbinding and Paper Workers* (Oxford: Clarendon Press, 1969). The history of trade union organization in the footwear trades has been well treated in Alan Fox, *History of the National Union of Boot and Shoe Operatives, 1874-1957* (Oxford: Basil Blackwell, 1958). For the brushmakers there is one of the earlier union histories, William Kiddier, *The Old Trade Unions* (London: Allen & Unwin, 1930).

Among a number of books which deal with different aspects of building trade unionism the most important are T. J. Connelly, *The Woodworkers, 1860-1960* (Manchester: Amalgamated Society of Woodworkers, 1960); John Oliver French, *Plumbers in Unity: History of the Plumbing Trades Union, 1865-1965* (London: Plumbing Trades Union, 1965); S. Higenbottam, *Our Society's History* (Manchester: Amalgamated Society of Woodworkers, 1939); William Samuel Hilton, *Foes to Tyranny* (Amalgamated Union of Building Trades Workers, 1963) and Raymond Postgate *The Builders' History* (London: Labour Publishing Co., 1923).

The organization of the coal-miners has been more thoroughly covered than that of any other major industrial group. Nationally, from the time of the formation of the Miners' Federation of Great Britain in 1888, the story has been told by Robert Page Arnot, *The Miners, 1889-1945*, 3 vols. (London: Allen & Unwin, 1949-61). (The earlier history is partly covered by the above mentioned work by R. Challinor and B. Ripley). The principal regional histories are; Ness Edwards, *The History of the South Wales Miners* (London: Labour Publishing Co., 1926); Eric Wyn Evans, *The Miners of South Wales* (Cardiff: University of Wales Press, 1961); Frank Machin, *The Yorkshire Miners: A History*, vol. 1 (Barnsley: National Union of Mineworkers, Yorkshire Area, 1958); Sidney Webb, *The Story of the Durham Miners, 1662-1921* (London: Labour Publishing Co., 1921); Edward Welbourne, *The Miners Union of Northumberland and Durham* (Cambridge: Cambridge University Press, 1923) James Eccles

Williams, *The Derbyshire Miners* (London: Allen & Unwin, 1962) and William R. Garside, *The Durham Miners 1919-1960* (London: Allen & Unwin, 1971).

The merit of James Bavington Jefferys', *The Story of the Engineers* (London: Lawrence & Wishart, 1945), is that the progress of trade unionism is related to the developments in the industry. For an allied industry there is the well written book by Hubert Jim Fyrth and Henry Joseph Collins, *The Foundry Workers* (Manchester: Union of Foundry Workers, 1959). Much less satisfactory is Arthur Pugh, *Men of Steel* (London: Iron and Steel Trades Confederation, 1951).

Organization of the postmen was minimal in the nineteenth century. Hence Henry G. Swift's *History of Postal Agitation* (new revised edn.) (Manchester & London: Percy Bros., 1929) deals only briefly with the period before 1907 after which unionization was rapid.

There is one reliable account of the pottery workers: William Henry Warburton, *History of Trade Union Organization in the North Staffordshire Potteries* (London: Allen & Unwin, 1931).

The main accounts of organization in the printing trades are Ellic Howe and Harold E. Waite, *The London Society of Compositors: A Centenary History* (London: London Society of Compositors, 1948); Sarah C. Gillespie, *A Hundred Years of Progress: The Record of the Scottish Typographical Association* (Glasgow: Robert Maclehose & Co., 1953) and Albert Edward Musson, *The Typographical Association* (Oxford: Oxford University Press, 1954).

The conditions of employment of shop assistants before union organization became important in the twentieth century are recalled in Percy Christopher Hoffman, *They also Served* (London: Porcupine Press, 1949). The history of the main organization of teachers (as well as that of its forerunner) is skilfully told in Asher Tropp, *The School Teachers* (London: Allen & Unwin, 1957).

Among the more important books about employment in the textile industry are Duncan Bythell, *The Handloom Weavers* (Cambridge: Cambridge University Press, 1969) (an indispensable work though not directly concerned with trade unionism). Norman H. Cuthbert, *The Lace Makers Society: A Study of Trade Unionism in the British Lace Industry, 1760-1960* (Nottingham: Amalgamated Society of Lace Making and Ancillary Workers, 1960); Margaret Stewart and Leslie David Stevenson Hunter, *The Needle is Threaded* (London: Heinemann, 1964) and Herbert Arthur Turner, *Trade Union Growth, Structure and Policy: A Comparative Study of the Cotton Unions* (London: Allen & Unwin, 1962).

Amongst transport workers the early development of trade unionism through the Amalgamated Society of Railway Servants was recorded at length by George Alcock, *Fifty Years of Railway Trade Unionism* (London: Co-operative Press, 1920), a book partly spoiled by a poor index. For early recruitment of railway labour and industrial relations before 1870 there is the authoritative work by Peter W. Kingsford, *Victorian Railwaymen* (London: Frank Cass, 1970). The official history of the National Union of Railwaymen and its predecessor the ASRS is Philip S. Bagwell, *The Railwaymen* (London: Allen & Unwin, 1963). This should be supplemented by Partha S. Gupta 'Railway Trade Unionism in Britain c 1880-1900', *Economic History Review* 2nd Ser XIX (1966) and by

Geoffrey Alderman, 'The Railway Companies and the Growth of Railway Trade Unionism in the late nineteenth century', *Historical Journal*, vol 14 1971. There is an ably written early account of the Associated Society of Locomotive Engineers and Firemen by John R. Raynes, *Engines and Men* (Leeds: Goodall & Suddick, 1921) and a less impressive later work, Norman McKillop, *The Lighted Flame* (London: Thomas Nelson & Sons, 1950). The history of the railway clerks has yet to be written, although there is a brief chapter on Railway Clerks Association in Robert Page Arnot and G. D. H. Cole, *Trade Unionism on the Railways* (London: Allen & Unwin, 1917). Dock and port labour, particularly in London, has been investigated in masterly fashion by John Lovell, *Stevedores and Dockers* (London: Macmillan, 1969) and by Walter Marcel Stern, *The Porters of London* (London: Longmans, 1960). The road haulage workers north of the border are the subject of Angela Tuckett, *The Scottish Carter* (London: Allen & Unwin, 1967).

On the fascinating aspect of trade union regalia there are two books: Robert Leeson, *United We Stand* (Bath: Adams & Dart, 1971) and John Gorman, *Banner Bright* (London: Allen Lane, the Penguin Press, 1973).

The Truck System
The principal authorities on the truck system in British industry are David Frederick Schloss, *Methods of Industrial Remuneration* (London: Williams & Norgate, 1892) and George Woodman Hilton, *The Truck System* (Cambridge: Heffer and Sons, 1960). Sidney & Beatrice Webb, *Industrial Democracy* 2 vols (London: Longmans Green & Co., 1897) is worth consulting on this, as on many other subjects. Information apart from that given in the parliamentary enquiries is not easily accessible, but among contemporary accounts there is David Bailey, *The Truck System* (London: Fred Pitman, 1859). The TUC Parliamentary Committee, *The Master and Servants, Payment of Wages (Truck) Bill* (London, 1872) and Stephen N. Fox and Clementina Black, *The Truck Acts — What they are and what they ought to do* (London: Women's Trade Union Association, 1894).

The Sweating System
There is no general work on the sweated trades of the late nineteenth century. Relevant shorter works include Beatrice Potter, 'Tailoring' in Charles Booth (ed.) *Labour and Life of the People* (London: Williams and Norgate, 1889); Fabian Society, *Sweating: its Cause and Remedy* (Fabian Tract 50) (London: Fabian Society, 1894); Beatrice Webb, *How to do away with the Sweating System* (Manchester: Co-operative Union, 1892); Fabian Society, *The Economics of Direct Employment* (Fabian Tract 84) (London: Fabian Society, 1898). A detailed study of somewhat later date of the industry which suffered most severely from sweated labour is Richard Henry Tawney, *Minimum rates in the Tailoring Industry* (London: L. S. E. and Ratan Tata Foundation, 1915). The system at its worst is described in Edith F. Hogg, 'The Fur Pullers of South London', *Nineteenth Century*, November 1897. The difficulty of preventing exploitation when work was done at home, rather than in a factory, is made clear in Evelyn Gibson Nelson, 'The putting out system in the English framework knitting industry', *Journal of Economic and Business*

History, vol. II No. iii, May 1930 and in M. H. Irwin, *Home Work amongst Women, Report of an enquiry conducted from the Glasgow Council for Women's trades* (Glasgow: The Council, 1897).

Co-operation and Profit-Sharing

The best modern account of the co-operative movement, placing its progress in the setting of the development of the economy and of the labour movement is G. D. H. Cole, *A Century of Co-operation* (London: Allen & Unwin, 1944). Also of value, though with much less historical content, is Arnold Bonner, *British Co-operation* (Manchester: Co-operative Union, 1961). The more important of the contempory accounts of nineteenth century developments are George Jacob Holyoake, *The History of Co-operation in England,* 2 vols (London: T. Fisher Unwin, 1906) and the same author's reminiscences in, *Sixty Years of an Agitator's Life,* 3rd edn. 2 vols (London: T. Fisher Unwin, 1893); James Malcolm Forbes Ludlow and Lloyd Jones, *The Progress of the Working Classes, 1832-67* (London: Stahan, 1867); Beatrice Potter, *The Co-operative Movement in Great Britain* (London: Sonnenschein & Son, 1891) and Benjamin Jones, *Co-operative Production* (Oxford: Clarendon Press, 1894). The decline of the early community idealism is traced in Sidney Pollard, 'Co-operation from community building to shopkeeping', in Asa Briggs and John Saville (ed.), *Essays in Labour History,* vol. 1 (London: Macmillan, 1960). Another very important aspect in the development of co-operation is dealt with in Bert James Youngjohns, *Co-operation and the State* (Loughborough: Co-operative Union Ltd., 1954).

The two leading contemporary works on profit sharing in the late nineteenth century are Sedley Taylor, *Profit Sharing between Capital and Labour* (London: Kegan Paul Trench & Co., 1884) and Thomas William Bushill, *Profit Sharing and the Labour Question* (London: Methuen, 1893). Most of the work by the foremost authority in this subject, D. F. Schloss, is to be found in the parliamentary papers but his classic, *Methods of Industrial Remuneration* (3rd edn., London: William & Norgate, 1898) should also be consulted.

Employers' Liability

A recent authoritative account is David Gordon Hanes, *The First British Workmen's Compensation Act, 1897* (New Haven and London: Yale University Press, 1968). Though primarily concerned with Joseph Chamberlain's Act, it also makes a critical examination of the Employers Liability Act of 1880. Of the contemporary works, Augustine Birrell, *Four Lectures on the Law of Employers' Liability at Home and Abroad* (London: Macmillan, 1897); Walter Cook Spens and Robert T. Younger, *Employers and Employed* (Glasgow: Maclehose & Sons, 1887) and Henry W. Wolff, *Employers Liability: what it ought to be* (London: King and Son, 1897) are the most valuable. A 'Powellite' protest against Joseph Chamberlain's 'Socialism' in introducing the right to insurance compensation for accidents is contained in John Buckingham Pope, *Conservatives or Socialists?* (London: Rivington, 1897). The railway companies' standpoint on the employers liability question has been examined by Geoffrey Alderman in *The Railway Interest* (Leicester: University Press, 1973).

Unemployment

Estimates of the volume of unemployment in the second half of the nineteenth century were made by Marie Dessauer-Meinhardt in two short articles 'Unemployment Records, 1848-59', *Economic History Review*, vol. X No. 1, February 1940 pp. 38-43 and 'Monthly Unemployment Records, 1854-92', *Economica*, n.s. vol. VII August 1940, pp. 322-26.

The story of how government met the emergency of unemployment arising from the interruption of trade caused by the American Civil War is told in William Otto Henderson, *The Lancashire Cotton Famine, 1861-65* (Manchester: Manchester University Press, 1939).

José Harris, *Unemployment and Politics: A study of English Social Policy, 1886-1914* (Oxford: Clarendon Press, 1972), is a recent study of outstanding merit. It has an extensive bibliography. Of great influence during the first three decades of the twentieth century was William H. Beveridge, *Unemployment: A problem of Industry* (London: Longmans Green & Co., 1912). The bibliography in Appendix D of this book is also of value to the student. The pamphlet by Alsager Hay Hill, *Our Unemployed* (London: TUC, 1868), is a reminder that unemployment was no new problem when the *Select Committee on Distress from Want of Employment* examined its causes in 1895-96. Preceding Beveridge's book by more than a decade was Geoffrey Drage, *The Unemployed* (London: Macmillan, 1894). The significance of the greater militancy of the unemployed in the years between Victoria's Jubilees is underlined in John Burns, *The Unemployed* (London: Fabian Tract No. 47, 1893) while the viewpoint of the recently established Independent Labour Party is set forth in Tom Mann, *The Programme of the ILP and the Unemployed* (London: ILP, 1895). Though primarily concerned with events in the twentieth century, Kenneth Douglas Brown's, *Labour and Unemployment* (Newton-Abbot: David & Charles, 1971), also touches on issues in the closing years of the preceding century.

The New Unionism and the Royal Commission on Labour

Full treatment of the development of labour organization in the principal industries, as well as an analysis of the outstanding features of the New Unionism is given in Hugh Armstrong Clegg, Alan Fox and Arthur Frederick Thompson, *A History of British Trade Unions since 1889*, vol. 1 (Oxford: Clarendon Press, 1964). Two chapters: 'The British Gas Workers' and 'General Labour Unions in Britain, 1889-1914' in Eric J. Hobsbawm, *Labouring Men* (London: Weidenfeld & Nicolson, 1964) are essential reading. Hugh Armstrong Clegg, *General Union: a study of the National Union of General and Municipal Workers* (Oxford: Blackwell, 1954), traces the subsequent development of unions originating in the period. The contemporary account of greatest value is Hubert Llewelyn Smith and Vaughan Nash, *The story of the Dockers Strike* (London: T. Fisher Unwin, 1890). The organization of dockers and sailors at Hull has recently been analysed in Raymond Brown, *Waterfront organisation in Hull, 1870-1900* (Hull: Hull University Press, 1972). A similar survey for Liverpool is by E. L. Taplin, *Liverpool Dockers and Seamen, 1870-1890* (Hull: Hull University Press, 1973). Three autobiographies written by major participants in the greatest strikes of these years are William Thorne, *My Life's Battles* (London: George Newnes Ltd., 1925), Benjamin Tillett,

Memories and Reflections (London: John Long Ltd., 1931) and Joseph Havelock Wilson, *My Stormy Voyage through Life* (London: Co-operative Printing Society, 1925). The part played by another leading participant is told in Dona Torr, *Tom Mann and his Times*, vol.1 (London: Lawrence & Wishart, 1956). There is a popular account of the match girls' strike and the dock strike in Ann Stafford, *Match to fire the Thames* (London: Hodder & Stoughton, 1961). A union which arose from the aftermath of the engineers' defeat in 1897 is the subject of Richard Hyman's, *The Workers' Union* (Oxford: Clarendon Press, 1971).

Although the organization of women workers became more important in the closing years of the nineteenth century very little has so far been written of these developments. An exception is Barbara Drake, *Women in Trade Unions* (London: Allen & Unwin, 1921). An outline of some value, particularly in view of the shortage of alternative sources of information, is the TUC's, *Women in the Trade Union Movement* (London: TUC, 1955). For further work in this subject one should consult Grenda M. Horne, 'The Liberation of British and American Women's History: A Survey of Recent Research', *Bulletin* of the Society for the Study of Labour History, No. 26 (Spring 1973).

The organizational strength of the employers was greatly increased in the 1890s but these developments have not as yet been subjected to extensive research. The shipowners are an important exception. Their organization, labour relations, and parliamentary influence has been examined in Leslie Hughes Powell, *The Shipping Federation: A History of the first Sixty Years 1890-1950* (London: London Shipping Federation, 1950). The foremost practitioner in the organization of free labour, William Collison, wrote about his activities in *The Apostle of Free Labour* (London: Hurst & Blackett, 1913). The only general work, V. L. Munns and W. E. J. McCarthy, *Employers Associations* (Royal Commission on Trade Unions and Employers Associations, Research Paper 7) is mainly about employers' associations at a much later date, but it is an authoritative account which is essential reading for the serious student of industrial relations. Most recent is Eric Wigham, *The Power to Manage* (Engineering Employers' Federation) (London, Macmillan: 1973).

The erosion of the legal rights of trade unions in the 1890s is the subject of an essay by John Saville, 'Trade Unions and Free Labour: the background to the Taff Vale decision', in Asa Briggs and John Saville (ed.), *Essays in Labour History* vol. 1 (London: Macmillan, 1960) and in Benjamin C. Roberts, *The Trades Union Congress 1868-1921* (London: Allen & Unwin, 1958) Chap. v.

The growth of socialism and the swing of union opinion to greater political activity is examined authoritatively in Henry Pelling, *Origins of the Labour Party* (Oxford: Oxford University Press, 1954). Other facets of the developments of socialism are considered in Margaret Cole, *The Story of Fabian Socialism* (London: Heinemann, 1961); Ann Freemantle, *This Little Band of Prophets: the story of the Gentle Fabians* (London: Allen & Unwin 1960); Edward R. Pease, *The History of the Fabian Society* (London: Allen & Unwin, 1925); Chushichi Tsuzuki, *H. M. Hyndman and British Socialism* (Oxford: Oxford University Press, 1961) and the same author's *Life of Eleanor Marx 1855-1898* (Oxford: Clarendon Press, 1967). The role of the ILP after its foundation in 1893 still awaits full analysis. Robert E. Dowse, *Left in the Centre: The Independent Labour Party, 1893-1940* (London: Longmans, 1966) is principally concerned to explain the reasons underlying the decline of the 'left wing' of the Labour Party after the Great War. Valuable, as giving an insight, through the life of F. W. Jowett, into the issues which brought the ILP into prominence in one of the areas in which it had most influence — the West Riding of Yorkshire — is Archibald Fenner Brockway, *Socialism Over Sixty Years* (London: Allen & Unwin, 1946).

Biographies

Besides the biographies of labour leaders mentioned above, there are now available the first two volumes of John Saville and Joyce M. Bellamy (ed.), *Dictionary of Labour Biography* (London: Macmillan, 1972 and 1973). This is likely to become an indispensable work of reference for information on leaders of the labour movement.

Index

Aberdare, 41
Abinger, Lord, 70
Accident insurance, 75, 76, 78-9
   and trade unionism, 77
Accidents:
   factory, 7
   industrial, 72
   mining, 21
   railway, 73, 76
Acts of Parliament:
   Arbitration, 1824, 33
      1872, 31, 32
   Artificers, 1563, 9, 15
   Combination, 1799, 9, 10, 11, 13
      1800, 9, 10, 11, 13
      1825, 15
   Combination Law Repeal, 1824, 9,
      14
   Conciliation, 1824, 33
      1867, 31
      1896, 33
   Conspiracy and Protection of
      Property, 1875, 42-3
   Corresponding Societies, 1799, 10
   Criminal Law Amendment, 1871, 9,
      40, 42
   Employers' Liability, 1880, 74
   Employers' and Workmen's, 1875, 43
   Factory, 1891, 60
   Friendly Societies, 1855, 34, 36
   Hosiery Manufacture (Payment of
      Wages), 1874, 54
   Industrial and Provident Societies,
      1852, 64
   Industrial Relations, 1971, 98
   Molestation of Workmen, 1859, 36
   Public Works (Manufacturing Dis-
      tricts), 1863, 81
   Trade Boards, 1909, 62
   Trade Disputes, 1906, 7, 9
   Trade Union, 1871, 9, 39, 42, 90
   Trade Unions (Protection of Funds),
      1869, 39
   Truck, 1817, 54
      1831, 46, 47, 54
      1896, 55
   Truck Amendment, 1887, 55
   Unlawful Oaths, 1797, 16, 17
      1819, 16
   Workmen's Compensation, 1897, 77,
      78-9
Agriculture:
   labour in, 8, 17, 43, 44, 78, 79, 83
   truck in, 46

Allan, W., 39, 40
Allen, W., 87
Amalgamated Association of Miners, 24
Amalgamated Society of Carpenters and
   Joiners, 22, 72
Amalgamated Society of Engineers, 21,
   22, 25, 63, 72, 83, 86, 100
Amalgamated Society of Railway
   Servants, 43, 73, 74, 91, 100, 101-2
Applegarth, R., 22, 38, 40
Apprenticeship, 14
Arbitration, 14, 20, 22, 26-34
   in boot and shoe manufacture, 30
   in cotton spinning, 30
   in hosiery, 30
   in lace making, 30
   employers' attitude to, 26, 29, 33
   unions' attitude to, 26, 29, 33
Asquith, H., 77
Associated Chambers of Commerce, 45

Baird, J., 50
Barnaby Rudge, 19
Bass, M. T., 73
Beaufoy, M., 87
Beehive, 35, 40
Besant, A., 94
Beveridge, W., 86
Bitter Cry of Outcast London, 57
Black lists, 16
Blackburn Power Loom Weavers
   Association, 45
Blackleg labour, 16
Blanketeers, 80
Board of Trade, 33
Boilermakers Society, 27, 36, 72
Bookbinders, 9
Boot and shoe manufacture, 30, 57
Booth, C., 57, 81
Bowerman, C. W., 61
Brace, H. A., 42
Bramwell, Baron, 36
Brassey, T., 34
Bray, J. F., 18, 23
Breeches makers, 13
Briggs Collieries, 67
Broadhurst, H., 79, 94
Bryant and May's, 94
Buckmaster, J. C., 23
Building Societies, 53
Building trade, 15, 16, 17, 19, 37, 45, 87
Burnett, J., 57, 58
Burns, J., 77, 81-2, 95

Burt, T., 91
Bushill, T. W., 66, 67
Buxton, S., 32, 60, 61

Cambrian Iron and Spelter Works, 48
Campbell, A., 37
Cardboard box making, 62
Carlyle, T., 19, 89
Carnbrae, 47
Carr, R., 7
Cassell, Messrs, 69
Castle, Mrs B., 8
Central Co-operative Agency, 64
Chain making, 62
Chamberlain, J., 77, 78, 82, 83, 84
Champion, H. H., 89
Charity Organisation Society, 82, 85
Chartism, 19
Chartism, 89
    and trade unionism, 21
Cheap Clothes and Nasty, 56
Cheshire, 11, 12
Christian Socialists, 8, 56, 63-4
Churchill, Lord Randolf, 88, 95
Civil War (U.S.A.), 35, 80
Classical economics, 14, 18, 26, 31, 51, 52
Clegg, H., 17-18, 21
Coal mining:
    employers' liability and, 72
    employment in, 90
    sliding scale, 31, 32
    truck in, 46
Cobden Treaty (1860), 80
Collective bargaining, 8, 21, 93
Combination laws, 9, 10, 11, 13-15, 19
Common employment, 70-4
Conciliation schemes, 23, 26, 29, 31, 32, 33
    extent of, 33
Conference of Amalgamated Trades, 40
Conseils de Prud'hommes, 30
Conspiracy, law on, 36, 41, 43
Contract, breach of, 36-7, 38, 43
Contracting Out, 75, 76, 77
Contributory negligence, 72
Co-operation, 24, 56, 62-6
Co-operative societies, 18, 62-3
Cotton spinners, 15, 16, 17
Coulson, E., 39, 40
Coventry, 80
Cross, R. A., 42, 74

Daily News, 61

De La Rue company, 68
Democratic Federation, 89
Derbyshire, 11, 46
Dickens, C., 19, 26
Disraeli, B., 19, 42
Dock, Wharf and Riverside Labourers' Union, 91, 94, 99
Dock workers, 92
'Document', the, 15, 16, 26, 27
Doherty, J., 2, 17, 19
Domestic servants, 78
Domestic system, 52, 53, 59
Dorchester, 17
Drunkenness, 53
Dublin, 20
Durham Miners' Association, 75

Education, 18
Electoral reform, 78, 82, 88-9
Employers' Associations, 16, 25, 37, 44-5, 75, 99, 100
Employers' Liability, 70-7
Engineering Employers' Federation, 100
Evans, F. W., 73
Eyre and Spottiswoode, 61

Fabian Society, 59, 89-90
Factory Acts, 59, 65
Fair wages contracts, 61-2
Fenwick, C., 91
Findlay, G., 73
Fines, 55
Frame rents, 49-51
Framework knitters, 12, 49-50, 51
Friendly Society of Agricultural Labourers, 17
Frost, J., 50
Fur pullers, 60-1

Galt, W., 76
Garibaldi, G., 34-5
Gas stokers' case, 41
Gas Workers' and General Labourers' Union, 91, 92, 94
Gaskell, E., 19, 27
General Builders' Association, 37, 48
General Railway Workers' Union, 91
George, H., 89
Germany, 77-8, 79, 95
Gladstone, W. E., 81
Glasgow, 19, 20, 40
Glasgow Cotton Spinners' Association, 20, 22

Glasgow Master Brickbuilders' Association, 45
Glasgow Sentinel, 35
Glasgow Trades' Council, 37, 44, 85
Gloucestershire, 54
Globe, The, 61
Gorst, Sir J., 83
Grand General Union of all Operative Spinners of the U.K., 17
Grand National Consolidated Trades' Union, 17
Graham, R. B. Cunninghame, 100
Great Depression, 1873-96, 31
Griffiths vs. *the Earl of Dudley,* 1881, 74-5
Guile, D., 10, 39, 40

Hampden clubs, 18
Hard Times, 27
Hardie, J. Kier, 85, 100
Harnott, R., 39
Harrison, F., 39, 42
Hawick, 28
Henson G., 12, 14
Hilton, G. W., 51
History of Trade Unionism (1894), 21
Hodgskin, T., 18, 23
Hogg, E. F., 60-1
Holder, Sir J., 74
Holmes, W., 101-2
Hornby vs. *Close,* 1867, 36
Horton, W., 18
Hosiery trade, 29-31, 46
    conciliation in, 29
    truck system in, 46, 49
Howell, G., 25, 31, 35, 39, 42, 94
Hughes, T., 39, 42
Hull, 100
Hume, J., 14, 51
Hutchinson vs. *York, Newcastle and Berwick Railway,* 1850, 71
Hyndman, H. M., 89

Immigrant workers, 57-8, 59-60
In Place of Strife, 8
Independent Labour Party, 86, 90
Industrial Relations Court, 98
Informers, 54-5
Intensity of labour, 7
Irish famine, 80, 81
Iron industry, 46, 80
    sliding scale, 31, 32
Iron Trade Employers' Association, 75
Ironfounders' Society, 10, 22-3, 72

James', Lord, arbitration, 1896, 33
Jennings, W., 51
Jewish Board of Guardians, 60
Jews, 57, 58, 59-60
Junta, the, 40, 41

Kenry, Lord, 57
Kettle, Sir R., 30, 31
Kingsley, C., 56, 57, 64

Labour Defended against the Claims of Capital, 18, 23
Labour Representation Committee, 87, 102
Labour's Wrongs and Labour's Remedies, 23
Lace making, 46, 62
Laisser-faire, 40, 54, 62
Lanarkshire, 46
Lancashire, 11, 12, 46, 80
Land Nationalization Society, 89
Land Reform Union, 89
Lansbury, G., 85
Lead mining, 46
Leeds, 12, 60
Liberal Party, 100
Lib-Labs, 100
Lichfield, Earl of, 39
Limited liability, 65, 66
Link, The, 94
Littleton, E. J., 54
Local Government Board, 82, 84
Loch, C., 85
Lock-outs:
    building trade, 26
    engineers, 15, 25
    textiles, 26
London, 26, 60
    Chamber of Commerce, 32
    dock strike, 1889, 32
    Trades' Council, 35, 37
    Unemployment in, 82
London County Council, 61
London Women's Trades' Council, 94
Long pays, 48, 49
Loveless, G., 17
Lowe, R., 35, 42
Luddism, 11-13
Ludlow, J. M. F., 8, 19, 63
Lyons vs. *Wilkins,* 1896, 101

Macclesfield, 80
McCulloch D., 14, 18
MacDonald, A., 42, 50, 72, 73, 74

Machine wrecking, 12, 13
Manchester, 17, 20, 25, 40, 60, 63, 80
Mann, T., 86, 87
Manning, Cardinal, 32
Mansfield, Lord, 9
Mansion House Fund, 82
Marshall, Prof. A., 8, 48
Marx, K., 2, 89
Mary Barton, 19
Master and servant laws, 34, 36-8, 43
Mather, W., 87
Maurice, F. D., 64
May Day, 92
Mayhew, H., 56
Mearns, A., 57
Mechanics institutes, 18
Mediation, 20, 27, 32
    employers' view, 27
Melbourne, Lord, 17
Merchant seamen, 72, 75, 78
Middlemen, 56, 58
Mill, James, 18
Mill, John Stuart, 24, 89
Millwrights, 9, 10
Miners' Advocate, 21
Miners' Association, 20, 22
Miners' Federation of Great Britain, 91
Mobility of labour, 52, 53
Morley, S., 34, 50, 74
Morning Chronicle, 56
Morris, W., 90
Mundella, A. J., 30, 34, 42, 50

Nail making, 46, 48, 51, 53, 57
Nasmyth, J., 26
National Agricultural Workers' Union, 97
National Amalgamated Sailors' and
    Firemen's Union, 91, 99
National Association of Coal, Lime and
    Ironstone Miners of Great Britain, 24
National Association of Operative
    Plasterers, 38
National Federation of Associated
    Employers of Labour, 45
National Labour Federation, 91
National Miners' Union, 24
National Union of Boot and Shoe
    Operatives, 60
Navigation Colliery, Mountain Ash, 41
Navvies', Bricklayers' Labourers and
    General Labourers' Union, 91
Neale, E. V., 64
'New Model' unions, 20, 21-5, 38-9
    and arbitration, 31
    friendly society benefits, 38-9

New unionism, 32, 65, 77, 90-3, 94, 95
Newton, W., 23, 24
Nine hours movement, 44
'Nobs', 16, 20
North and South, 27
North Eastern Railway, 33
North of England Iron Manufacturers'
    Association, 45
Northern Star, 21
Nottinghamshire, 11-12

Odger, G., 31, 35, 40
O'Grady, J., 79
Oldham Limiteds, 66
Out workers, 7
Overtime, 14, 24-5, 86
Owen, R., 18, 62, 63

Paris and Orleans Railway, 66, 69
Parliamentary reform, 13
Paterson, E., 93
Pattison, W. P., 53
Pawnbrokers, 46-7
Pensions, 39
Petty foggers, 48, 52
Picketing, 16, 34, 36, 43, 88, 92
Piecework, 25, 28
Place, F., 13, 15, 18
Politics in trade unions, 23, 34-5
Poll tax, 58
Portland stone, 46, 49
Postal services, 22
Postgate, R., 19
Potato famine, 80
Potter, Beatrice, 56, 58, 60
Potter, George, 40
Preston, 26
Priestly vs. *Fowler*, 1837, 70
Principles of Political Economy (J. S.
    Mill), 24
Profit-sharing, 64, 66-70
    extent of, 68
    in France, 66, 69
    ratio of bonus to profits, 69
    and industrial unrest, 66-7
    trade unions and, 67-8
    and wage rates, 67-8
Profits, 31
Progress and Poverty, 89
Public Ownership, 99
Public utilities, 90, 93
Punch, 58

Railway Companies' Association, 73
Railway interest, 73
Railways, 16, 33, 46, 74
    and truck system, 46, 48
Railwaymen, 43, 72, 100
Rattening, 38
Redemptionists, 64
Reform Bill, 1866, 35
Reg. vs. *Bunn and others,* 1872, 41
Reg. vs. *Druitt,* 1867, 36
Ricardo, D., 14, 51
Ritchie, C. T., 83
Roberts, W. P., 21, 73
Rochdale Equitable Pioneers, 63, 65
Royal Commissions:
    Labour, 1891, 32-3, 87, 88, 95-101
    Labour Laws, 1874, 42
    Mines, 1842, 21
    Railway Accidents, 1876, 73-4
    Trade Unions, 1866-7, 10, 22, 31,
        38, 39-40, 88
    Truck System, 1871, 46, 47, 48-9,
        50, 55
Ruskin, J., 66

St. Martin's Hall Conference Committee,
    40
Schloss, D. F., 56, 66, 68, 70
Scottish Tailors' Society, 60
Seagoing Firemen's Friendly Associa-
    tion, 76
Second International, 92
Secular Sunday Schools, 18
Select Committees:
    Combination Laws, 1825, 15
    Combinations of Workmen, 1838,
        16, 19-20
    Contracts of Service between Master
        and Servant, 1865-6, 37
    Distress from Want of Employment,
        1895, 84, 87
    Employers' Liability Act Amend-
        ment Bill, 1876, 75, 76
    Framework Knitters' petition, 1812,
        12
    Government Contracts (Fair Wages
        Resolution), 1896, 61
    Masters and Operatives, 1856-60, 23,
        28, 29
    Railway Labourers, 1846, 46
    Stoppages of Wages in Hosiery
        Manufacture, 1854-5, 49, 54
    Sweating System, 1887-90, 56, 57,
        61
    Truck Acts, 1842, 46

Self improvement, 18
Shaw, G. B., 27
Sheffield, 37, 39, 40
Sheffield Outrages, 35, 39
Shetland Islands, 46
Shipping Federation, 99, 100
Shipwrights, 23
Silk weavers, 80
Sliding scales, 31
    effects on trade unionism, 32
Smith, A., 8, 14
Smith, H. Llewellyn, 85-6
Social Democratic Federation, 81, 86,
    89, 90
Socialism, 24, 89, 90, 91
Socialist League, 90
Society for Promoting Working Men's
    Associations, 64
South Metropolitan Gas Co., 67
South Wales, 46, 54
Sportsman, The, 61
Staffordshire, 46, 52-3
Standard of living, 8
Statute of Artificers, 1563, 9
Strikes, 14-5, 35, 88
    in building trade, 15, 16, 22, 37
    in cotton industry, 19
    in docks, 32
    hosiery trade, 29-30
    statistics, 32
    in textile industry, 20
    truck system and, 50
    unions' policy towards, 22, 39
Sub-contracting, 56 57-8, 59, 61
Sweating system, 56-62
    in chain making, 57
    in cutlery trade, 57
    definitions of, 56
    'Fair wage' contracts, 61-2
    in nail making, 57
    sub-contracting, 56, 58, 59
    in tailoring, 56, 57
    trade unionism and, 59, 60
    in wholesale trading, 58, 59
Sybil, or the Two Nations, 19

Tangye, R., 66
Tailoring trades, 56, 57, 59, 62
Taylor, S., 66
Teachers, 43-4
Temperton vs. *Russell,* 1893, 101
Thames Ironworks, 67
Thompson, W., 18, 62
Thorne, W., 85, 87, 91
Tillett, B., 92, 99

Times, The, 61, 75, 87-8, 95, 101
Tolpuddle labourers, 16-17
Tommy shops, 47, 49, 50, 51, 52, 54, 55
Trade Boards, 62
Trade cycle, 80, 90
Trade unions:
    amalgamations, 98
    funds, 34, 35-6
    general unionism, 90-1
    legal position, 34, 35-6, 40, 41-2, 98-9, 101
    membership, 8, 34, 90-1, 99
    picketing, 16, 34, 36, 43, 101
    and politics, 23, 34-5, 89
Trades Councils, 35, 44
    Edinburgh, 44
    Glasgow, 37, 44, 85
    London, 35, 44
    Manchester and Salford, 40
    Sheffield, 44
Trades Union Congress:
    affiliations to, 90
    and federations of trades, 101
    and immigrant labour, 60
    'new unionists' in, 99
    origins of, 40-1
    Parliamentary Committee, 31, 40, 42, 94, 101
    and profit sharing, 67-8
    and unemployment, 86, 87
    women in, 93, 94
    and workmen's compensation, 79
Trades Union Directory, 1867, 34
Transport, employment in, 90
Tremenheere, H. S., 48, 52
Trollope, G. F., 26
Trollope vs. *London Building Trades' Federation,* 1896, 101
Truck system, 7, 14, 45-55
    extent of, 46, 55
    in hosiery trade, 49, 50
    in nail making, 46, 48, 51, 53
    prosecutions under, 54
    and small firms, 50
    Social and economic effects, 52-3
    in textile manufacture, 46-7, 49, 52
    in trade depression, 47, 48, 52
    and wage cutting, 48, 52
    workmen affected by, 46, 55

Turnbook days, 53

Unemployment, 13, 80-8
    causes of, 83
    extent of, 85, 99
    public works and, 81, 82
    relief, 83
    remedies for, 86
    statistics, 80, 85
    technological, 83
    and trade cycle, 86, 87
    and wage rates. 87
United Kingdom Postal Clerks Association, 94
Unskilled labour, 90
Unto this Last, (1862), 66
U.S.A., 60, 78, 95

Violence in industrial disputes, 11, 12, 13, 15, 19, 38
Voice of the People, 17

Wages, 13, 31, 56
Walker, R., 50
Watkin, E., 73
Webb, S. and B., 10, 17, 21, 60, 76, 93, 98
West Ham, 83
West of Scotland Power-Loom Female Weavers' Society, 93
What a compulsory eight-hour day means to the workers, 86
White, G., 9
Wilson, J. Havelock, 76, 91
Wilson vs. *Murray,* 1868, 71
Women workers, 55, 93-4
    in trade unions, 93
    in T.U.C., 93, 94
Women's Protective and Provident League, 93
Women's Trade Union League, 93
Woolcombers, 9
Working Bakers' Association, 64
Working Builders' Association, 64
Working day, 44, 77, 86, 92-3
Working Shoemakers' Association, 64